Women, Men and Books
Issues of Gender in Yiddish Discourse

LEGENDA

LEGENDA is the Modern Humanities Research Association's book imprint for new research in the Humanities. Founded in 1995 by Malcolm Bowie and others within the University of Oxford, Legenda has always been a collaborative publishing enterprise, directly governed by scholars. The Modern Humanities Research Association (MHRA) joined this collaboration in 1998, became half-owner in 2004, in partnership with Maney Publishing and then Routledge, and has since 2016 been sole owner. Titles range from medieval texts to contemporary cinema and form a widely comparative view of the modern humanities, including works on Arabic, Catalan, English, French, German, Greek, Italian, Portuguese, Russian, Spanish, and Yiddish literature. Editorial boards and committees of more than 60 leading academic specialists work in collaboration with bodies such as the Society for French Studies, the British Comparative Literature Association and the Association of Hispanists of Great Britain & Ireland.

The MHRA encourages and promotes advanced study and research in the field of the modern humanities, especially modern European languages and literature, including English, and also cinema. It aims to break down the barriers between scholars working in different disciplines and to maintain the unity of humanistic scholarship. The Association fulfils this purpose through the publication of journals, bibliographies, monographs, critical editions, and the MHRA Style Guide, and by making grants in support of research. Membership is open to all who work in the Humanities, whether independent or in a University post, and the participation of younger colleagues entering the field is especially welcomed.

ALSO PUBLISHED BY THE ASSOCIATION

Critical Texts
Tudor and Stuart Translations • *New Translations* • *European Translations*
MHRA Library of Medieval Welsh Literature

MHRA Bibliographies
Publications of the Modern Humanities Research Association

The Annual Bibliography of English Language & Literature
Austrian Studies
Modern Language Review
Portuguese Studies
The Slavonic and East European Review
Working Papers in the Humanities
The Yearbook of English Studies

www.mhra.org.uk
www.legendabooks.com

STUDIES IN YIDDISH

Legenda *Studies in Yiddish* embrace all aspects of Yiddish culture and literature. The series regularly publishes the proceedings of the International Mendel Friedman Conferences on Yiddish Studies, which are convened every two years by the European Humanities Research Centre of the University of Oxford.

PUBLISHED IN THIS SERIES

1. *Yiddish in the Contemporary World*
2. *The Shtetl: Image and Reality*
3. *Yiddish and the Left*
   ed. by Gennady Estraikh and Mikhail Krutikov
4. *The Jewish Pope: Myth, Diaspora and Yiddish Literature*, by Joseph Sherman
5. *The Yiddish Presence in European Literature: Inspiration and Interaction*
   ed. by Joseph Sherman and Ritchie Robertson
6. *David Bergelson: From Modernism to Socialist Realism*
   ed. by Joseph Sherman and Gennady Estraikh
7. *Yiddish in the Cold War*, by Gennady Estraikh
8. *Yiddish in Weimar Berlin: At the Crossroads of Diaspora Politics and Culture*,
   ed. by Gennady Estraikh and Mikhail Krutikov
9. *A Captive of the Dawn: The Life and Work of Peretz Markish (1895-1952)*,
   ed. by Joseph Sherman, Gennady Estraikh, Jordan Finkin, and David Shneer
10. *Translating Sholem Aleichem: History, Politics and Art*,
    ed. by Gennady Estraikh, Jordan Finkin, Kerstin Hoge and Mikhail Krutikov
11. *Joseph Opatoshu: A Yiddish Writer between Europe and America*,
    ed. by Sabine Koller, Gennady Estraikh and Mikhail Krutikov
12. *Uncovering the Hidden: The Works and Life of Der Nister*,
    ed. by Gennady Estraikh, Kerstin Hoge and Mikhail Krutikov
13. *Worlds of Yiddish Literature*,
    ed. by Simon Neuberg and Diana Matut
14. *Children and Yiddish Literature: From Early Modernity to Post-Modernity*,
    ed. by Gennady Estraikh, Kerstin Hoge and Mikhail Krutikov
15. *Three Cities of Yiddish: St Petersburg, Warsaw and Moscow*,
    ed. by Gennady Estraikh and Mikhail Krutikov

Managing Editor
Dr Graham Nelson, 41 Wellington Square, Oxford OX1 2JF, UK
www.legendabooks.com

Women, Men and Books

Issues of Gender in Yiddish Discourse

EDITED BY
GENNADY ESTRAIKH AND MIKHAIL KRUTIKOV

Studies in Yiddish 16
Modern Humanities Research Association
2019

*Published by Legenda
an imprint of the Modern Humanities Research Association
Salisbury House, Station Road, Cambridge CB1 2LA*

*ISBN 978-1-78188-577-2 (HB)
ISBN 978-1-78188-578-9 (PB)*

First published 2019

All rights reserved. No part of this publication may be reproduced or disseminated or transmitted in any form or by any means, electronic, mechanical, photocopying, recording or otherwise, or stored in any retrieval system, or otherwise used in any manner whatsoever without written permission of the copyright owner, except in accordance with the provisions of the Copyright, Designs and Patents Act 1988, or under the terms of a licence permitting restricted copying issued in the UK by the Copyright Licensing Agency Ltd, Saffron House, 6–10 Kirby Street, London EC1N 8TS, England, or in the USA by the Copyright Clearance Center, 222 Rosewood Drive, Danvers MA 01923. Application for the written permission of the copyright owner to reproduce any part of this publication must be made by email to legenda@mhra.org.uk.

Disclaimer: Statements of fact and opinion contained in this book are those of the author and not of the editors or the Modern Humanities Research Association. The publisher makes no representation, express or implied, in respect of the accuracy of the material in this book and cannot accept any legal responsibility or liability for any errors or omissions that may be made.

Trademark notice: Product or corporate names may be trademarks or registered trademarks, and are used only for identification and explanation without intent to infringe.

© *Modern Humanities Research Association 2019*

Copy-Editor: Dr Alastair Matthews

CONTENTS

	List of Contributors	ix
	Introduction: Women, Men, and Books: Issues of Gender in Yiddish Discourse MIKHAIL KRUTIKOV	1
1	The Old Yiddish *Šeder Nošim* and the *Querelle des Femmes* ARNAUD BIKARD	7
2	The Marxist Theory of Primeval Matriarchy in Yiddish Intellectual Discourse: Gender between Anti-Religious Radicalism, Orthodox Judaism, and a New Metaphysics of *Yidishkayt* ROLAND GRUSCHKA	19
3	'Mother, in the chain of generations, I am the broken link between you and my child': The Experience of Being a Mother and a Daughter in Yiddish Poetry by Women JOANNA LISEK	36
4	*Yidishe Dikhterins, Nice Jewish Girls*: Creating Communities in Jewish Literary History ZOHAR WEIMAN-KELMAN	65
5	The Best-Selling Shomer and his Fear of Emancipated Women GENNADY ESTRAIKH	80
6	Dreams of a Jewish Queen: A Literary Itinerary of National-Sexual Desires, from the Book of Esther to Aaron Zeitlin's *Esterke* RONI MASEL	93
7	Between Talmud and Feminism: Bashevis Singer's Playful Jugglery in his Bilingual Corpus VALENTINA FEDCHENKO	108
8	The Forbidden Fruit: Gender and Desire in David Hofstein's Early Poetry SABINE KOLLER	123
9	'Ikh hob lib shlangen': Virility and Di Yunge EITAN KENSKY	139
10	Gendered War in Aharon Reuveni's *Yerusholayim in Shotn fun Shverd* YAAKOV HERSKOVITZ	152

11 The *Kmoy*-Conquest of South America: Yankev Botoshansky and
    the Masculine Imaginary of Yiddish Literature   162
    WILLIAM GERTZ RUNYAN

12 The 'Bathroom Crisis' in the Shtetl: Transgender Identity and
    Homoerotic Anxiety in Isaac Bashevis Singer   173
    ALEXANDRA TALI HERZOG

    Index   191

LIST OF CONTRIBUTORS

Arnaud Bikard is Associate Professor, Vice Chair of the Hebrew and Jewish Studies Department, Institut National des Langues et Civilisations Orientales (INALCO), Paris

Gennady Estraikh is a Professor at the Skirball Department of Hebrew and Judaic Studies, New York University

Valentina Fedchenko is Postdoctoral researcher, Institut National des Langues et Civilisations Orientales (INALCO), Paris

William Gertz Runyan is a Ph.D candidate, University of Michigan, Ann Arbor

Roland Gruschka is Professor of Jewish Literatures at the Hochschule für Jüdische Studien Heidelberg

Yaakov Herskovitz is a postdoctoral fellow at the Frankel Institute for Advanced Judaic Studies, University of Michigan, Ann Arbor

Alexandra T. Herzog is Assistant Director of the American Jewish Committee (AJC) New England

Eitan Kensky is Judaica and Hebraica Curator, Stanford University Library

Sabine Koller is Professor of Slavic-Jewish Studies, Department of Slavic Studies, Regensburg University

Mikhail Krutikov is Professor of Slavic and Judaic Studies, and Chair, Department of Slavic Languages and Literatures, University of Michigan. Ann Arbor

Joanna Lisek is an Adjunct Professor, Department of Jewish Studies, University of Wroclaw

Roni Masel is a Ph.D candidate, New York University

Zohar Weiman-Kelman is an Assistant Professor in the Department of Foreign Literatures and Linguistics, and The Blechner Career Development Chair in East European Jewish Culture, Ben-Gurion University of the Negev, Beersheba

INTRODUCTION

Women, Men, and Books: Issues of Gender in Yiddish Discourse

Mikhail Krutikov

Historically, the gender division in Yiddish was arguably the strongest among European languages. For centuries, Yiddish has been — and in some communities it still is — commonly perceived as the women's tongue, as opposed to Hebrew as the language of men. This clear-cut dichotomy has been recently explored, questioned, and challenged by a number of distinguished scholars, and we hope that our collection will contribute to the ongoing discussion in this regard. The specificity of Yiddish gender constructions attracts a broad academic community with diverse scholarly and intellectual interests, as well as cultural and political commitments, taking Yiddish away from the somewhat marginal position it occupies both in general literary studies and in Jewish studies. Like most of the previous publications in the Studies in Yiddish series, this collection represents a selection of case studies which stem from diverse research projects, and therefore does not aim at a systematic, let alone comprehensive, coverage of the subject. It should be read as a report on the field and an invitation to carry out further research.

There is one particular aspect, however, which was mentioned during the discussions at the workshop behind the volume and will undoubtedly be noticed by the reader: the relative weight accorded to the issue of masculinity. As the organizers of the workshop and the editors of the volume, we have to admit that this was not our intention. But it does make this collection different from most gender-related studies on Yiddish, which tend to focus on women. This brings us to another peculiar aspect of Yiddish culture: while its main consumers were women, it was produced mostly by men. We hope that paying more attention to men as creators of Yiddish culture will be helpful for a better understanding of gender dynamics in Yiddish literature. At the risk of provoking further criticism in dichotomist thinking, we decided to structure the chapters according to the gender principle as articulated in the title of the volume. The chapters in the first part deal predominantly with women as creators and characters, while the second part focuses on men. However, this binary is unsettled and challenged by the concluding paper, which deals with transgender issues. Books are everywhere.

The traditional gender division in the premodern period is addressed by Arnaud

Bikard in his discussion of the medieval poetic compilation known as *Šeder nošim* [The Order for Women], a lengthy rhymed compilation which portrays in great detail the private and public daily life of Ashkenazi women in Italy at the beginning of the sixteenth century. He makes a case for a re-evaluation of this complex and multilayered text, which has been neglected by previous scholars, by examining it through the lenses of ambiguity inherent in medieval literature: although the (male) author declares that the primary purpose of his work is a concern for women's spiritual life, he often treats them disparagingly as inferior human beings. Bikard argues that the poem should be interpreted according to the rules and conventions of the popular Renaissance *querelle des femmes* genre, which combines irony, playfulness, and philosophical sophistication. It both mocks and praises women, but ultimately acknowledges their essential role in the epic struggle of the Jewish people for survival.

Moving into the modern period, Roland Gruschka examines a peculiar application of the concept of prehistoric matriarchy in Marxist theory to the history of ancient Judaism. In the works of Yiddish socialist and anarchist thinkers such as Philip Krantz, Benjamin Feigenbaum, and Abba Gordin, Gruschka identifies the influence of nineteenth-century philosophical and ethnographic ideas about matriarchy and prehistorical society, arguing that these Yiddish thinkers became, in some limited ways, forerunners of contemporary gender theorists. While Feigenbaum and Krantz largely followed the Marxist mainstream in their secularist interpretation of gender as a class-based construction, Gordin provocatively sought to combine Marxist radicalism with religious metaphysics, struggling on two fronts against radical secularism and religious traditionalism. While often inconsistent and controversial, these largely forgotten Yiddish thinkers challenged the essentialist approach to gender, particularly in the linguistic and social spheres, long before such critique became a widely accepted notion in gender studies.

The evolution of traditional Jewish matriarchy in the modern age is the theme of Joanna Lisek's chapter. The image of the *yidishe mame* as a strong and loving matriarch who reigns supreme over her household is among the most popular Jewish cultural stereotypes. Lisek explores the multitude of responses by Yiddish women poets to the assaults of modern ideas and practices on the traditional lifestyle, especially with regard to pregnancy, childbirth, and nursing. While Celia Dropkin downplays the specifically feminine aspect of pregnancy and childbirth, emphasizing the general mystery of the emergence of a new human life in another human body, Pessie Hershfeld celebrates both as the fulfilment and quintessence of womanhood. Rosa Yakubovitsh presents the moment of breastfeeding as a sacred ritual binding together the mother and her child, but the same time is not free of anxiety and fear for the child's life, which is amplified by the underlying allusions to the blood libel. The traditional bond between mothers and daughters is affirmed by Miriam Ulinover, but becomes problematic for Kadia Molodowsky. Modernity invades the intimate traditional family sphere in the form of pogroms and massacres, which figure prominently in Khana Levin's graphic depictions of violence during the Russian Civil War. And yet, despite its richness and diversity of poetic expression, women's creativity was historically neglected by the predominantly male Yiddish literary establishment, which tended to segregate women's poetry into a separate section.

The segregation of women in the male-dominated Yiddish canon is challenged in Zohar Weiman-Kelman's critique of Ezra Korman's 1928 anthology *Yidishe dikhterins*. She emphasizes the significance of female Yiddish poetic voices of the past mediated by contemporary feminist translators and theorists as an impulse for the consolidation and restoration of cross-temporal female collectivity by reclaiming its literary tradition. Building her argument on contributions by Irena Klepfisz, Kathryn Hellerstein, Adrienne Rich, and Anita Norich, and polemically engaging with an intervention by Avraham Novershtern, Weiman-Kelman discusses the challenges faced by cultural projects aimed at overcoming women's marginalization and restoring their place in Jewish history, drawing parallels between Yiddish and lesbian writers and 'identifying the lesbian over and against its historical erasure'. She turns to the essays and poetry of Kadia Molodowsky, and reads them as a sustained defence of women's creativity against the patriarchal discourse dominant in Yiddish letters of the time, as is exemplified in Molodowsky's polemics with Melech Ravitch.

One of the most striking examples of the male-dominated discourse are the novels by arguably the most popular nineteenth-century Yiddish author, Shomer (Nokhem Meyer Shaykevitch), who, thanks to Sholem Aleichem's devastating critique, became notorious as the epitome of *shund* (trash). Gennady Estraikh analyses the misogynist stereotypes in Shomer's 1888 chapbook entitled *Halb-mentsh halb-affe; oder, Vu zukht man dem emes?* [Half-Human, Half-Ape; or, Where Can One Find Truth?]. This sensational story set in East Prussia caricatures emancipated women by endowing them with dehumanizing animalistic features with racist overtones and blaming them for ruining men's lives. As Estraikh demonstrates, Shomer employs Darwinian language for representing the evolution from traditional Jewish society to modernity, squarely placing all the blame for the defects and deficiencies of the latter on women's aspirations to education and emancipation. Estraikh argues that, despite his harsh critique of Shomer, Sholem Aleichem largely shared his prejudice regarding women's place and role in society.

As a purveyor of cultural stereotypes, Shomer figures prominently also in the chapter by Roni Masel, which explores the intersection of nationalism, gender, and sexuality in Yiddish and Hebrew literary adaptations of the legend about the Polish king Casimir the Great and his Jewish beloved, Esterke. Following the Yiddish literary historian Chone Shmeruk, Masel traces two opposing interpretive trends, one that celebrates the love of the two as a symbol of Polish–Jewish symbiosis, and another that reflects anxiety over assimilation. Masel's analysis focuses on two different versions of Aaron Zeitlin's drama *Esterke un Kazimir der groyser: Ahasver in Poilin* [Esterke and Casimir the Great: Ahasver in Poland] (from 1932 and 1967 respectively). She demonstrates that the later version radically revised the earlier one by collapsing the fantasy of national salvation through Jewish femininity and the dream of a Jewish–Polish symbiosis.

Not dissimilar to Shomer's bias is the representation of gender 'anomalies' in the works by Isaac Bashevis Singer, as Valentina Fedchenko demonstrates in her analysis of the original newspaper publications of his novels *Sonim: Geshikhte fun a libe* and *Neshome-ekspeditsyes*, known in their abridged English versions as *Enemies: A Love Story* and *Shosha*. While female characters often lack psychological depth in the English versions of Singer's works, Fedchenko argues, some of the original Yiddish versions do portray more complex and controversial female figures who represent the challenges of American modernity as perceived by the author and his intended Yiddish readership. One of these figures is Nancy Isbel, the fourth female character in *Enemies*, who has been erased without a trace from the English edition. Her lesbian sexuality, anagrammatically embedded in her last name, distorts the clear-cut gender divisions inherent in the traditional Jewish worldview and ultimately brings about the collapse of the male protagonist, Herman Broder, making his disappearance at the end of the novel more understandable. The Yiddish version of the character of Shosha is more ambiguous and less 'naturally' feminine than her English counterpart, which further complicates the plot and structure of the novel. While the English versions of Singer's works tend to portray a more conservative image of Eastern European Jewish society, with fixed gender boundaries catering to the expectations of his English-speaking readership, the Yiddish originals are more explicit in addressing the challenges of American reality. As a result, the English versions of his works are often shorter and more dynamic, their characters are less complex and ambiguous, and philosophical and theological digressions are mostly absent. The Yiddish versions, meanwhile, reveal Singer's deeply seated misogynist bias and fear of modernity, which, Fedchenko suggests, may have come from the controversial *fin-de-siècle* Austrian thinker Otto Weininger.

Modernity presented challenges to the traditional Jewish concept of masculinity as well. Sabine Koller traces the development of the erotic metaphorical repertoire in David Hofstein's modernist poetry of the 1910s and 1920s. His poetic imagery combined the synaesthetic richness of immediate sensual perception with manifold references to European art and literature, in particular to Russian literature. In his meticulously crafted erotic metaphors, Hofstein aspired to bring together sound, vision, and the heritage of world culture, expanding the thematic and formal boundaries of Yiddish verse. While his main cultural aspiration was one of European universalism, he was also seeking to incorporate into his poetic language allusions to the biblical tradition, which sometimes assumed a disguised form, as Koller demonstrates by analysing the multilayered metaphorical structure and mimetic representations of the female body in his early love poems. This expressive exuberance gives way to restrained minimalism in his later works, which reflect Hofstein's existential philosophical concept of the woman as the guarantor of the continuity of life. Hofstein's creative use of the Yiddish poetic idiom, enriched by imagery borrowed from secular European and traditional Judaic sources, Koller concludes, breaks the traditionally entrenched gendered division between Yiddish and Hebrew, appropriating Yiddish for masculine discourse.

While Hofstein enthusiastically embraced the new masculinity of Jewish modernity, his American modernist counterparts were more circumspect in their treatment of virility. As Eitan Kensky argues in his analysis of the prose, poetry, and criticism of the Di Yunge group, modernist authors such as Mani Leib and Dovid Ignatov distanced themselves from the assertive embrace of masculinity that was prominent in both Zionist and American cultures. This hesitancy can be explained as a strategy of resistance to assimilation driven by the fear that a full 'realization' of man's virility could lead to a loss of his identity. The seductive danger of assimilation is embodied in the open eroticism of American female characters in Yiddish literature, which threatens to destroy the Jewish male protagonist. The expanse and intensity of the American space with its erotic allure additionally destabilizes the identity of the young Jewish male, forcing him to seek asylum in the familiar Jewish sphere. This new American Yiddish perception of virility differs from the old Eastern European masculine ideal, which was traditionally associated with marriage and children. In America, virility becomes problematic as it is linked with the perceived danger of identity loss. The early American Yiddish modernists, Kensky concludes, were still unable to confidently bring together the concepts of being 'American', 'Jewish', and 'Man', advocating restraint in passion.

Moving from America to Ottoman Palestine, Yaakov Herskovitz examines gender tensions in the writing of the Yiddish/Hebrew author Aharon Reuveni. The experience of World War I and displacement affected his representation of female characters, turning them into auxiliary devices in the service of men in difficult circumstances, Herskovitz argues in his reading of Reuveni's novel *Yerusholayim in shotn fun shverd* [Jerusalem in the Shadow of the Sword]. The plot of the novel revolves around an attempt to avoid being drafted into the Ottoman military during World War I, which would put the protagonist's life in mortal danger. Despite self-sacrificing actions by several women, the protagonist eventually fails to escape from military service, largely due to his own weakness, and ends up committing suicide. But even in his death, this selfish and manipulative man preserves more dignity than the self-sacrificing women who willingly denigrate themselves for his sake. Rather than upholding the gender hierarchy based on the presumed man's moral and intellectual authority, the war, in Herskovitz's reading of the novel, collapses it. The character weakness of the protagonist, which is pronounced in the Yiddish version, challenges the ideal of masculinity promoted by Zionist ideology and questions readings of the novel based on its Hebrew version.

William Runyan's chapter invites us to follow the prolific Yiddish writer Yankev Botoshansky to the exotic remote location of Tierra del Fuego in southern Patagonia. Runyan argues that, by assuming the persona of an adventurous explorer, popular during the interwar years, Botoshansky seeks to uphold and upgrade the image of the Jewish male. His report was reprinted in the leading literary weekly, the Warsaw-based *Literarishe bleter* [Literary Pages], fashioning a Yiddish man of letters as a brave traveller traversing inhospitable wild terrain. Botoshansky's reportage exemplifies a trend towards globalization in Yiddish literature which was articulated by a number of interwar critics and theorists, most notably Borekh Rivkin. Responding to the growing interest of Yiddish readers in exotic travel and colonial exploits, and building on the legacy of the nineteenth-century Enlightenment, the Yiddish press across the globe promoted the image of the new Jewish man of the world. By contrast, some of Botoshansky's other works, such as the novel *Buenos Ayres*, emphasized obstacles to mobility for women whose ability to move was controlled by men.

The closing chapter, by Alexandra Tali Herzog, investigates, using queer theory, representations of gender performance and sexual identity in three stories by Isaac Bashevis Singer. She demonstrates that Singer engaged Talmudic concepts of gender in creating a set of colourful characters with blurred and fluid gender identities. While often provocative in portraying cross-dressing, androgyny, and transgender individuals, Singer ultimately sought to reinforce norms rather than deconstruct differences, which reflects an anxiety regarding same-sex relationships, Herzog argues.

Like most of the previous volumes in this series, the present one is an outcome of a workshop at the semi-annual Mendel Friedman Conference on Yiddish, generously endowed by his son, the late Jack Friedman. The editors express their gratitude to Graham Nelson for his unwavering support and encouragement; to Kerstin Hoge for her momentous contribution in organizing and conducting the August 2016 workshop, 'Gender in Yiddish: Life and Literature'; and to Alastair Matthews for meticulous copy-editing of the volume.

CHAPTER 1

The Old YiddishŜeder Nošim and the Querelle des Femmes*

Arnaud Bikard

Old Yiddish literature seems, at first sight, to be characterized by the regularity of its patterns, models, and themes: its historians present a dozen clearly defined genres (Bible translations, Bible commentaries, moral and hagiographic works, practical guides to religious conduct, secular and religious epics, etc.).[1] The relationship of literature to women seems, overall, even more clearly defined in Old Yiddish. Although they are, more often than not, the declared addressees of the works, the apparent care for the spiritual life of women does not preclude an obvious disparagement of human beings whose access to knowledge is severely limited by their (traditional) ignorance of Hebrew. If we go further and look at the content of the numerous moral guides that have been preserved, the role of women appears strictly defined by religious laws and by the respect and submission they owe to their husbands.[2]

However, newly discovered texts and a closer attention to the diversity of Old Yiddish sources challenge the notions we have had about this literature and its relationship to women. We thus need to qualify the overall picture previous scholars have given.

A Gem of Old Yiddish Literature, Recently Rediscovered

The work I intend to discuss in the present article is one of the most remarkable poetic creations in Old Yiddish. It is a long poem, composed of more than 1200 verses organized in rhyming couplets (akin to the German *Knittelvers*), which presents itself as a praise of women. The poem has been little studied so far because it has long remained hidden in a manuscript from the first half of the sixteenth century kept at Cambridge University Library.[3] In 1928, Max Weinreich partly described it in his *Bilder fun der yidisher literatur geshikhte* [Sketches from the History

---

* This research was supported by the Russian Foundation of Science, project 15-18-00062, 'Formation of Culture in Diaspora', St Petersburg State University. The transcription used for Old Yiddish texts is the one currently used nowadays in Germany; see Erika Timm, 'Transkriptionszeichen', in *'Paris un Wiene': Ein jiddischer Stanzenroman des 16. Jahrhunderts von (oder aus dem Umkreis von) Elia Levita*, ed. by Erika Timm with Gustav Adolf Beckmann (Tübingen: Niemeyer, 1996), pp. cxlviii–cl. When I refer to modern Yiddish works and concepts, the standard YIVO transcription is used.

of Yiddish Literature], but the great scholar unwittingly contributed to the relative indifference this work has met with on the part of the academic community until very recently.[4] He presented the manuscript in question without clearly identifying its three parts. Although this codex contains three completely different works (as was frequently the case with Old Yiddish manuscripts, which can sometimes be described as small portable libraries),[5] Weinreich did not distinguish its first and second parts, thus conflating a classical treatise about the religious duties of women (*khale, nide, hadlokes haner*) and a complex half-serious, half-comic poem on the merits of the fair sex.[6]

There is actually a huge gap between the two compositions. The first (occupying fols 4^r–44^v) belongs to the traditional genre of practical guides for women that helped them to comply with the divine commandments in their everyday life. Written in rhymed prose (probably in order to facilitate memorization), it does not have any aesthetic ambitions and does not aim at entertaining. This is the oldest witness of a very popular genre which flourished over the centuries and was supposed to inspire, among women, the fear of God and the hatred of sin.[7] This type of work considers women both as crucial for the salvation of this world (through their respect for *mitsves*, or good deeds done from religious duty) and as having to atone for Eve's sin and for the Fall from Gan Eden. The elaborate title page has been preserved and reads *Śeder nošim* [The Order for Women]; the name of the female addressee of this manuscript, Zurt, is noted in the letters *shin* and *mem*.[8]

The second part of the manuscript (occupying fols 53^r–83^r; the introduction and the conclusion have been lost) is a mostly comic work, written in a rich and refined language showing a level of poetic elaboration which was rarely reached in Old Yiddish. I have, in fact, never encountered such a high degree of poetic craftsmanship except in the case of Elia Levita (Elye Bokher), and have therefore — and on the basis of philological, linguistic, and stylistic arguments — proposed attributing this poem to that great grammarian and poet.[9]

The poem was published from the manuscript, translated into English, and accompanied by an extensive commentary in 2011 by two Canadian researchers, Harry Fox and Justin Jaron Lewis, under the title *Many Pious Women*. Their work deserves praise because they have made accessible this important poem through their edition and translation and because they have brought a great deal of relevant information in their notes and commentaries. But it also raises a series of questions and has met with some criticism.[10]

The first problem of Lewis and Fox's edition concerns the overall characterization of the work. It is presented as a hagiographic, didactic poem, but it is clearly far from being such.[11] This erroneous description is reflected in the title the two scholars have decided to give the poem (which has come to us deprived of a name): *Many Pious Women*. Such a title is very problematic: apart from being generally foreign to the ways of naming works in Old Yiddish, it does not adequately reflect the comic, entertaining quality of the poem. I have thus decided to keep the old name under which it was known, albeit while being erroneously confused with the preceding work in the manuscript: *Śeder nošim*. The title is used for lack of a better one. It has the advantage of pointing to the partly parodic nature of the work.[12] Furthermore, if we keep in mind that the work has little to do with the traditional, pious genre of *vrou'énbüchlein*, this title has the advantage of adequately reflecting the content of the poem. Significantly, the word *Seder* designates in Old Yiddish not only a precise order, a set of rules, but also a way of living, a set of traditions and customs, as illustrated in the way Elia Levita justifies the lack of hospitality of Venetian Jews in a satirical prologue (Canto 7) of *Paris un Wiene*: 'Werś aso sò tragtś ir śeder' [If things be so, this is the way their customs want it].[13]

An Ironic Voice Praising (or Satirizing?) Contemporary Ashkenazi Women and Biblical Heroines

One of the intentions of the poem we are studying is to offer a vivid description of the lives and customs of Ashkenazi women in Italy at the beginning of the sixteenth century. About a third of the poem, namely its not fully preserved beginning and end (1–205, 1082–1220),[14] offers collective or typical portraits of women in their ordinary, day-to-day activities and at important times of their life, such as childbirth and weddings. The first part focuses on the private sphere and the last on the public one. The central, longer part of the poem (206–1081) presents, in a quite haphazard order, a series of biblical (and para-biblical) figures such as Jochebed, Miriam, Tamar, Ruth, Deborah, Judith, and Esther. Unifying the different parts of the work — the ones dedicated to contemporary women and the one dealing with female biblical heroes — the voice of the mischievous poet-narrator is omnipresent and plays with the expectations of the reader or listener.

As a whole, the poem is unusually complex for Old Yiddish poetry: it is built like a triptych whose central panel depicts scenes from the Bible, while the lateral panels portray the artist's contemporaries (thus comparable to many paintings of the same age). The pictorial analogy might also help us understand the nature of this puzzling work: the poem is characterized by its comic features, which are sharper in the parts relating to the life of contemporary women but remain very much present in the treatment of biblical figures. Such a phenomenon can be observed, for example, in the paintings of Brueghel the Elder, where biblical figures do not radically differ from Flemish peasants. In our poem, the carnivalesque spirit, in its Bakhtinian sense, dominates.[15]

I shall quote a fragment, dealing with childcare, to illustrate the tonality of the poem:

> Eś wer nit wundér vor löut si sòltén sich selwért schechtén
> Asò vil habén si mit den kindérn an vechtung.
> Si kònén nit mit ru' eśén ain biśén
> Iśt dàś bèseicht òdér bèschiśén.
> [...]
> Izundér krazt eś den grint,
> Den vaint eś wen eś sich schint,
> Den wil eś habén di hend
> Di mu' hòt kain end.
> [...]

> Sȯltén si nun dȧś alś gėdenkén,
> Ė si manén nemén si sȯltén sich ė dér-trinkén
> Un sȯltén sich ė ligén zu ainém durch štekén
> Ė si zu ainém man sȯlt schmekén.

[It would be no wonder if they cut their own throats — such trials they have with their children. They cannot eat one bite in peace: the child has peed or pooed. [...] Now it is scratching a scab. Then it cries when the skin peels off. Now it wants to have her hands. [...] If they remembered all this, they would rather drown themselves rather than taking husbands; they would rather lie with a dried-out stick than ever taste a man.][16]

Reading such an excerpt, which combines realism with blatant humour, one immediately understands why it is problematic to designate such a poem as hagiographic or didactic. The author constantly evokes the carnal, material sphere. He uses all the techniques of caricature: accumulation, exaggeration, and unexpected associations. His taste for detailed description, for the evocation of everyday life, decidedly marks his comic orientation.[17]

Theses verses are representative of the whole work, and it would probably never have been defined as hagiographic were it not for the playfulness of the poet, who mischievously sends contradictory signals to his reader. His complex use of irony blurs the ultimate goal of the poem: if his declared intention, repeated over and again, is to praise women, his tongue-in-cheek attitude makes the reader wonder repeatedly whether his real aim is not actually to satirize them. A series of stereotypical female failings, always denounced in the misogynous medieval tradition, are thus caricatured at specific points of the poem without ever being explicitly presented as sins: greed, extravagance, coquetry, vanity, and concupiscence. But at other moments, sometimes very close to the previous ones, real qualities are brought out: dedication to children and to communal life, and courage against adversity. The ambiguity is not only conveyed through the juxtaposition of failings and positive qualities: it is sometimes difficult to decide whether the poet deems a specific feature positive or negative. Women's overwhelming sexual desire, once more a traditional misogynous cliché, is frequently alluded to (with a touch of ribaldry), and especially so in the section dealing with biblical women. But this trait is clearly presented as a virtue in accordance with the commandment 'grow and multiply' that makes possible the survival of the Jewish people.[18] Where does irony begin and where does it stop?

It is not easy to tell. A few verses after the excerpt I have just quoted, we read:

> Ich zėl al undzérė nošim
> Wol as di lebéndigén kédošim
> Si habén in disér welt wol as vil in paz
> Si šterbén al tag nöun mȯl as ain kaz.

[I count all our womenfolk as living martyrs. In this world they have so many troubles: they die nine times every day, like a cat.][19]

Despite the solemnity of the expression 'living martyrs', the subsequent comparison with cats makes us brutally fall from the realm of sanctity to that of folklore and superstition. This kind of palinode regularly surprises the reader, as in the conclusion of an earlier section about labour pains:

> Hetén si nun nit andér zóròss wen di bèsundér
> So wer eś doch kain w'undér
> Daś si asò lebéndik in gàn edén kemén doch
> As ain ku in ain möus loch.

[If they had no other troubles but these in particular, it would still be no wonder if they entered alive into Paradise, like a cow into a mouse hole.][20]

As I have already mentioned, this kind of ambiguity concerns not only the lateral panels of our triptych, the ones depicting contemporary women and supposedly singing their praise, but also the central panel, which deals with biblical stories. It has an epic flavour since it insists on the victories of the Jews against their enemies and on the central role women played at certain crucial moments in Jewish history. The merits of the women vary in their nature: they ensure the birth of prophets and kings (Moses from Jochebed, David from Ruth); they fight for virtue and righteousness, even showing the men how they should behave (the Sin of the Golden Calf, Bathsheba and Solomon); they fight and defeat the enemies of Israel (Jael, Judith, Esther). Overall, they appear as essential actors in the whole epic of Israel's survival. Their exploits are sometimes moral and sometimes physical, but, more than anything else, they can rely on ruses to overcome men. Our poet remains generally faithful to the biblical stories, of course enriched with Midrashic content, but his tone is always light-hearted, playful, and familiar.[21]

When Tamar, disguised as a harlot, leads Judah to have intercourse, the whole scene is presented in the form of a lively negotiation in which the sly woman knows how to defend her interests. Judah has promised to give her a kid as a reward:

> Si sagt ich bin eś wol kòntent,
> Gib mir ain màškòn biz man mir dàś kizlén sent,
> Wen ich tanz nit sólchè tenz
> Öuf bòrg un öuf grèdenz.

[She told him, 'I am well content with that; give me a pledge until the kid has been sent to me, because I do not dance this kind of dance on loan or on credit'.][22]

And, when the deal is made, the poet makes a playful and quite sceptical allusion to the Midrashic story according to which Tamar and Judah have actually married before going to bed:[23] 'Ich waiś nit wi' man zu der broche rif | Tantò dàś thàmàr der bòuch öuf-lif' [I do not know how the wedding was proclaimed, but Tamar's belly swelled!].[24]

The few quotations I have presented illustrate the poetic quality of the language used in Šeder nošim. It is with an exceptional freedom that the poet uses the different registers and the different components of his Italian Old Yiddish. Mixed and rich rhymes — *in paz* (compare It. *impaccio*) and *kaz*, or *tenz* and *grèdenz* (compare It. *credenza*) — and the use of idiomatic phrases, proverbs, concision, and pointed witticisms: the quality and the originality of the writing prove that the poet, whoever he might have been,[25] had at his disposal a sufficiently developed literary tradition to which he could refer and with which the original addressees of his work were, at least in part, familiar. If we want to understand the meaning of a literary creation that employs such complex discursive and poetic strategies, we need to understand what might have been the original conditions of its reception, first of all by situating it within the landscape of literary production in Old Yiddish.

An Unusually Sophisticated Poetic Construction and Tonality

Ŝeder nošim is a unique combination of two genres that are usually separated in the tradition: (1) the genre of Midrashic epics (such as the famous Šému'el-buch and the Melochim buch),[26] which retell the stories of whole books or episodes from the Bible, integrating material from the Midrash, in a familiar, idiomatic language influenced by the tradition of Christian, mostly German, chivalric romance; and (2) the genre of satire in general, and all the genres using some techniques typical of satire that combine realistic description with comic exaggeration (the early *purim špilén* and the secular tales, such as those collected in the *Kü' buch*).

In both respects, the poet has distanced himself from the features we observe in all the other works which have survived. Contrary to all the Midrashic epics we know, Ŝeder nošim does not follow one single biblical source. Instead, it combines different figures and episodes in a series of juxtaposed portraits.[27] Our poet offers, in the biblical part of his work, a catalogue of remarkable heroines, following a model unknown to traditional Jewish writing but concurrently popular in Italian literature, at least since the composition by Boccaccio of his famous defence of women, *De claris mulieribus* (1361–62). The biblical and Midrashic stories are treated no more for their own sake but instead as *exempla* brought to illustrate the issue at stake, namely: do women deserve praise?

Ŝeder nošim retains some lexical and stylistic features from the traditional Midrashic epics. The biblical figures are depicted as knights and counts, the women are ladies. Most importantly, the glorification of women aims at illustrating their role in the preservation of the Jewish people. But, at the same time, the juxtaposition of the different heroines does not really obey any chronological or thematic logic, and the constant humour deflects the tone of the moments of epic pathos. Thus, when Jochebed is praised for having brought Moses into the world, a long and traditional enumeration of the merits of the prophet is presented. But the final casual comment returns, quite nonchalantly, to the real object of the section — the fact that Jochebed convinced Amram to have sex and thus made possible the birth of Moses:

> Er bracht unś di hailik tòro v̄un dem himél her àb
> Un' bat gòt daś er unś den màn gab
> Er špaist unś wachtilén un' macht unś ain-brunén
> Mir hatén gluk wàś mir bei' im bėgónén
> Er štund unś bei' in al unzérém nót
> Ŝiḥòn un' 'òg schlug er öuch zu tòt
> Er wer bòz dò hintén blibén.

[He brought the holy Torah down to us from heaven, and prayed to God so that He gave us the manna. He fed us quails and made a well for us. We were lucky in whatever we began with Moses. He stood by us in all our hardship. He also struck Sihon and Og dead. It would have been bad if he had stayed behind!][28]

The tongue-in-cheek attitude of the poetic voice, the (quite sophisticated) familiarity of his language, never allows the reader to take admiration, or any other emotion, too seriously.

The passages on contemporary women are also different from the satires or tales we know. The poetic work does not seem to be linked to any specific occasion (the celebration of Purim or of a wedding),[29] it does not parody a liturgical text like most of the first *purim špilén*,[30] and it does not borrow from existing collections of tales like the *Kü' buch* did. This increases the immediacy of the descriptions put forward by the poet, who seems to have had one main interest: to portray the women, at the beginning of the poem, as he knew them in their domestic life and then, at the end of the poem, at social occasions — festivities, weddings, funerals, and circumcisions. His descriptions are particularly lively. Sometimes they rely on exaggeration and caricature, as when the women are depicted coming to *shul* for Shabbats with a thick layer of make-up compared to *kharoyses*,[31] or when they are presented trembling for the child on the eve of the ritual of his circumcision (a night traditionally called *di weiś*). On the latter, the poet comments jokingly: 'Si habén ouf irém herzén ain gróś laidén | Si v̄urchtén man mócht kind zu v̄il ab-schnaidén' [They have one great anxiety in their hearts: they fear that the child may get too much cut off].[32]

On the whole, however, the descriptions, humorous as they may be, are devoid of the sharp criticism we ordinarily meet in satire. It seems, at times, that the main objective of the poet is to give a sympathetic description of the women's lives and customs with the careful eye of a folklorist *avant la lettre* — as, for example, when he describes in detail all the customs of weddings, from the braiding of the bride's hair (*vlechtén*) through the main feast (*di mai*) to the merry procession accompanying the newly wed couple to their room (*rumplén*).

Hatred of or Support for Women?

When a poet uses such complex rhetorical strategies, how can we really fathom his intentions? Can we ultimately determine what vision of women this work conveys? In order to answer these questions, we need to take into consideration a poetic tradition that had its heyday in the Renaissance, especially in Italy. It is usually referred to by its French name: the *querelle des femmes* (dispute over women's nature). We need to answer the following question: what motivated our poet to write a praise of women (even if this praise sometimes turns to satire)? The only reasonable answer is that he was aware of the existence of this literary debate, which was well known to Italian Jews at that time. Its influence is reflected in a series of Hebrew poems written among the Italian intellectual elite by poets such as Abraham da Sarteano, Elia da Genazzano, or Yehuda Sommo.[33] These poems

Fig. 1.1. *Book of Customs (Sefer Minhagim)* (Venice, Giovanni di Gara: 1600). The Bodleian Libraries, The University of Oxford, Opp. 4° 1004, fol. 39v. Kindling Sabbath Candles

constituted a protracted debate between poets, involving probably a dozen writers over several decades. The poems follow the same rhythmic and metric patterns (changing through time) and refer to one another, with a 'misogynist' inciting the defenders of women to respond. Most of those poems rely on the rhetorical device of the *exempla*, delivering catalogues of famous women taken both from the Bible and from Greek and Latin mythologies and literatures. Invective and humour are common ingredients of the genre. Our Yiddish work was obviously not addressed at such an educated and privileged elite and therefore does not integrate, as the Hebrew poems do, foreign figures such as Dido or Semiramis. But it clearly assumes the form of a praise of women, albeit mischievous and quite ambiguous.

Did such a debate penetrate Old Yiddish literature in Italy? Probably not in a comparable form. We do not have any other work than *Šeder nošim* that exclusively addresses the question, and it is impossible to say, from this single poem, whether the author was engaged in a debate with other poets. Traditional medieval misogyny is very much present in Old Yiddish literature. We hear its echoes, for example, in stories from the *Kü' buch* dealing with marital infidelity, in the retelling of the story about the widow of Ephesus, or in the depiction of an unfaithful wife adapted from the *Mashal hakadmoni*.[34] This early misogyny was also noticed by Israel Zinberg, in relation to the somewhat later *Zucht-špigél*, but it still deserves to be fully investigated.[35] The work under consideration here does not represent this early, unambiguous, stereotyped misogyny. It sometimes relies on it, for example when it alludes to women's coquetry or concupiscence, but it always modifies the reader's perception of those allusions through the general framework of praise and pity for the women's miseries. Is the author serious when he deplores the lack of education of the women who do not even know the dates of the special Shabbats (so that they cannot show their most splendid garments!)?[36] The allusion to women's extravagance belongs to traditional misogyny, but the way the poet laments women's ignorance blurs the message.

Only one other known work of Old Yiddish literature plays the same kind of ingenious game: Elia Levita's *Paris un Wiene*. In the prologue of Canto 4 (strophes 168–84), one character, Odoardo, delivers a long monologue denouncing women's sins, vanity, and cruelty, and dwells at some length on women's coquetry, depicting the whole arsenal of women's cosmetics. The poet has mischievously noted, at the beginning of this long speech, that the words that follow are not his, but the character's. At the end of this indictment, he criticizes Odoardo:

> Ich sag öuch wol: er hàt nit recht,
> Dàś er rėdėt aso herb un' herbér.
> Sein der bösén v̄ünf, sekś, sibén, echt,
> Di' selbén štròf er un' v̄ér-derb er!
> Er sein dàrgėgén hundért lecht
> Di do sein gėtröu' un' vrum un' erbér.
> Ich sag wol 'lecht' un' wilś nit bėzöugén;
> Wen sagėt ichś gėwiś, so möcht ich löugén.

[Indeed, I tell you that he is not right to speak so harshly and even more so: if there are five, six, seven, or eight of the wicked ones, let him reprimand and condemn them, but there are on the other hand perhaps a hundred who are true, honest, and honorable. Indeed, I say 'perhaps' and do not wish to provide evidence, for if I were to say it for certain, I might be wrong.][37]

Here again, we are confronted with a defender of women that might be worse than an accuser. If it is hard to grasp the sources of inspiration for *Šeder nošim*, because we know so little about its context of composition, the situation is different for *Paris un Wiene*. This long secular epic, adapted from an Italian poem, lies under the direct influence of Ariosto and emulates its great model when it comes to dealing with the *querelle des femmes* (one of the strophes of the above-mentioned prologue was directly and masterly translated from *Orlando Furioso*). The way Ariosto deals with this already old debate, pretending to be a servant of the fair ladies, while actually resorting to an elaborate and comic misogynist discourse, resembles what we observe in *Paris un Wiene* and, in a different way, in *Šeder nošim*.[38]

As a consequence, even if we cannot say that the *querelle des femmes* actually entered Old Yiddish literature, as it did Hebrew literature in Italy, it clearly impregnated (at least) these two Yiddish works in a very sophisticated way. For *Šeder nošim*, the rhetorical use of the catalogue of famous women (compare *De claris mulieribus*), which is the main technical device used in the works associated with the *querelle* at the time (in Italian, in Hebrew, and in other languages), and which is generally foreign to Jewish literature, strongly suggests direct inspiration from Italian literature (perhaps through Hebrew). But our poet is not a simple follower.

His work is more original than most of the Hebrew poems involved in the *querelle*. He reinterprets the genre with a lot of freedom for the popular audience of the Jewish Ashkenazi population of northern Italy. At the end of the day, it is hard to answer plainly the question of whether the poet of Šeder nošim is a hater or a supporter of women. If satire and mockery are obvious all through the poem, praise does not disappear; and women are given a central role in Jewish history through the genealogy of biblical heroines. Moreover, the lively portraits of the poet's contemporaries are imbued with genuine tenderness and with a rare and precious attention for women's everyday lives and worries.

Gender studies have recently devoted great efforts to analysing and understanding the meaning of such a dispute and have argued that, behind the rhetorical games, it implied a great deal of seriousness.[39] We still need a comprehensive study of the echoes of the *querelle des femmes* in Jewish literature, which could enable us to better assess the role played by rhetorical conventions in the works that reflect it. This is all the more important given that the *querelle* originates very early among Jews, with Judah ibn Shabbetai and the beginning of the thirteenth century, if not before. For now, it is clear that this debate inspired some of the most interesting and enjoyable works of the period, in Hebrew and — as Šeder nošim eloquently demonstrates — also in Yiddish.

Notes to Chapter 1

1. In order to grasp the regularity of patterns and forms in Old Yiddish literature, it is sufficient to look at the tables of contents of the classic histories of the interwar period: Max Erik, *Geshikhte fun der yidisher literatur fun di elteste tsaytn biz der haskole-tkufe* (Warsaw: Kultur Lige, 1928); Max Weinreich, *Bilder fun der yidisher literaturgeshikhte* (Vilna: Tomor, 1928); Israel Zinberg, *Di geshikhte fun der literatur bay yidn*, 8 vols (Vilna: Tomor, 1929–37), VI (1935): *Alt-yidishe literatur*. See also the more recent overview in Jean Baumgarten, *Introduction to Old Yiddish Literature*, trans. by Jerold C. Frakes (Oxford: Oxford University Press, 2005).
2. The first engagement with the question of the traditional relationship of Old Yiddish works to women is the well-known essay by Shmuel Niger, *Di yidishe literatur un di lezerin* (Vilna: Vilner farlag, 1919). It is marked by the incipient state of research on the subject and reflects a perception relevant to the nineteenth century and the beginning of the twentieth century. For a better-informed evaluation of the role of women in Old Yiddish literature, see Chava Turniansky, 'Meydelekh in der alt-yidisher literatur', in *Jiddische Philologie: Festschrift für Erika Timm*, ed. by Simon Neuberg and Walter Roll (Tübingen: Niemeyer, 1999), pp. 7–20*; Chava Turniansky, 'Old Yiddish Language and Literature', in *Jewish Women: A Comprehensive Historical Encyclopedia* <https://jwa.org/encyclopedia/article/old-yiddish-language-and-literature> [accessed 3 November 2017]. Turniansky, in her rich contributions, does not deal with the question of the literary construction of women's figures in fiction and poetry; this lies at the core of the present article.
3. The last text in the whole manuscript is dated 1504 and was written in Mestre, but watermarks point instead to a larger span of time for the composition of the manuscript, which was certainly written in northern Italy in the first half of the sixteenth century; see Harry Fox, 'Introductory Essays', in *'Many Pious Women': Edition and Translation*, ed. and trans. by Harry Fox and Justin Jaron Lewis (Berlin and New York: De Gruyter, 2011), pp. 1–126 (pp. 12–15).
4. The manuscript in question is kept at Cambridge University Library (Or. Add. 547). It is described in Weinreich, pp. 145–48.
5. See Nokhem Shtif, 'A geshribene yidishe bibliotek in a yidish hoyz in Venetsye in mitn dem

zekhtsentn yorhundert', *Tsaytshrift*, 2–3 (1928), 141–58. Shtif deals with a particularly rich manuscript kept at Oxford (Cod. Neubauer 1217, Can. Or. 12).
6. Even though he perceived the originality of the latter text; Weinreich, pp. 146–47, quotes whole fragments of it as if they actually belonged to the traditional ethical guide for women (quotations which, as we shall see, could not possibly have belonged to an ethical religious treatise). The distinction between the two works has been made harder by missing folios (45–52, 82) that correspond precisely with the beginning and the end of our poem.
7. This genre of how-to books for women has been studied by Agnes Romer-Segal, 'Yiddish Works on Women's Commandments in the 16th Century', in *Studies in Yiddish Literature and Folklore* (Jerusalem: Hebrew University, 1986), pp. 37–59. See also Edward Fram, *My Dear Daughter: Rabbi Benjamin Slonik and the Education of Jewish Women in Sixteenth-Century Poland* (Cincinnati: Hebrew Union College Press, 2007).
8. This page can be seen in *Yiddish in Italia*, ed. by Erika Timm and Chava Turniansky in collaboration with Claudia Rosenzweig (Milan: Associazione Italiana Amici dell'Università di Gerusalemme, 2003), p. 62. An excerpt of the first part of the manuscript (the actual women's guide) is printed in *Early Yiddish Texts 1100–1750*, ed. by Jerold C. Frakes (Oxford: Oxford University Press, 2004), pp. 115–19.
9. This question is fully discussed in the fifth chapter of my monograph on Elia Levita's Yiddish oeuvre: Arnaud Bikard, *La Renaissance dans les rues du ghetto: L'Œuvre poétique yiddish d'Élia Lévita (1469–1549)* (Turnhout: Brepols, forthcoming).
10. Chava Turniansky, 'Review of Harry Fox and Justin Jaron Lewis, eds. *Many Pious Women: Edition and Translation*', *Renaissance Quarterly*, 65 (2012), 1273–74. I do, in part, agree with Turniansky's criticism, but was surprised by the fact that, bothered as she was by the shortcomings of the book, she did not underline the exceptional quality of the work itself and did not try to position it within the landscape of Old Yiddish literature.
11. One reads, for instance, on the back cover of Fox and Lewis: 'this hagiographic work on the lives of biblical women'.
12. The confusion of the title with that of the preceding work is not embarrassing in a broader context because the term *Šeder nošim* is generic, like *Mitsvass nošim* or *Vrou'enbüchlein*, for designating the traditional Old Yiddish guides for women. I thus use this title in a different, somewhat ironic way to name the highly individual poem under study.
13. *Paris un Wiene*, p. 109 (my translation).
14. I segment the text here on the basis of the Fox–Lewis edition using line numbers (which the edition does not, however, itself include). One should not forget that some parts are missing and that the numbers do not adequately reflect the poem as it was originally composed.
15. Mikhail Bakhtin, *Rabelais and his World*, trans. by Helene Islowsky (Bloomington: Indiana University Press, 1984).
16. *Many Pious Women*, pp. 172–74. Unless otherwise indicated, the translations of this work are those by Justin Jaron Lewis in the edition quoted.
17. The description of everyday life as comic is a well-known convention of medieval literature which persists in the Renaissance. One can compare this passage with the very similar one (in terms of content) in Teofilo Folengo's macaronic epic *Baldus*, ed. by Emilio Faccioli (Turin: Einaudi, 1989), VI. 510–16, where a mother describes her predicament: 'In this way, I need to deal with everything at the same time | As soon as the pan boils I take it from the brands | Meanwhile I am mixing porridge for the pig | I calm the baby with milk, I clean the diapers | From their shit, I quiet the older kid with bread, | Suddenly I shout "pit, pit" | And the hens run to peck their usual seeds.'
18. Harry Fox rightly speaks of 'redemption through sex' ('Introductory Essays', p. 51).
19. *Many Pious Women*, p. 174.
20. *Many Pious Women*, pp. 166–67.
21. The Midrashic elements brought by our poet are well known and did not require an unusual amount of erudition. Many of them are present in Rashi's commentary. The various sources are presented well in the notes to the Fox–Lewis edition.
22. *Many Pious Women*, pp. 184–85.

23. This interpretation is notably given in the later *Ze'enah u-Re'enah: Part 1*, ed. and trans. by Morris M. Faierstein (Berlin: De Gruyter, 2017), p. 285.
24. *Many Pious Women*, p. 184 (my translation).
25. I will not dwell on the question of attribution here. I would like merely to say that Elia Levita is the only poet in Old Yiddish literature who used such a broad range of poetic techniques with such mastery. The elaboration of rhymes is a good example; the revolution introduced by Levita in this field has been clearly demonstrated by Benjamin Hrushovski, 'The Creation of Accentual Iambs in European Poetry and their First Employment in a Yiddish Romance in Italy (1508–09)', in *For Max Weinreich on his Seventieth Birthday*, ed. by Lucy S. Dawidowicz (The Hague: Mouton, 1964), pp. 108–46.
26. The great Old Yiddish epics, such as the *Šému'el-buch* or the *Melochim buch*, have distinct comic episodes, but the general tone is serious. It would be interesting to study the representation of women figures in these epics. Some clearly reflect misogynous perceptions; cf., for example, the vivid dialogue, full of insults, between the women in the episode of the Judgement of Solomon, in *Das Altjiddische Epos Melokim-Bukh*, ed. by Leo Fuks, 2 vols (Assen, Van Gorcum, 1965), I, strophes 200–04.
27. All the other Midrashic epics systematically follow the biblical source they adapt (and some associated Midrashim). The versification, the tonality, and the number of Midrashim involved can vary, but the writing principle is always the same: following faithfully one sacred source. For a useful summary of the development of the genre, see Chone Shmeruk, *Prokim fun der yidisher literatur-geshikhte* (Tel Aviv: Peretz; Jerusalem: Hebrew University, 1988), pp. 179–99.
28. *Many Pious Women*, pp. 182–83.
29. Whereas the rhymed adaptations of the stories of Judith and Esther, composed a little later by Gumprecht von Szczebrzeszyn, were clearly associated with the celebration of Hanukkah and Purim respectively, both stories are, in *Šeder nošim*, presented in an enumeration and have a rhetorical function, not a social, paraliturgical one. Edition: Moritz Stern, *Lieder des venezianischen Lehrers Gumprecht von Szczebrszyn (um 1555)*, ed. by Moritz Stern (Berlin: Hausfreund, 1922). The kale-lider (wedding songs) of the sixteenth century often describe some of the traditions linked to marriage (cf., for example, *Early Yiddish Texts*, pp. 385–93). Our poet does this in passing, before evoking the traditions of circumcision, funerals, and so on.
30. Evi Butzer, *Die Anfänge der jiddischen 'purim shpiln' in ihrem literarischen und kulturgeschichtlichen Kontext* (Hamburg: Buske, 2003).
31. A traditional paste made of a mixture of fruit and nuts eaten at the Passover dinner and symbolizing the mortar used by the Jewish slaves in Egypt. Cf. *Many Pious Women*, p. 228.
32. *Many Pious Women*, pp. 236–37.
33. Dan Pagis, 'Ha-pulmus ha-shiri 'al tiv ha-nashim bevoah be-tmuroth be-shirah ha-'ivrit be-Italiah', *Jerusalem Studies in Hebrew Literature*, 9 (1986), 259–300.
34. *The 'Book of Cows': A Facsimile Edition of the Famed 'Kuhbuch', Verona 1595*, ed. by Moshe N. Rosenfeld (London: Hebraica, 1984), pp. 51–53, 95–109.
35. Zinberg, VI, 302–04.
36. *Many Pious Women*, pp. 228–30.
37. *Paris un Wiene*, p. 67. The translation is taken from *Early Yiddish Epic*, ed. and trans. by Jerold C. Frakes (Syracuse: Syracuse University Press, 2014), p. 343.
38. Nicolas Ivanov, 'Le Roland Furieux et la querelle des femmes au XVIe siècle', *Revue du seizième siècle*, 19 (1932–33), 262–72.
39. See, for example, in France, the work of the SIEFAR (Société Internationale pour l'Étude des Femmes de l'Ancien Régime), <http://www.siefar.org/> [accessed 6 November 2017].

CHAPTER 2

The Marxist Theory of Primeval Matriarchy in Yiddish Intellectual Discourse: Gender between Anti-Religious Radicalism, Orthodox Judaism, and a New Metaphysics of *Yidishkayt*

Roland Gruschka

In early twentieth century, the canonical Marxist theory on the origin of family and matrimony, which had been created by Friedrich Engels (1820–95) and August Bebel (1840–1913), and which was propagated and vulgarized by anti-religious radicals such as Benjamin Feigenbaum (Binyomin Faygenboym, 1860–1923) and Philip Krantz (Yankev Rombro, 1858–1922), gave new impulses to the discourse on women's rights in the Yiddish-speaking world and confronted Jewish intellectuals with gender-related issues.

As is well known, canonical Marxism embraced the thesis of prehistorical or ancient clan matriarchy as a necessary stage in human development. With all its novelty, this bold theory provoked varied and multifaceted responses among Jewish intellectuals, and became an impulse for rethinking the conditions of Jewish life and even for reconceptualizing Jewishness. This chapter will focus on three of these endeavours: on the educational leftist activism of Benjamin Feigenbaum and Philip Krantz; on Abba (or Abe) Gordin's (1887–1964) anarchistic philosophy of *Yidishkayt*, which employs gender aspects as categories of a highly speculative metaphysics; and on the apologetic *oeuvre* of the Orthodox rabbi Nachman (Nakhmen) Shemen (1912–93). First, however, some brief remarks about the Marxist theory of primeval or ancient matriarchy (and its ideological predecessors) are necessary.

The Marxist Theory of Primeval Matriarchy

For Marx and Engels, the 'first class-oppression [in history coincided] with that of the female sex by the male' in patriarchy.[1] According to Engels, before the establishment of private property and patriarchy, mankind was organized in matrilineal clans of kinship, in which much authority rested on the women (such a matrilineal formation with so-called *Mutterrecht*, 'mother-right', should not be confused with 'women's rule' in the naive-Romantic sense). Based on such diverse sources as the works of the Swiss conservative historian Johann Jacob Bachofen (1815–87; *Das Mutterrecht*, 1861) and of the American anthropologist Lewis H. Morgan (1818–81; *Ancient Society*, 1877), Engels developed a complex theory of the gradual progression of mankind from initial, primitive-communist and matriarchal savagery via barbarism towards — patriarchal — civilization, which he outlined in his treatise *Der Ursprung der Familie, des Privateigentums und des Staats* [The Origin of the Family, Private Property and the State] (1884; rev. and expanded edn 1892).[2] Later, the leader of the German Social Democratic Party, August Bebel (1840–1913), integrated Engels's ideas and theories into the expanded version of his own comprehensive study of the situation of women in the past, present, and future, known today as *Die Frau und der Sozialismus* [Woman and Socialism] (1st edn 1879).[3]

Despite their materialist outlook, neither Engels's nor, all the more so, Bebel's depictions of matrilineal societies are entirely free of romanticizing overtones.[4] It has been argued that this romanticist trait facilitated the reception of their studies, as well as Morgan's and Bachofen's, in Germany in such a way that in liberal middle-class circles the theory of ancient matriarchy became a controversial issue associated with various, not necessarily leftist, forms of utopianism.[5] In the US, however, the discussion of these theories seems to have extended beyond a small circle of academic specialists only after the turn of the century. In fact, English-speaking readers and intellectuals for a long time seem to have preferred to engage in a discussion solely of Morgan's and Bachofen's theses and those of their academic critics — often without even mentioning the Marxist school of thought.[6]

The subsequent career of the Marxist theory of ancient matriarchy in academia proper is beyond the scope of my study. Small wonder, however, that Morgan read through the eyes of Engels became, in Andrei A. Znamenski's words, an intellectual 'household god' of Soviet ethnography — highly revered, but over the years tacitly revised.[7] In other countries, the response was more varied. Leading anthropologists in the US and Britain (for instance, Bronisław Malinowski) arrived at an outward rejection of Morgan's evolutionist model, but were ultimately unable to replace it with a compelling theoretical scheme covering the entire multitude of family systems and kinship rules found among 'savage' peoples.[8] Critical modifications and revisions of Engels's theory from within the Marxist school, such as those voiced by the German Social Democratic theoretician and ethnographer Heinrich Cunow (1862–1936), an academic outsider, found much acclaim in Left intellectual circles at the beginning of the century, but in the end fell into oblivion.[9]

The American-Yiddish Reception of Morgan's, Engels's, and Bebel's Writings on Matriarchy

Yiddish intellectuals of the socialist and anarchist camps closely followed the Marxist discourse on primeval matriarchy and the evolution of human society. In part, their reception of Engels's and Morgan's theories was affected by the specific situation in their countries of residence, which made study material in certain

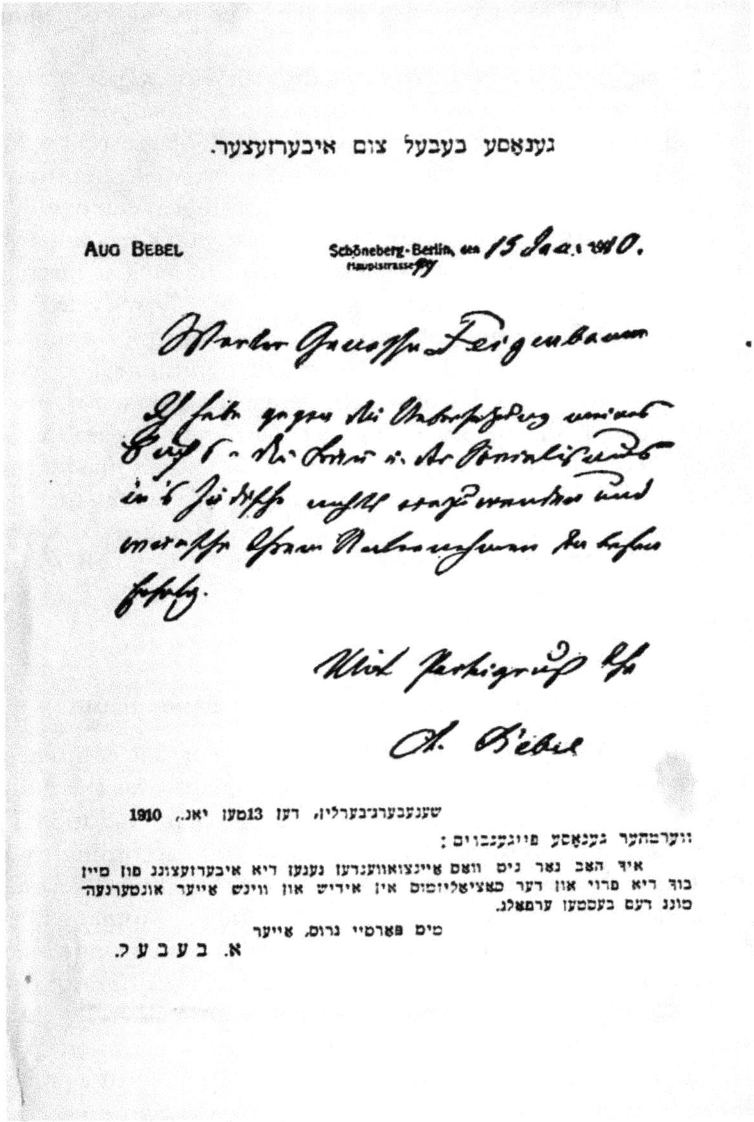

גענאָסע בעבעל צום איבערזעצער.

AUG BEBEL

Schöneberg-Berlin, den 15 Jan. 1910.
Hauptstrasse 97

Werter Genosse Feigenbaum

Ich habe gegen die Übersetzung meines Buchs „Die Frau u. der Sozialismus" ins Jüdische nichts einzuwenden und wünsche Ihrem Unternehmen den besten Erfolg.

Mit Parteigruß Ihr

A. Bebel

שענעבערג־בערלין, דען 13טען יאנ., 1910

ווערטהער גענאָסע פייגענבוים:

איך האב גאר ניט וואס איינצואווענדען געגען דיא איבערזעצונג פון מיין בוך דיא פרוי און דער סאציאליזמוס אין אידיש און ווינש אייער אונטערנעהמונג דעם בעסטען ערפאלג.

מיט פארטיי גרוס, אייער

א. בעבעל.

FIG. 2.1. August Bebel's letter to Benjamin Feigenbaum:
Schöneberg-Berlin, den 15. Jan. 1910,
Werter Genosse Feigenbaum,
Ich habe gegen die Übersetzung meines Buchs „Die Frau und der Sozialismus" ins Jüdische nichts einzuwenden und wünsche Ihrem Unternehmen den besten Erfolg. Mit Parteigruß, Ihr A. Bebel
[Dear Comrade Feigenbaum: I have no objections to the translation of my book 'Woman and Socialism' into Yiddish and wish you the best success in your endeavour. With Party-greetings Yours, A. Bebel]

periods difficult to obtain to varying degrees, and of course also depended on their individual levels of education.[10]

In 1900–1903, however, the New York Yiddish socialist writer and theoretician Philip Krantz published his ambitious materialist study *Di kulturgeshikhte: Der mentsh un zayn arbet* [Cultural History: Man and his Labour].[11] The second volume of this work dealt with the origin of human society and more or less entirely relied on Engels's and Bebel's theoretical outline, which Krantz supplemented with excursions based on his autodidactic studies of anthropological literature and in which he presented the historical narrative of the development of ancient matriarchy as an already well-established scientific fact.[12] Krantz obviously regarded the Marxist theory of matriarchy and the origin of family as a useful historical counter-narrative that could effectively challenge Jewish religious traditions, and consequently employed it in analyses of episodes of the Bible that he included in his work.[13] In the years that followed, the theory of ancient matriarchy became established in the Yiddish intellectual discourse of the political Left, and also had a certain place in the repertoire of Yiddish educational and propaganda works that popularized socialist ideas, in particular in brochures and articles that addressed women's rights and women's issues.[14] (Noteworthy, however, is the fact that not all Yiddish authors writing on the women's question included explicit references to Engels and Bebel in their publications.)[15]

At the Threshold of Gender Awareness: Benjamin Feigenbaum

A major figure in the American-Yiddish labour movement who combined advocacy for the women's cause with an outspoken militant atheism was the radical activist Benjamin Feigenbaum.[16] In 1904, Feigenbaum authored an educational pamphlet, *Libe un familyen-leben loyt idishkayt* [Love and Family Life according to *Yidishkayt*], disputing the reasonableness and consistency of both Halakhic law and Christian morals concerning marriage.[17] As his biographical sketch of Morgan's life and works in the Yiddish socialist educational journal *Di tsukunft* demonstrates, Feigenbaum had already acquainted himself with Engels's treatise on the origin of family in the 1890s.[18]

When, two decades later, Jewish cultural organizations intensified their activities to produce genuine, high-quality Yiddish translations of socialist political theory for study,[19] Feigenbaum translated (or rather, adapted) the two canonical works of Marxism as *Di froy un der sotsializmus* (1916), even authorized by Bebel himself,[20] and *Di familye amol un haynt* (1918).[21] Feigenbaum supplemented his Yiddish translations of Engels's and Bebel's works with broad introductions and annotations dealing with the specific situation among Jews, and in extensive footnotes illustrated the theory with examples taken from the Hebrew Bible. As an appendix to his translation of Engels's *The Origin of Family*, Feigenbaum included a critical account of the theory in the light of Heinrich Cunow's more recent anthropological studies.[22]

In passing, Feigenbaum, Krantz, and other Yiddish intellectuals writing about women's rights touched upon a number of subjects and problems that, generations later, became the intellectual starting points of modern gender theory, such as, for instance, the phenomenon of language representing gender hierarchies. This is not to say that the Yiddish socialists and anarchists had elaborated a full-fledged gender theory *avant la lettre*. However, what can be said is that, under the influence of Bebel's and Engels's writings, Feigenbaum, at least, developed a sort of raised awareness for the gender-related issues on which he reflected in his theories. One example must suffice here. In *Woman and Socialism*, August Bebel remarked:

> Wie in der französischen Sprache der Mensch und der Mann durch ein und dasselbe Wort, 'l'homme', bezeichnet werden, und ebenso in der englischen durch 'man', so kennt das französische Recht den Menschen nur als Mann, und ganz ähnlich war es bis vor wenigen Jahrzehnten in England, woselbst die Frau sich in sklavischer Abhängigkeit vom Manne befand.
>
> [In the French language, as in the English language, human being and the male are denoted by the same word, '*l'homme*' — man. In the same way, the French law only recognizes the man as a human being, and, until a few decades ago, this was true also of England, where women were maintained in abject dependence.][23]

Following Bebel's observation, Benjamin Feigenbaum discussed the various common Yiddish expressions used for women, and came to the conclusion that the vocabulary of the Yiddish language of his time defined women solely in terms of their relations to men.[24] For instance:

> [Af] yidish iz nor do: a meydl, a kale, a vayb (fun a man), a vaybl, a yidene, an almone, a grushe, an agune, an ishes-ish u.z.v. [...] a vort vos zol badaytn irgendvelkhe fun zey ale, nit batrakhtndik derbay vos zi iz far a man, iz alzo nito.
>
> [[In] Yiddish, there are only [expressions such as]: a[n unmarried] girl, a bride, a wife (of a husband), a young wife, a Jewess, a widow, a divorced woman, an abandoned woman, a housewife, etc. [...] A term denoting any of them regardless of what she is in relation to a man, thus does not exist.][25]

According to Feigenbaum, the term *froy*, the only word in Yiddish that could denote a female human being regardless of her age, marital status, or ethnic or religious affiliation (Jewish vs non-Jewish), was a recently borrowed loanword from German literary language, one whose introduction into Yiddish literary language had to be explained and justified to a self-educating lay readership. His thoughts and observations regarding the colloquialisms of Polish Jews compared to those of Litvaks (Jews from Lite)[26] give a glimpse of the cultural problems regarding gender roles and gender images with which Feigenbaum, as the translator of a key work of socialist propaganda into Yiddish, had to cope:

> Ba di poylishe yidn iz do a vort, vos men banutst af dem zelbn bagrif, vos 'froy' af daytsh, in algemeynem zin: dos iz — 'nekeyve'. Ba di litvakes iz dos ober a shendlekher vort. Un afile ba di poylishe yidn ken men dos vort nit gebroykhn, vayl dos iz shoyn vider tsu algemeyn, es drikt nemlekh oys ales vos iz a 'zi', say ba mentshn, say ba khayes. [...] Bay di mer veltlekhe poylishe yidn gebroykht men oykh af dizen bagrif dos vort 'froyentsimer'. Dos iz ober oykh ba di litvakes nit onshtendik. Gemore-lerners bahelfn zikh do mit a gemorevort; zey zogn 'an ishe'. Natirlekh ken men dos vort in folks-yidish oykh nit gebroykhn.[27]

[Among Polish Jews there is an expression used for the same concept denoted by *Frau* in German, with a general meaning: that is — *nekeyve*. For Litvaks, this is an abusive word. And even among Polish Jews, one cannot use this expression, because its meaning is, on the other hand, far too broad, for it denotes anything female [literally, 'anything that is a "she"'], among human beings as well as among animals. [...] Among the more secular Polish Jews, one also uses for this [general] concept the term *froyentsimer* [compare German *Frauenzimmer*]. However, for Litvaks this word likewise does not sound decent. Students of the Talmud [in this case] employ an expression taken from the Gemara; they say *an ishe*. Of course, one cannot use this expression in folksy Yiddish either [because of its possibly derogatory connotations].]

Accordingly, Feigenbaum chose *froy* and *vayblekh* as translation words, because there was no other genuine Yiddish equivalent for German *Frau*, 'woman', and *weiblich*, 'female'.

The educational activities of Feigenbaum, Krantz, and other anti-religious radicals were not without success. In the Yiddish Left, Bebel's and Engels's theories became the starting point for any new theory on women's issues. In the 1920s and 1930s, however, many secular Yiddish cultural activists outside the Moscow-oriented communist camp developed an increasingly positive, affirmative attitude towards Jewish tradition and *Yidishkayt*. The most original thinker in this respect, perhaps, was the libertarian 'inter-individualist' anarchist Abba Gordin, who in 1926 fled from Soviet Russia to the US, where he became one of the main contributors of the anarchist newspaper *Di fraye arbeter-shtime* [The Free Voice of Labour], and the founder and central figure of the utopianist Yidish-etishe gezelshaft (Jewish Ethical Society) in New York.[28]

Abba Gordin

In his three-volume magnum opus with the ambitious title *Di kritik fun reynem gloybn* [Critique of Pure Faith] (New York, 1937–39), Gordin attempted to integrate the Marxist narrative of ancient matriarchy and other gender-related topoi (such as gender hierarchies expressed in language) into his own speculative theory in order to surpass Marxism.[29] Gordin's theoretical approach may be characterized as a unique form of psychohistory in a leftist-anarchist key with some quite nationalist-biologist undertones.[30] In his narrative, that is to say, the progression of socio-economic formations follows more or less canonical historical materialism, whereas the cultural life of ethnic groups is strongly determined by their respective psychologies or, as one might rather say, *Volksgeist*. However, the decisive historical struggles, in Gordin's view, seem to take place within the minds of class-bound individuals, depending on their ability to proceed from collectivism via egoism towards a genuine inter-individualism.[31] In this context, religion (understood in a broad sense) becomes a determining factor of human destiny, not as a delusion or an 'opiate for the masses' that has to be abandoned on the path of human liberation, but as a possible cultural resource for the long-term development of a genuine humanist morals, ethics, and world order.

In Gordin's writings, a speculative counter-history of the Jewish People and its spirit unfolds, an attempt at unearthing (or inventing) hidden or lost traditions of Jewish thought and Jewish life, or at uncovering 'subconscious' traits in Jewish collective memory. Gordin makes the Jews the bearers and epitome of an idea of redemption that, not surprisingly, symbolically prefigures his own anarchist vision of a redemption of world, nature, and spirit altogether, a vision inspired by Charles Fourier's utopianism. Thus, he sees the Jewish People as both a social avant-garde and a messianic force in history.

With the entire project, Gordin conducted a struggle on two fronts: against the Jewish traditionalists and, all the more, against leftist radical critics of Judaism and anti-religious activists like Feigenbaum. Small wonder, then, that the Marxist theory of an ancient matriarchate was for him a pivotal element of history that had to be rewritten. Although references to socialist literature are surprisingly sparse in many of Gordin's writings and he rarely engages in detailed discussion of other authors, his narrative is obviously a reply to certain claims made by Feigenbaum or, respectively, by Bebel and Engels.³²

A few examples must suffice here. Feigenbaum had criticized Jewish tradition because it defined the status of women solely in relation to men. Abba Gordin turns this criticism upside down. In biblical Hebrew, he asserted, the word for 'woman', *ishah*, was not derived from *ish*, 'man' (as declared in Genesis 2. 23), but quite the opposite:

> ober es volt zikh beser shikn tsu zogn, az er heyst 'ish', vayl er shtamt op fun der 'ishe', un zi heyst 'ishe', vayl zi git akhtung afn fayer un tsulib dem, vos der man gehert tsu ir, 'isho' meynt i 'ir fayer', i 'ir man'.

> [however, it would be better to say that he is called *ish* because he descended from the *ishah*, and she is called *ishah* because she takes care of the fire and because the man belongs to her; *ishah* [written אשה *alef-shin-hey*, in defective spelling] means both 'her fire' and 'her man'.]³³

Gordin's arguments draw some inspiration from a highly selective and idiosyncratic reading of rabbinical and Kabbalist literature. As is well known, the substitution and reinterpretation of Hebrew letters is an essential element of both rabbinical hermeneutics and Kabbalist philosophy. However, even when quoting from these sources, Gordin employs the traditional texts in an associative manner via analogy as an illustration and legitimation for his own original, so to speak 'deconstructivist', plays on words. (Compare, for instance, Gordin's etymology of Hebrew *ish/ishah*, quoted above, with the well-known exegesis in Chapter 12 of *Pirke de-Rabbi Eliezer*.)³⁴

According to Engels (who agreed with Bachofen on this point), the prehistoric overturning of gender hierarchies was reflected in the mythologies of the ancient peoples, in particular in myths that emphasize the confrontation of the old and the new order, and, in part, legitimize the break between them.³⁵ Gordin agrees with these theories only insofar as ethnic groups other than the ancient Hebrews are concerned, and attempts to prove that the Jewish People was a unique historical exception. In Gordin's reading of the Bible, the biblical patriarchy draws its legitimation from prehistoric matriarchy, and this dependence is symbolically mirrored in the biblical episode in which God renamed Abraham the Patriarch (cf. Genesis 17. 5).

> Un der umshtand fun opshvakhn di rigoritetn fun mantsbil-hershaft vert ongedayt durkh dos simbolish aranshteln a h' [*hey*], a simen-nekeyve in Avroms nomen. Dos meynt tsu zogn, az a kompromislekhe linye, a sintetishe, filveynik, form fun foter-muter-hershaft, oder rikhtiker fun a foter-hershaft mit garanties, a muter-element in same foter-rekht aleyn. [...] Ale di, velkhe zaynen veyniker derfarn in hilkhes-hanhole fun biologishn un politishn kerper, hobn gedarft onboygn zeyere kep un tsuboygn zeyere vilns tsu der fiziologisher un psikhologisher oyberhershaft, der umtsvayflhafter natirlekher oytoritet, tsu der matriarkhie un shpeter-tsu, durkhgeyendik a serye transformatsyes un derivatsyes, tsu der patriarkhie.
>
> [And the condition of weakening the hardships of men's rule is indicated by the symbolic insertion of a h' [ה *hey*], a feminine marker, in Abraham's name. This means to say that a line of compromise [is established], a synthetic, more or less, form of father-mother-rule, or, correctly speaking, of a father-rule with guarantees, a mother-element in the very core of father-right itself. [...] All those less experienced in the rules of conduct of the biological and political body had to bow their heads and bend their wills to the supreme physiological and psychological rule, to the unquestioned natural authority, to matriarchy, and later, undergoing a series of transformations and derivations, to patriarchy.][36]

This 'uncovering' of the Hebrew feminine suffix ה- *hey* as a marker of the female gender is one of Gordin's key 'techniques' for tracing back concepts of ancient matriarchy in biblical and rabbinical sources and other authoritative texts of Judaism.

Abba Gordin even goes as far as to insinuate that the traditional Jewish names for God may have been derived from no-longer known, hypothetical, matriarchic goddesses that historically preceded the traditional Jewish concept of God. The ending of the Tetragrammaton, he stated, was a feminine suffix marker which fitted a god 'philologically and egologically [an expression coined by Gordin that does not concern us here] more female than male';[37] God's older name *Shaday* was, according to him, derived from an expression for the maternal breast; and the divine name *Elohim* contained the letter *hey*, which also allowed him to speculate about its etymology.[38] For Gordin, however, the Jewish God ultimately represented a synthesis of the male and the female principle, just as, in Jewish tradition, elements of an old matriarchy had been preserved in a patriarchal garment and in the past enabled the transformation from the one social formation to the other.[39] Moreover, Gordin construed the Tetragrammaton in itself as a prefiguration of this synthesis and, in a way, also of his political-cultural programme that was to be realised in the course of history: the Tetragrammaton, he asserted, 'iz an ikhtum, vos iz a zikhtum, a "zi-ikh", a "zikh"',[40] in other words, is an *ikh*, 'I', that integrated in itself a *zi*, 'she', resulting in a reciprocal *zikh*, 'oneself, each other'.

The question of whether Gordin's numerous (and lofty) speculations and flights of fancy would withstand the test of historical linguistics or could ever be validated or falsified by prehistoric anthropology, does not concern us here. Since his approach to religion is, as already mentioned, basically psychohistorical, it is more or less irrelevant for Gordin's argumentation whether the Bible — understood according to the Jewish tradition as encompassing both the *Toyre shebeksav* and *Toyre shebal-pe*, the Written Torah and the Oral Torah — was an accurate recording of actual historical events or rather merely a faraway mythological or ideological reflection of them. Rather, Abba Gordin reads the Bible as a kind of recorded collective psychosocial memory of mankind as a whole and of the Jewish People in particular, a document that, on a somewhat hidden level, preserves and maintains a kind of collective human moral consciousness. For instance, in his interpretation of the 'Ets-khayim-mitos' [Myth of the Tree of Life], as he preferred to call the biblical episode of the Fall of Man (Genesis 3), Gordin asserted that the historical defeat of matriarchy and the subsequent subjugation of the woman as a wife and mother continued to torment the conscience of mankind up to the present day, and that the biblical narrative was intended both to provide an explanation for and to remind Man of this painful historical turn.[41] However, in Gordin's narrative of world history, the Jewish People stands out in its ability to create the desperately needed synthesis of the male and the female principle and to provide a means to reconcile the antagonism of men and women,[42] and therein lies for him, although he does not state it explicitly, the chosenness of the Jewish People.

Despite his outspoken materialist phraseology, Gordin's thinking more often than not extends into philosophical idealism, in particular insofar as gender roles are concerned. Gordin's argumentation implicitly operated with a dichotomist scheme of 'tsvey elementn, azoy tsu zogn, dos menlekhe un dos vayblekhe'[43] — that is, a dialectics of 'the male' vs 'the female' metaphysical principles, from which, in the end, any progression of social formations emerges. For Gordin, motherhood epitomizes the 'female element' of reproduction, organic growth, passivity, and so on, whereas paternity stands for the 'male element' of activity, procreation, organization, technical rationalism, and, somewhat surprisingly, the ability of genuine leadership.[44] Because of the complex modes of production in the technical-industrial age, he reasoned, any attempt at a restoration of matriarchy — be it understood in the literal sense as women's rule or in an abstract-metaphysical sense as a social order in which the forces of reproduction prevail over the principle of rational organization and management — was doomed to fail.[45] It is noteworthy that the anti-communist Abba Gordin declared the Bolshevik 'dictatorship of the proletariat' one of these futile endeavours.[46]

With this dualism, Gordin's philosophy, deliberately or not, comes close to Johann Jacob Bachofen's conservative-romanticist idealism of *Das Mutterrecht* of 1861.[47] In Bachofen's scheme, paternality and maternality appear not only as rules of descent and social order but also as metaphysical principles. Paternality he associated with individualism, rationalism, and technology; maternality epitomized the telluric forces of organic growth, reproduction, and sensualism.[48] The institution of modern patriarchy Bachofen regarded as an achievement in terms of civilization.[49] In contrast to Bachofen, however, Gordin's narrative does not end with the submission of the woman to the man, but with a vague but emphatically proclaimed vision of a synthesis of these antagonistic principles in a new social order based on 'mutual aid' between the sexes (as well as between the other social powers governed by these gendered principles).[50] Gordin devoted much effort to prove that the seeds for such a synthesis were somehow prefigured in the historically developed ways of *Yidishkayt*, even if those seeds still had to be rediscovered.[51]

Responses from the Religious Milieu

Once the narrative of a primeval and ancient matriarchate had been established as a topic of the discourse on women's issues in secular Jewish circles, it became, after a period of ignorance, to a certain extent also known in the traditionally religious Orthodox milieu, and, in the course of time, politically conservative and religiously Orthodox Yiddish newspapers occasionally seem to have touched upon this theory in their articles.[52] A small number of Orthodox intellectuals and Jewish community activists even found a way to integrate the core idea of this theory into their worldview and to alleviate or neutralize its potential anti-religious implications. As a rule, they more or less accepted the idea of a prehistoric stage of matriarchy, but either ignored, discarded, or disputed the materialist explanations of its origination given by Engels, Bebel, and Morgan. Moreover, they treated the Jewish nation as an exceptional case in world history, as a people that had been basically patriarchal from its beginnings.

In 1927–28, the Białystok merchant and Jewish community activist Yisroel-Dovid Vays (1868–?) edited a series of educational pamphlets entitled *Der hoyz-lerer* [The Home Tutor].[53] As a *lamdan* (traditionally learned Jew) and private teacher, he wanted to show his readers a way to adapt to modern life without losing Orthodox Jewishness. During the interwar period, Białystok, an industrial Polish city with a strong Jewish minority, was a vibrant centre of multifaceted Jewish culture, where Left groups had a continuous presence.[54] Therefore it seems plausible to assume that Vays had acquired his knowledge of the theory of primeval matriarchy from newspapers or from direct encounters with socialist-anarchist propaganda, even if he only heard it from some unruly juvenile pupils of his. Among other educational and devotional writings, *Der hoyz-lerer* included (in instalments) a lengthy, excursive tractate on the important role of the woman in Judaism, in which the author briefly touched upon the issue of matriarchy.[55] Vays had no problem in accepting a prehistorical matriarchate or 'mother-right' formation, and treated it as a proven fact, but nowhere did he unequivocally indicate whether he also imagined the ancient Hebrews of the Bible as one of the peoples that had passed through this stage in the course of history.[56] The main objective of his tractate, however, was to present the heroines of the Hebrew Bible as an inspiration for the modern Jewish woman to observe *Yidishkayt* and chastity and to be a worthy spiritual companion to her husband. In Vays's narrative, the Jewish woman had sunk in her status in the course of history, but solely because ordinary Jews, both men and women, had become oblivious to their great past and the role that the virtues of the Jewish heroines had once played in it — virtues of self-devotion that, according to him, enabled the Jewish woman to be the centre and economic pillar of the Jewish family. In the end, Vays's tractate was a reaffirmation of the traditional conception of gender roles.

In 1930, Shlomo Ashkenazi (1904–92), a Misrakhi Zionist activist, journalist, and later prominent Israeli folklorist and religious writer, published in Yiddish his monograph *The Rights of the Woman as Spouse and Human Being*, a study comparing women's rights in various cultures with the status of women according to the Halakhah.[57] Ashkenazi's study is a defence of Judaism against the allegation of legitimizing a backward suppression and denigration of the Jewish woman, and was written in response to an article on that theme in the Polish-Jewish newspaper *Nasz Przegląd*.[58] In an introductory chapter, Ashkenazi briefly summarized the theory of a matriarchal formation in the history of mankind according to the writings of Bachofen, Morgan, Engels, Bebel, and Cunow.[59] Although Ashkenazi noted the existence of matrilineal rules among 'fil vilde felker un shvotim' [many [contemporaneous] savage peoples and tribes],[60] and seems to agree at least with the general outlines of the theory, he nevertheless did not relate it to Jewish history in any specific way, nor did he employ it as a heuristics (e.g. in the explanation of the cultural backgrounds of diverse biblical laws). Whereas Bebel and Engels are frequently referred to in the chapters dealing with ancient and contemporary Gentile nations, all of his statements regarding the Jewish People are entirely based on Halakhic sources, and his legalist division of its history into epochs follows, in principle, the chronological scheme established in the teachings of traditional Orthodox rabbinic Judaism.[61] It was certainly due to the author's non-polemical attitude in dealing with and defending Jewish religious tradition and the Halakhah that his work was issued by the card-carrying Yiddishist, left-leaning, and secularist publishing-house Yidish-bukh.[62]

In theory, the concept of a primeval matriarchy could be reconciled with the traditional Orthodox religious interpretation and exegesis of the Bible if the exegete situates the matriarchal epoch vaguely between the times of Adam and Eve and the times of Abraham the Patriarch, and if the materialist model of social evolution is replaced with an explanation conforming with Jewish religion. This idea, which might, in a vaguely developed manner, have been implied in Vays's and Ashkenazi's trains of thought, was later taken up and employed against the radicals' arguments by the Toronto Orthodox rabbi and Yiddish religious writer Nachman Shemen, who in the 1960s, under the aegis of the Argentinian branch of YIVO, authored a compendious and, in part, apologetic treatise on the topic of women in Judaism.[63] In principle, Shemen accepted the concept of a primeval matriarchy and its progression to patriarchy, even though he obviously rejected Engels's materialist foundation as well as some delicate postulates of Morgan's theory.[64] When contrasting their evolutionist schemes with Jewish tradition and the development of Jewish law, he explicitly refrained from overt polemics.[65] However, for him as an Orthodox rabbi, the status of the Bible as divine revelation was beyond question, and within the framework of traditional Jewish exegesis he implicitly employed the books of

Genesis and Exodus as records of actual historical events.[66] Shemen's chronological scheme is occasionally vague. In his monograph, he did not systematically outline his own theory, but rather relayed it to the reader by associating quotations from rabbinic literature with exegetical remarks and excursions. As he argued, the Jewish family (at least as depicted in the Torah), from its very beginnings, had always been somehow basically patriarchal but granted to women a respectable legal status that was hardly found among other ancient nations, no matter whether these societies were matriarchal or patriarchal.[67] Morgan himself had classified the ancient Hebrews of the Bible as a federation of patrilineal tribes that only in recent times had passed the stage of matrilineal clans.[68] (In contrast to him, Engels was a little more cautious on this subject.)[69] Rejecting the underlying materialist-evolutionist model, Shemen altered this thesis and reinterpreted the biblical episodes that Morgan employed as evidence. In Shemen's view, the institution of patriarchy among the Hebrews was not motivated by economical interests but solely by the wish to establish a healthy and civilized family system as a firm base for the People of Israel, which conformed with the divine will.[70] In the evolution of Jewish religious law, Shemen discerned a kind of gradual progression that inevitably led to the establishment of the modern rules and morals of strict monogamy and a kinship system with rules of marriage that became universal in the civilized world.[71] However, the Mosaic amendments of hereditary right in the case of the daughters of Zelophehad (Numbers 27. 1–11, 36. 1–13), which Morgan had explained as a reflection of a process of transition from the matrilineal to the patrilineal clan system, was mentioned by Shemen merely as an illustration of the progressive traits of Hebrew patriarchy.[72] Shemen dealt in a similar vein with the more delicate stories of the Bible, such as those of Lot and his daughters (Genesis 19. 30–38) or of Amnon and Tamar (II Samuel 13. 1–22) — stories which the anti-religious radicals Feigenbaum and Krantz, in support of Engels's arguments, did not fail to remind their readers of.[73] Shemen either dismissed these stories as belonging to a stage predating Mosaic Law or explained them as negative examples illustrating the importance of moral conduct.[74] In the tradition of rabbinical hermeneutics and biblical exegesis (and as an alternative to Engels's materialism), Shemen himself proposed a speculative idea on the origin of Hebrew patriarchy. Since men were natural 'builders' and 'creators', he stated, the 'legal-juridical' bonds between sons of the same father had been stronger than those between sons of the same mother, and this relationship had found its expression in the Hebrew term for 'son', *ben*, derived, he argued, from the same root as *binyan*, 'building'.[75]

In commenting on the various theories of ancient matriarchy from Bachofen to Engels, Shemen also engaged in a discussion of Abba Gordin's ideas, and even conceded that he found 'a sakh emes' [much truth] in Gordin's theses regarding matriarchy among 'felkershaftn in a primitiver stadye' [tribes at a primitive stage [of development]].[76] It would be a mistake, however, to assume that Shemen in any way appreciated Gordin's method and programme of reinterpreting and reaffirming Scripture and rabbinical literature. On the contrary, for him, Gordin was nothing but an atheist well disguised in his secularized *Yidishkayt*, whose speculations distorted the established rabbinical-Jewish readings of Bible and Talmud in a primitive, pseudo-scholarly manner that could easily be refuted.[77] Obviously, Shemen felt that Gordin's speculative flights of fancy were a travesty rather than an enhancement of the traditional approach of rabbinical hermeneutics. Moreover, he must have been particularly offended by Gordin's manneristic habit of spelling out the Tetragrammaton in all his treatises.

Shemen stated that the plan for his monograph originated as early as the 1940s.[78] For all this, one may assume that Gordin's writings had been no less an impulse for taking up his work than other, card-carrying atheists, Marxists, and critics of religion such as Benjamin Feigenbaum, and that Shemen developed his own exegesis of the Bible in part in (negative) response to Gordin's thoughts. In the end, Shemen's work is a document of a long-lasting argument of the Orthodox-Jewish milieu with cultural theories popular among the Yiddish Left and, no less so, with its protagonists.

Conclusion

As we have seen, in Yiddish socialist and anarchist circles, the response to Engels, Morgan, and Bebel was varied. In the early twentieth century, Benjamin Feigenbaum and Philip Krantz canonically followed Engels's and Bebel's materialism. For them, that is to say, more decisive than the woman's 'nature' was the woman's social role — which was defined by the modes of production and therefore subject to fundamental, revolutionary change. In the 1930s, Gordin declared women's and men's natures an emanation of an eternal metaphysical dualism that would inevitably be part of any modes of production in past, present, or future. Whereas Feigenbaum and Krantz envisioned a universal-secularist socialist world revolution, and therefore zealously attacked Jewish tradition and particularism in all its forms, Gordin's first concern was a reaffirmation of a Jewish cultural and ethnic identity that was able to play a vital role in his utopianist-anarchist hopes for the redemption of the entire universe. It is one of the paradoxes of Yiddish intellectual history that the canonical Marxist theory of primeval matriarchy (and other topoi of Marxist discourse on women's rights) served both of these highly divergent and competitive endeavours so well.

An entirely different response came from the Orthodox rabbi Nachman Shemen. Accepting the concept of a primeval matriarchy became for him a starting point for elaborating on and emphasizing the unique role of the Jewish People and its Halakhic tradition in world history. In the end, Shemen was also eager to demonstrate, against Feigenbaum's criticism and Gordin's theories, that his own reading of Jewish tradition had a better answer to the women's question.

Notes to Chapter 2

1. Friedrich Engels, *The Origin of the Family, Private Property and the State* (New York: International Publishers, [n.d.]), p. 54.
2. The expanded version of 1892 (the book's fourth printing) became the canonical base for numerous study editions, such as Friedrich Engels, 'Der Ursprung der Familie, des Privateigentums und des Staats', in Karl Marx and Friedrich Engels, *Werke*, 44 vols (1956–2018), XXI (Berlin [GDR]: Dietz, 1962), pp. 25–173, with Engels's preface to the fourth edition on pp. 473–83 and annotations by the editors on pp. 552–62. Readers in North America, who had already acquired some knowledge of Morgan's ideas and findings from the radical press, were introduced to Engels's theory through the English translation by Ernest Untermann, a socialist émigré from Germany: Frederick Engels, *The Origin of the Family, Private Property and the State*, trans. by Ernest Untermann (New York: Kerr, 1909 [first published in 1902]).
3. The book was published in numerous editions and versions, and continuously updated by the author. The fiftieth, expanded, 'jubilee edition' of 1909, which was declared the definitive one by Bebel himself (cf. the foreword), became the canonical version. The present chapter refers to the German text in August Bebel, *Die Frau und der Sozialismus*, 62nd edn (Berlin [GDR]: Dietz, 1973), and the English translation in August Bebel, *Woman and Socialism: 50th, Jubilee Edition*, trans. by Meta L. Stern (Hebe) (New York: Socialist Literature Co., 1910).
4. Cf. e.g. Eduard Bernstein's criticism in his 'Bemerkungen über Engels' Ursprung der Familie', *Sozialistische Monatshefte*, 4.8 (1900), 447–57 (pp. 452–53).
5. Cf. e.g. Ute Frevert, *Frauen-Geschichte: Zwischen Bürgerlicher Verbesserung und Neuer Weiblichkeit* (Frankfurt a.M.: Suhrkamp, 1986), p. 136.
6. According to Ernest Untermann, the names of Morgan, Bachofen, and Marx had been 'practically unknown' in the US at the beginning of the century; see his 'Translator's Preface' to Engels, *Origin of the Family*, trans. by Untermann, pp. 5–7 (p. 5). Untermann explained this fact, in the same vein as before him Engels with respect to Morgan, as a kind of conspiracy of the capitalist elites in order to suppress the development of revolutionary thinking. Cf. Untermann, *passim*; Engels, *Origin of the Family*, trans. by Untermann, pp. 12, 25; Engels, 'Ursprung der Familie', pp. 473, 481–82. Certainly, Untermann's and Engels's accusations have to be taken with a grain of salt. However, it is noteworthy that, for instance, the prolific and much-read British writer Catherine Gasquoine-Hartley (*c*. 1867–1928), in her books on women's issues such as *The Age of Mother-Power: The Position of Woman in Primitive Society* (New York: Dodd, Mead & Co., 1914), moderately advocates women's rights but carefully focuses her discussion on works not associated with the socialist cause.
7. Andrei A. Znamenski, '"A Household God in a Socialist World": Lewis Henry Morgan and Russian/Soviet Anthropology', *Ethnologia Europeana*, 25 (1995), 177–88. See also Hans-Jürgen Hildebrandt, 'Zur Bedeutung Lewis Henry Morgans für die gegenwärtige ethnologische Diskussion', in Hans-Jürgen Hildebrandt, *Rekonstruktionen* (Göttingen: Edition Re, 1990), pp. 92–125 (pp. 119–23).
8. On this development, see Hans-Jürgen Hildebrandt, 'Das Matriarchat: Zur Geschichte und Struktur eines Problems', in Hildebrandt, *Rekonstruktionen*, pp. 256–71 (pp. 256–57); Hildebrandt, 'Zur Bedeutung Lewis Henry Morgans', pp. 92–93, 116–19. Cf. also the sources cited by Chris Knight, 'Early Human Kinship Was Matrilineal', in *Early Human Kinship*, ed. by N. J. Allen and others (Oxford: Blackwell, 2008), pp. 61–82 (in particular pp. 69–73).
9. Cf. e.g. Heinrich Cunow, *Die Marxsche Geschichts-, Gesellschafts- und Staatstheorie: Grundzüge der Marxschen Soziologie*, 2 vols (Berlin: Vorwärts, 1920–21), II (1921), 82–142.
10. On the Yiddish socialist activists' and writers' varying levels of formal education, see e.g. Tony Michels, *A Fire in their Hearts: Yiddish Socialists in New York* (Cambridge: Harvard University Press, 2005), pp. 83, 119, 145–50.
11. On Krantz, see Elias Schulman, 'Krants, Filip', in *Leksikon fun der nayer yidisher literatur*, ed. by the Congress for Jewish Culture, 8 vols (New York: CYCO, 1956–81), VIII (1981), ed. by Berl Kagan and others, cols 243–49; Michels, pp. 63, 96–105, 118, 148, 194–96, 211.
12. Cf. e.g. Philip Krantz, *Di kulturgeshikhte: Der mentsh un zayn arbet*, 3 vols, 5th edn (New York:

International Library Publishing Co. [= A.M. Evalenko], 1900–03), II (1903), 15–45; III (1903), 238.
13. See e.g. Krantz, II, 50, 123–24.
14. Cf. e.g. Mikhail Zametkin, 'Shpurn fun evolutsion', *Di tsukunft*, [14].3 (1909), 327–33 (p. 331); Sofie Bogatin, 'Di froy in alterthum', *Di tsukunft*, 13.9 (1908), 531–39.
15. Cf. e.g. Katherina Yevzerov-Merison, *Di froy in der gezelshaft* ([n.p.]: [n. pub.], 1907), published by the Germinal group, a revised version of a journal article of 1900.
16. On Feigenbaum, see Michels, pp. 84–85, 117, 183–84; Leyb Vaserman, 'Faygenboym, Binyomin', in *Leksikon fun der nayer yidisher literatur*, VII (1968), ed. by Ephraim Auerbach and others, cols 338–41.
17. Benjamin Feigenbaum, *Libe un familyen-leben* [sic] *loyt idishkayt* (New York: Hillman, 1904).
18. Benjamin Feigenbaum: 'Luis Morgan un vos er hot ufgeton fir di [sic] visnshaft', *Di tsukunft*, 5.2 (no. 33) (1896), 65–73 (1–9).
19. Michels, pp. 148–49, 175.
20. August Bebel, *Di froy un der sotsializmus*, trans. by B. Feigenbaum (New York: Forverts, 1916). Feigenbaum's translation closely followed the version of the 'jubilee edition' of 1909. For a facsimile of Bebel's letter granting permission to translate his work, see p. [iii].
21. Friedrich Engels, *Di familye amol un haynt*, free, annotated trans. with appendix by B. Feigenbaum (New York: Forverts, 1918).
22. Benjamin Feigenbaum, 'Di nayeste visnshaft vegn entviklung fun der familye (tsugabe fun dem iberzetser)', in Engels, *Di familye*, pp. 323–53.
23. Bebel, *Die Frau und der Sozialismus*, p. 310; translation from Bebel, *Woman and Socialism*, p. 273. Cf. also Bebel, *Di froy un der sotsializmus*, p. 377.
24. Benjamin Feigenbaum, 'Forvort fun iberzetser', in Bebel, *Di froy un der sotsializmus*, pp. xxvi–xxx (pp. xxviii–xxx).
25. Ibid., p. xxix.
26. Lite is the Yiddish name for the Jewish cultural area covering the territory of the historical Grand Duchy of Lithuania (including today's Belarus) and some minor adjacent territories.
27. Feigenbaum, 'Forvort fun iberzetser', pp. xxix–xxx.
28. On Abba Gordin, see Paul Avrich, *The Russian Anarchists* (Princeton: Princeton University Press, 1967), pp. 176–80, 201–03, 222, 237, 249–50, 252–53; Moshe Goncharok, *Vek voli: Russkii anarkhizm i evrei (XIX–XX vv.)* (Jerusalem: the author, 1996) <http://www.jewniverse.ru/RED/gonchrok/index.htm> [accessed 22 February 2017]; Lilian Türk, 'Religiöser Nonkonformismus und Radikale Yidishkayt: Abba Gordin (1887–1964) und die Prozesse der Gemeinschaftsbildung in der jiddisch-anarchistischen Wochenschrift *Fraye Arbeter Shtime* 1937–1945' (doctoral thesis, Martin Luther University of Halle-Wittenberg, 2014) <urn:nbn:de:gvb:3:4–23057> [accessed 1 February 2017].
29. Abba Gordin, *Idishe etik*, Di kritik fun reynem gloybn, 1 (New York: Yidish etishe kultur-gezelshaft, 1937); *Gruntprintsipn fun idishkayt*, Di kritik fun reynem gloybn, 2 (New York: Yidish etishe kultur-gezelshaft, 1938); *Di froy un di bibl*, Di kritik fun reynem gloybn, 3.1 (New York: Yidish-etishe gezelshaft, 1939); *Idisher velt-banem*, Di kritik fun reynem gloybn, 3.2 (New York: Yidish-etishe gezelshaft, 1939).
30. Cf. also Kenyon Zimmer, *Immigrants against the State: Yiddish and Italian Anarchism in America* (Urbana: University of Illinois Press, 2015), p. 193.
31. On these concepts in Gordin's philosophical system, cf. e.g. Gordin, *Gruntprintsipn fun idishkayt*, pp. 103, 139, 297–98. Cf. also Simkhe Hamburg, 'Di filosofye fun Abe Gordin', *Khayfe: Yorbukh far literatur un kunst*, 2–3 (1965), 163–64; Türk, pp. 62–80.
32. Cf. Gordin, *Idisher velt-banem*, pp. 27–28, 275.
33. Gordin, *Di froy un di bibl*, p. 35.
34. *Pirkê de Rabbi Eliezer*, trans. by Gerald Friedlander (New York: Bloch, 1916), p. 88: 'What did the Holy One, blessed be He, do? He put His name [YH] between their (names), saying: If they go in My ways and keep all My precepts, behold My name is given to them, it will deliver them from all distress. If they do not walk (in My ways), behold I will take away My name from their (names) and they will become *êsh* (fire). And fire consumes fire [...].'

35. Cf. Engels, 'Ursprung der Familie', pp. 475–76; Engels, *Origin of the Family*, trans. by Untermann, pp. 14–17; Engels, *Di familye*, pp. 4–6. See also Johann Jakob Bachofen, *Das Mutterrecht* (Stuttgart: Krais & Hoffmann, 1861), pp. xxvii, 55.
36. Gordin, *Di froy un di bibl*, pp. 156–57.
37. Ibid., p. 17.
38. Ibid., pp. 17–18.
39. Cf. e.g. ibid., pp. 16–26, 156–57.
40. Ibid., p. 18. This play on words works only in Yiddish (and German) and is quite untranslatable into other languages.
41. Ibid., pp. 36–37.
42. Ibid., pp. 37–38.
43. Gordin, *Idisher velt-banem*, p. 30.
44. Ibid., pp. 29–32. Cf. also Gordin, *Di froy un di bibl*, pp. 18, 36.
45. Gordin, *Idisher velt-banem*, pp. 31–32.
46. Ibid. On Gordin's anti-communism, see also his *Communism Unmasked* (New York: Hord, 1940).
47. For the following, cf. e.g. Bachofen, pp. v–xxxiii, 20–23, 55, 60. See also Hans-Jürgen Hildebrandt, 'Johann Jakob Bachofen', in Hildebrandt, *Rekonstruktionen*, pp. 138–64 (pp. 154–58).
48. Cf. e.g. Bachofen, pp. xxvii–xxviii.
49. It should be noted here, however, that Bachofen's teleology of historical formations was not a simplistic linear one; cf. e.g. Bachofen, p. xxx; Hildebrandt, 'Bachofen', p. 157. Moreover, Hildebrandt, 'Bachofen', pp. 157–58, has argued that Bachofen conceived the metaphysical gender dualism not as absolute but (in the sense of a philosophical immanentism) as in principle subject to limited modification.
50. Gordin, *Idisher velt-banem*, p. 32; Gordin, *Di froy un di bibl*, pp. 37–38.
51. Cf. also Türk, pp. 102–12.
52. See, for instance, B. Kalish, 'Heyrath un familye', *Der Morgn-zhurnal*, 16 August 1922, p. 5. Kalish's article gives a basic introduction to the different concepts of marriage, matrimony, and family among the peoples of the world (with most examples taken from the indigenous nations of North America). According to the phraseology and terminology employed, the author must have read Morgan, Engels, or some other, albeit popularized, anthropological literature relying on them. Quite remarkable for the politically conservative, religiously Orthodox *Morgn-zhurnal* is, for instance, the following indirect reference to Marxism: 'Es iz afile faran a svore, az di ekonomishe badingungen un di ekonomishe produktsions-formen bashtimen alts in mentshlekhn lebn un sheypen ale formen un idealn fun lebn' [There is even the opinion that the economic conditions and the economic forms of production determine everything in human life and shape all forms and ideals of life].
53. Yisroel-Dovid bar Shmuel-Meir ha-Cohen Vays, *Der hoyz-lerer: Lektsyes geshildert in lebns-bilder vi azoy zikh zelbst tsu kenen lernen un hobn oykh a blik af der tsukunft [...]*, 1–5 (1927–28). On this author, see 'Vays, Yisroel-Dovid', in *Leksikon fun der nayer yidisher literatur*, III (1960), ed. by Ephraim Auerbach and others, col. 398. From no. 6 on, the title of *Der hoyz-lerer* was changed to *Undzer kultur* [Our Culture]; see Yisroel-Dovid bar Shmuel-Meir ha-Cohen Vays, 'A por verter tsum lezer', *Undzer kultur*, 6 (1928), pp. 81–84 (p. 82). It is not known how many issues were published.
54. Cf. Avrich, pp. 42–48; *Natsionale un politishe bavegungen ba yidn in Byalistok*, ed. by Herman Frank and others (New York: Shulsinger, 1951).
55. Yisroel-Dovid bar Shmuel-Meir ha-Cohen Vays, 'Di froy', *Der hoyz-lerer*, 4 (1927), 49–64; 5 (1928), 65–80.
56. Cf. Vays, 'Di froy', pp. 50, 52, 62–63, 71.
57. Shloyme Ashkenazi, *Di rekht fun der froy als vayb un mentsh* (Warsaw: Yidish-bukh, 1930). On this author, see 'Ashkenazi, Shloyme', in *Leksikon fun der nayer yidisher literatur*, I (1956), ed. by Shmuel Niger and others, col. 193; David Tidhar, *Entsiklopedyah le-halutse ha-yishuv u-vonav*, 19 vols (Tel Aviv: the author, 1947–71), XIV (1965), 4446; Moshe Krone, 'Yamim yedabru — al r' Shlomo Ashkenazi', *Gevilin*, 4 (Tammuz 5751 [1992 CE]), 81–87.

58. Cf. Ashkenazi, p. 14; Krone, p. 86.
59. Ashkenazi, pp. 11–18, in particular pp. 14–18.
60. Ibid., p. 17.
61. Cf. ibid., pp. 11–14.
62. Cf. Krone, p. 86.
63. Nakhmen Shemen, *Di batsiung tsu der froy, loyt Tanakh, Talmud, Yahades un literatur-shtudyes*, 2 vols (Buenos Aires: YIVO, 1968–69); for the following, cf. in particular I (1968), 213–60. Noteworthy is the fact that Shemen included not only Engels, Bebel, and Morgan in his references, but also Shlomo Ashkenazi and Abba Gordin.
64. Cf. e.g. Shemen, I, 221, 227, 231, 232.
65. Shemen, I, 226, 253 n. 12.
66. Cf. Shemen, I, p. xi.
67. Cf. Shemen, I, 214–16, 227–28, 229, 234, 235–36.
68. Lewis H. Morgan, *Ancient Society* (New York: Holt, 1877), pp. 366–71, 465–66, 470, 499, 506–07, 544–48; Lewis H. Morgan, *Die Urgesellschaft*, trans. by Wilhelm Eichhoff and Karl Kautsky (Stuttgart: Dietz, 1891), pp. 309–11, 394–95, 397, 427, 432–34, 468–71.
69. Cf. e.g. Engels, 'Ursprung der Familie', 58; Engels, *Di familye*, pp. 87–88; Engels, *Origin of the Family*, trans. by Untermann, p. 66.
70. Cf. e.g. Shemen, I, 231–32.
71. Cf. Shemen, I, 214–15, 220, 227, 229–30, 233–34.
72. Shemen, I, 232, 239; II (1969), 39–41, 213, 235. Cf. also Shemen's appraisal of levirate marriage as a historical institution of social security for childless Jewish widows (I, 232–33).
73. Cf. e.g. Engels, *Di familye*, pp. 51, 55; Krantz, II, 50.
74. Cf. Shemen, I, 117–19, 136–37, 218; II, 12.
75. Shemen, I, 220, 254 n. 29.
76. Shemen, I, 221.
77. Shemen, I, 221, 254 nn. 8 and 10.
78. Cf. Shemen, I, p. ix.

CHAPTER 3

❖

'Mother, in the chain of generations, I am the broken link between you and my child': The Experience of Being a Mother and a Daughter in Yiddish Poetry by Women*

Joanna Lisek

A *Yidishe Mame*

The established ideal of a man in Judaism — a Talmudic scholar spending the entire day on studying the sacred texts in a *bet ha-midrash*, removed from everyday matters — forced Jewish women to assume roles traditionally perceived as male. This was also associated with the shift of the division between public and private spheres. A synagogue and a house of study were the spaces that men associated with prestige and power. A woman's position there was marginal. However, the sphere of economics and trade was open to her. Furthermore, girls had wider access to secular education and foreign languages than their brothers, since the girls' education was not subject to strict rabbinical control.

As a result, Jewish women were often much better prepared to interact with the outside community than their husbands.[1] Women's domination in Jewish everyday life in Eastern Europe was also reinforced by marriages contracted at a very early age,[2] and combined, with the *kest*, an arrangement widespread among well-off (*balebatishe*) Jews. According to this custom, the in-laws financially supported the son-in-law up to seven years after the wedding to provide him with Talmudic education during that time. A teenage husband — usually less physically developed than his wife and barely able to fulfil the obligations of the wedding night — was placed in a house of strangers, where he was often considered as an additional financial burden. Thus dominated, he stepped aside, escaping into the world of Talmudic disputes. Sometimes, the young wife would even take on the role of a mother to her juvenile husband.[3] The above factors contributed to the literary representation of a *yidishe mame* as a strong dominating woman who reigns not only

---

* This article was translated from the Polish by Agnieszka Legutko, who also — unless otherwise indicated — made the philological translations from the poems. The quotation in the title is from Bertha Kling, *Lider* (New York: [n. pub.], 1935), p. 41.

over the domains of current family matters but also over her husband, who is often out of touch with practical life.

Another very significant factor, widely propagated in the press and in literature, emerged in the late nineteenth century as a result of the intensified processes of acculturation and assimilation on the one hand, and the awakening of Jewish national aspirations on the other, partly a consequence of the increased anti-Semitism and partly a reaction to the wave of pogroms in Eastern Europe. The factor in question was the representation of the Jewish mother as the guardian of *yidishkayt* (Jewishness). Civilizational changes, waves of emigration, and revolution in social life and customs weakened the impact that traditional Jewish institutions and ties within the Jewish community had on the process of shaping the younger generation. As a result, the home became the guarantor of preserving Jewish identity, and it was ruled by the woman, herself most exposed to the influence of the assimilation trends.[4] Therefore, a special emphasis was placed in the public discourse on exposing the key role of the mother in raising the faithful sons and daughters of Israel. Even women's periodicals published in the early twentieth century, or the later feminist press that pointed out the necessity of change in the situation of women in traditional Jewish society, wanted to see the Jewish woman as the combination of a modern woman, aware of her worth and rights, and a *yidishe mame*, perceived as the guardian of domestic peace and joy.[5]

An explicit deconstruction of this traditional image of the Jewish mother and motherhood takes place in the domain of women's Yiddish poetry, which flourished between 1888 and 1939,[6] thus becoming an important medium for the manifestation of change in women's status in Jewish society and the challenges of revolution in social life and customs.

Pregnancy, Birth, and Breastfeeding as Themes of Women's Yiddish Poetry

The transformation of the representation of the mother in women's Yiddish poetry is associated with a new manner of addressing pregnancy. The voice of the pregnant woman was not foreign to Yiddish literature and did not constitute a taboo. The collections of *tkhines* (women's prayers) contain many texts that are supplications of a woman expecting a child. An expecting mother prays for protection during pregnancy, for an easy childbirth, health and wisdom for her offspring, and so on.[7]

Celia Dropkin's poem 'Du kenst' [You Can] is a complete departure from the tradition of *tkhines*.[8] The pregnant woman — the speaker of the poem — addresses not God but the father of the child. Furthermore, this is not the voice of a woman who humbly accepts the difficulties of pregnancy and expects the soon-to-be-born child with hope and joy. On the one hand, the poem is a reproach or a grievance against the father, who is not affected by the direct consequences of the conception of a child, thanks to which he can go around 'free and happy'.[9] On the other hand, the poem depicts a mother focusing her attention on herself and her body, not on the child. This candid expression of anxiety, remorse, and even bitterness is a novelty in Yiddish poetry, and it constitutes an audacious rejection of the idealized and simplified image of the pregnant woman. Dropkin, who herself gave birth to six children, divulges the price a woman has to pay for carrying and giving birth to a child. She daringly brings up the theme of terror evoked by her body's transformation during pregnancy. The child is presented as a parasite that grows in the woman's body, feeding on its bone marrow and blood. This alien being rampantly prevailing inside the woman's body is described almost as an aggressor 'drilling through her breasts'. The pregnant woman feels ugly with her disfigured limbs. Motherhood deprives her of her sex appeal and her breasts become 'fountains of milk'. This is accompanied by the constant fear of the inevitable pain: the birthing bed is referred to as 'the inquisition bed', the place of torture. The asexuality of motherhood is underscored once again through the juxtaposition of a dream about the woman's body stretched out on the bed and the vision's designation as the image of lying in the pains of childbirth. This poem-complaint ends with the woman's direct address to the inside of her own body, to the mysterious life growing there. Dropkin deliberately avoids using such words as 'child' and 'mother' in this poem, thus emphasizing the fact that the relationship between the woman and the being growing inside her is not obvious and easy to identify. Human life maturing in the body of another human being and at her expense remains a mystery here:

> Du kenst arumgeyn fray un freylekh,
> Ven in mir langzam, langzam vakst a lebn,
> Geflantst fun undz.
> Vos hot mies ibergeandersht mayne glider
> Un zoygt mayn markh un blut,
> Un egbert mayne brist
> Far milkh fantanen?
> Vos kholemt zikh mir azoy oft
> Di inkvizitsye bet,
> Vu oysgeshtrekt lig ikh in shvere laydn?
> O, soydesdiker lebn, vos vakst in mir!

> [You can go around, free and happy,
> While inside me life is slowly, slowly growing,
> Planted by us.
> What has so uglily distorted my limbs,
> And is sucking my marrow and blood,
> And is drilling through my breasts
> For milk fountains?
> Why do I so often dream of
> The inquisition bed
> With myself lying outstretched in terrible pain?
> Oh, the mysterious life that grows in me!][10]

Yet modern Yiddish women poets do not always depict pregnancy as a burden, the experience of which essentially differentiates the scope of sovereignty of women and men. In the poem 'Oyfbli' [The Bloom], Pessie Hershfeld takes delight in childbearing,[11] which guarantees the preservation of humankind. Her poetic study of pregnancy and childbirth depicts a personal (through the first-person speaker of the poem) experience of carrying inside and bringing to the world a child as state of being chosen which grants women near-divine status:

> Ikh hob zikh oyfgeknipt, un tsaytik, vi der boym in feld,
> Hob oyfgenumen mit freyd dem zomen fun der velt.
> Un vi der boym balodn shver, vos vigt zikh um in feld,
> Knoylt in mir, shprotst un blit der doyer fun velt.
> [...]
> Az peyn fun geboyrn zol brengen oyf der velt
> Dos likht gevuntshene, dos likht gegarte!
>
> [I branched out and matured like a tree in the field,
> I joyfully accepted the seed of the world,
> And like a tree swaying heavy with fruit
> Swirls, sprouts, and blooms in me the duration of the world.
> [...]
> Let the birthing pain bring to the world
> The desired light, the longed-for light!]¹²

Hershfeld also brings the issue of motherhood into the sphere of sexuality, but, in contrast to Dropkin, pregnancy is for her the fulfilment and quintessence of womanhood. Fertility and pregnancy are depicted not as a distortion of the woman's body but as its blooming, with the child as its desired fruit:

> Vi vunderlekh tsu filn in zikh di last fun yunge frukht,
> Ven glider zaftikn un tsaytikn mit lebediker freyd.
> O, bentsh in mir durkh shvangershaft di bliendike frukht,
> Mayn kind zol oyfgeyn far der velt — a brenendike freyd.
>
> [It is wonderful to feel inside me the burden of a young fruit,
> When the limbs are juicily ripening with vital joy.
> Oh, I am blessed by the bearing of a blooming fruit,
> Let my child rise for the world — an ardent delight.]¹³

The poet also introduces the image of the woman's body on the birthing bed, but while in Dropkin's poem this was the 'inquisition bed' of torture, here we find allusions to the bed as a site of ecstasy. Hershfeld depicts birth in the categories and means of an erotic poem. In this presentation, the act of childbirth is, as it were, a continuation of sexual intercourse, hence the allusions to 'caressing', a 'thicket of desires', and the body's 'limbs', which 'float' like 'song-filled songs':

> Blit mayn froyenlayb af tsikhtikn geleger;
> Ful mit tsuzog otemt haynt di nakht.
> Tsertlt zikh mayn layb af tsikhtikn geleger
> Fun zunike bagern oyfgebrakht.
>
> Viklt oyf mayn layb tsebleterte bagern
> Mit toyznt benkshaftn bavakht.
> Glider mayne, zingendike lider,
> Benkendike shvomen in der shtiler nakht ...
>
> Tsiterdike shoen fun mayn lebn!
> In dinste fedim plontert ir mikh ayn.

> Ven dinste freyd un umbavuster troyer,
> Vi royter oyfgeshoymter gliendiker vayn,
> Tseshoymen ale mayne yunge glider
> Mit zisn payn!
>
> [My womanly body blossoms on the clean bed;
> The night is breathing tonight with the fullness of promise.
> My body is caressing itself on the clean bed,
> Bent with sunny yearnings.
>
> The thicket of desires veils my body
> Guarding thousands of longings.
> My limbs, song-filled songs,
> Longing, float into the quiet night ...
>
> The trembling hours of my life!
> Entwining me in thin threads.
> When the silky joy and unintentional sadness,
> Like the red frothy glittering wine
> Stirs all my young limbs
> Sweet pain!][14]

If it were not for the rest of the poem, one might think this passage is a poetic attempt to capture a moment of intimacy between a man and a woman. However, in the following stanzas, this lustful, longing woman's body becomes transformed by the emphatically repeated simple word 'ma-ma':

> Ven lebn tsitert oyf in mames trakht
> Un shpart zikh tsu derzen Gots velt;
> Ven in dervartung flatert oyf dos harts,
> Vi vayse flaterlekh arum dem likht vos helt;
>
> Ven shoen in loyf fun zeyer gang,
> Vi yunge dershrokene feygl,
> Patshn ritmish mit di fligl oys
> Ma-me, ma-me, ma-me;
> Tsiterdike shoen klingen oys —
> Ma-me, ma-me, ma-me ...
>
> [When the life trembles in the mother's womb
> And pushes its way through to see God's world;
> When in anticipation, the heart flutters
> Like white butterflies around bright light;
>
> When the hours racing at their own speed,
> Like young fearful birds,
> Rhythmically beat time with their wings:
> Ma-ma, ma-ma, ma-ma;
> Quivering hours are ringing:
> Ma-ma, ma-ma, ma-ma ...][15]

The pain of ecstasy turns out to be the pain of labour, which is a mysterious union of suffering and joy — a mystical experience connecting corporality with transcendence:

O, shtil gebet, flis fun mayne lipn
Tsu alts vos eybik iz, tsu alts vos lebt,
Az payn fun geboyrn zol nit zayn umzist.

[A silent prayer, a stream from my mouth,
To everything that is eternal, everything that is alive,
Let the pain of birthing not be in vain.][16]

Rosa Yakubovitsh's poem 'Tsu zoyg-kind' [To the Suckling Baby] is marked by a similar spirit of delight over the miracle of motherhood.[17] In this poem, the moment of breastfeeding a child is brought into the context of a ritual, into the sanctified sphere. The eyes of the newborn baby gulping down milk are here compared to kiddush wine. The milk, on the other hand, emphasizes the organic bond between the mother and the child, since it is described as the flow of her life. She indeed gives the newborn a piece of her own being, which sustains the child:

Ikh otem ayn vi luft dayn kindish tsart bavegn,
Oyf mayn antplektn hartsn ven du rust,
Ikh trink vi kidesh-vayn dem shtral fun dayne oygn,
Ven du, du zoygst mayn lebns-iberflus.

[Like air, I breathe in your childlike delicate movements,
When you are resting on my exposed heart,
Like kiddush wine, I drink in the rays of your eyes,
When you, you are sucking my life's flow.][18]

The poem nonetheless introduces a note of anxiety: the nursing mother with the newborn at her breast seems to be entirely alone amidst the night and the unfriendly outside world. The child's vulnerability and trust fill her with apprehension, as if she fears that she would not be able to protect the child against the threatening reality surrounding them:

Es shtralt mir fun dayn oyg dayn umbagrenetst fartroyen,
Vi umbaholfn, kind mayn kleyns, biztu —
Un kh'veyn in mitn nakht, — in droysn soves voyen
Un roybn mir mayn muterlekhe ru.

[Boundless faith radiates to me from your eyes,
My little child, how vulnerable you are —
I'm crying therefore in the middle of the night — owls are hooting outside,
Robbing me of my maternal rest.][19]

The interpretive context for the anxiety expressed here seems to be offered in another poem by Yakubovitsh, 'Di shrek' [Fear],[20] published in the collection *Mayne gezangen* [My Songs] in the immediate vicinity of the poem just discussed. The child and kiddush wine also appear in 'Fear', but the situation depicted is very different. Fear is the leitmotif here. Similarly to the previous work, the woman speaker of this poem is in her house, during Passover. The world blossoms in springtime, yet she is haunted by fear, and the external world appears to be hostile and dangerous. She knows that someone — a stranger — could come at any moment and accuse her of ritual murder. Therefore, the bottle of Passover wine fills her with fear. This bottle could become the basis of accusations that it is not wine but 'blood of an innocent child'. This is an evident allusion to blood libel — false accusations, occurring repeatedly across the centuries, that Jews would puncture a Christian child in order to draw his or her blood, allegedly required for the production of matzoh or wine. The fear of suspicions of drinking Christian blood was so widespread that white wine was allowed to be used during the Seder instead of the traditional sweet red wine. Ritual murder accusations customarily intensified during the festival of Passover and could even lead to pogroms. The woman speaking in this poem — and breastfeeding her child in solitude in the previous one — is afraid of a pogrom.

> Mir yomert in mayn harts:
> Vos vil fun mir der shrek?
> S'iz peysekh oyf der velt un sheyn,
> Di velt zet oys, vi oysgebodn fayn,
> Nor vintn shtifn do un dort on grenets un on breg,
> Vos vil fun mir der shrek?
> Dort in der shank in flash der royter vayn
> Er nemt mir tsu mayn ru,
> Kh'hob moyre, s'kon nokh kumen ver fun veg,
> A fremder beyzer man,
> Un zogn kon er, zogn —
> Gerekhter got, der tog zol nisht batogn, —
> Az ikh, ikh mit peysekh-meser hob gekoylet gor
> A kristlekh kind ———

> [The heart is wailing in me:
> What do you want from me, Fear?
> The world grows beautiful for Passover,
> The world looks newly bathed,
> Only the boundless winds are raging limitlessly.
> What do you want from me, Fear?
> There, in the cupboard, red wine is in the bottle,
> It takes my peace away,
> I fear someone will come from the road,
> A strange evil man
> And — God the just, let this day never dawn, — and he can say, yes, — say —
> That I, I killed with a Passover knife
> A Christian child —][21]

The tragic absurdity of the accusations is underscored in Yakubovitsh's work by the juxtaposition of these two poems: one poem features an archetypal image of the mother breastfeeding her child, while in the other poem she is accused of puncturing a Christian child to death. On the one hand, we can see a woman giving life to a child with milk; on the other hand, an anti-Semitic image of a Jewish woman pouring out the substance of life — blood — from a Christian child. The motifs of milk, wine, and blood are combined in an interesting way in these poems. Milk and blood are the elixir and the ur-matter of life, while many cultures have identified wine with blood. The poem 'Fear,' however, rejects the metaphorical understanding of wine with the reality of accusations against the Jews. In the poem, the accusation based on the connection between wine and blood is literal in character and transcends the metaphor, thus generating fear.

Abortion

The period in which women's Yiddish poetry flourished introduced a new way of talking about motherhood that connected it with the problem of abortion. The opening of a poem by Kadia Molodowsky from the 'Froyen lider' [Women-Poems] sequence ('These are the spring nights | When up from under a stone, a grass blade pushes forth from the earth'),[22] looks like one of many trite poems about the spring in which nature awakening to life evokes a sentimental mood in the speaker of the poem. However, Molodowsky's poem plays with the poetic convention: the well-worn theme of the poem becomes the pretext for taking up not-in-the-least-bit romantic subjects. The arrival of spring serves as the background against which to depict women's sexual and maternal instincts, here interwoven into one unity:

> Un ale glider fun a froy betn zikh tsu veytik fun geburt.
> Un froyen kumen un leygn zikh vi kranke shof
> Bay krenitses oyf heyln zeyer layb.
> Un hobn shvartse penimer
> Fun langyerikn dorsht tsum kinds geshrey.
>
> [All of a woman's limbs beg for the hurt of childbirth.
> And women come and lie down like sick sheep
> By wells to heal their bodies.
> And their faces are dark
> From long years of thirsting
> For the cry of a child.][23]

The comparison between women coming into the field in order to give in to men and the sick sheep turns the women into passive victims of their own biology, which here acquires a somewhat animalistic character. This is also a subversive biblical allusion, since in the Torah wells were often a site of meetings which then led to marriages (e.g. Rebecca meets Eliezer, seeking a wife for Isaac, at a well, and Rachel meets Jacob at a well too). In Molodowsky's poem, these meetings are not of a matrimonial character: they are only a means of satisfying one's lust. The sexual encounter between a man and a woman is depicted through a reference to the archetype of ploughing the earth, which reinforces the female passivity and biologicity exposed earlier, surrendering to the brutal strength of masculinity, which is symbolized by the knives cutting through the black earth:

> S'iz nekht azoyne frilingdike do,
> Ven s'vakst unter a shteyn a groz fun dr'erd
> Un s'bet der frisher mokh a grine kishn oys
> Unter a sharbn fun a toytn ferd.
>
> [These are the spring nights
> When up from under stone, a grass blade pushes forth from the earth,
> And the fresh moss makes the bed of a green cushion
> Under the skull of a dead horse.][24]

The reference to the archetype of woman — the earth ploughed in the spring — also introduces the aspect of fertility. These biblical-archetypal images are drastically juxtaposed with the hospital reality of white beds with women seeking to abort their pregnancy, the fruit of spring's blood passions:

> Un froyen shvangere tsu vayse tishn fun shpitol
> Kumen tsu mit shtile trit
> Un shmeykhlen tsum nokh nisht geborenem kind
> Un efsher nokh tsum toyt.
>
> [And pregnant women approach
> White tables in the hospital with quiet steps
> And smile at the yet-unborn child
> And perhaps even at death.]²⁵

Motherhood perceived in terms of libido and ending in abortion is a clear deconstruction of the *yidishe mame* myth.

The problem of being a future mother unable to carry the baby to term and give birth to it is at the centre of the poem 'Di froy' [The Woman], Khana Levin's feminist manifesto.²⁶ This poet, who was born in 1900 in Ukraine and who later served as a soldier in the Red Army, must have seen the ruthless images of massacres in the years 1917–19. This extremely drastic work, which opens her debut poetry collection, is a cry for the rights of women, whose bodies always become spoils in times of historical unrest. Levin writes not only about the rapes carried out by men but also about the massacres of pregnant women. It is characteristic that, in her dissatisfaction with a description of events from an observer's point of view (such accounts of pogroms have a long tradition in Jewish poetry), she, striving for subjectivity, makes one of the victims of male barbarism the speaker of the poem instead:

> Vemen,
> Vemen zol ikh mayn vey fartroyen?
> Ikh kon nit zoygn mer in shtumenish mayn vund!
> Ale nakht ikh ze in kholem froyen,
> Un yedere baveynt a kind.
>
> Un ver mit mir mayn tsorn vet tseteyln?
> Ver vet fargringern mayn shvern vor?
> Yede nakht ikh ze in kholem froyen,
> Shlept men zey tsum toyer far di hor ...
> Ongeshlaydert froyen af di tishn.
> Fardreyte kni tserayst a fremde hant.
> Emervayz men trogt af shvartse mistn
> Shtiker kinder-layb un froyen-shrek un shand ...
>
> Shver iz mir,
> Un ikh shem zikh klogn,
> Vayl mayn land iz sheyn
> Un yomtevdik farton.
> Freydn in mayn land —
> Zangen ful mit korn,
> Nor mir,
> Un af mayn kheylek

Puste kumen on ...

Ikh hob dokh oykh gezeyet un geakert
Far zikh
A zangele
A fuls ikh hob fardint.
Es tor azoy nit zayn,
Es tor azoy nit kumen,
Az muter-layb zol zayn a trune farn kind! ...

[Before whom,
Before whom am I to bare my pain?
No longer can I silently suck on my wound! —
Each night I dream of women,
And each bewails a child.

Who will share with me my anguish?
Who will relieve me in this harsh world?
Each night I dream of women,
Pulled by their hair to the door ...
Women thrown on tables.
Their knees pulled apart by strange hands.
Thrown onto the rubbish pile at every moment
Are bits of children's and women's bodies — terror and shame ...
It is hard,
But I am ashamed to wail,
Because my country is beautiful
And the joy of a festive morning
Awakes in my country —
Ears full of grain,
But for me
And for my fate
Empty ...

I too ploughed and sowed,
For myself
The little ear
I toiled hard.
It should not be so,
It should not happen so,
That the mother's body becomes a coffin for the child! ...][27]

The poem reaches a violent strength of expression through the introduction of an almost naturalistic depiction of tormented women, whose tragedy is seen from two perspectives: that of the loss of a child, and that of the loss of an element of humanity, that is, shame and the possibility of controlling the fate of one's own body. Similarly to Molodowsky's poem, this work features a reference to the world of nature — the grain full of ears brings to mind a woman's pregnancy. The child growing in the woman is affectionately referred to as a 'little ear' of grain, but, in contrast to the aforementioned poem by Molodowsky, it is the woman herself who has 'ploughed and sowed', thus becoming the 'soil' for the new life. The man does not appear here as the one who decides about conception; it is the woman herself who has 'toiled' to grow a person inside her. Yet this hardship turns out to be in vain — her body has become a coffin for her child. The women are entirely alone in their tragedy: their husbands have grown blind to the rapes carried out on their own wives, finding an effective anaesthetic in alcohol. They do not preserve the memory of the babies killed in the womb. Women, on the contrary, have their bodies marked by the stamp of tragedy, and retain the memory of the death that occurred inside them. Levin brutally speaks of the tragedy that can be comprehended only by women who have experienced the death of another person in their own living bodies:

> Mener unzere zaynen gevoynt unz zen mit fonen
> Un oystrinken a nakht on khoyv far morgn, — blind.
> Nor froyen narish layb fargesn vet nit konen
> Dem prostn glik fun hodeven a kind.
>
> Iz ful mayn yeder glid mit vildn vey un yomer,
> Un shtikn zikh mit vey — mer hob ikh nit keyn koy(e)kh.
> Kh'bin ufgerufn zayn fun helstn dor a mame,
> Un bashert iz mir — im palmesn in boykh.
>
> [Our husbands have grown used to seeing us with our lords,
> They drink all night on a tab till morning, — blind.
> But the naive female body cannot forget
> The simple joy of the growing baby.
>
> Every particle of my body is full of wild despair and lament,
> The pain chokes me — I have no strength left.
> I was called upon to be the mother of the brightest generation,
> But I am destined — to dissect it in my belly.][28]

A woman emerges from such a traumatic experience mutilated, no longer able to treat her relations with a man as before, anxious about and fearful of sex: 'A pair of joined lips causes me pain, | Anxiety strikes, like sweat of nights thick as honey.'[29] At the end of the poem, Levin changes her strategy — she moves from the individual speaker to the collective. She speaks on behalf of women who are faced with the possibility of asserting their own rights. A crack has appeared in the patriarchal history of humanity, and the foundations of the system of subordination of one gender to another seem to be temporarily shaken; therefore, it is necessary to seize the moment and 'Cast off the burden | Of our sex':

> Mir zaynen ale in urloyb,
> Mir zaynen af a vayle —
> Farshikerte fun megn folgn dem geshlekht.
>
> Kumt a leybikhe tsum leyb in tsayt fun libe,
> Kumt a fuksikhe tsum fuks nokh froy- un mame-rekht,
> Un mir —
> Derhoybene fun doyres — 'man un froy' zikh rufn,
> Bam tsoym fun leyb
> Bafrayen mir dem last
> Fun dem geshlekht.

> [We are all on a vacation,
> For a moment we are
> Drunk from the chance to respond to the call of sex.
> The lioness comes to the lion at the time of love,
> The vixen comes to the fox for the rights of women and mothers
> And we —
> Chosen from generations — calling ourselves 'man and woman',
> At the lion's cage
> Cast off the burden
> Of our sex.][30]

Levin's poem breaks all the taboos associated with motherhood. Furthermore, the figure of the woman-mother, which served in the 1920s as a shield in anti-feminist discourse, here becomes an active participant in the feminist rebellion and the main subject of its aspirations.

Mothers and Daughters in Yiddish Poetry

Yiddish women poets who enter a generational dialogue with their own mothers and who take up the subject of motherhood as their own — or generally understood — women's experience deconstruct the traditional stereotype of the *yidishe mame* in a different way.[31] The origins of this motif in women's Yiddish poetry can be found in the Yiddish folk-song genre that contains collections of works based upon or featuring a dialogue between a mother and a daughter. Furthermore, feminist critique perceives the relationships between mothers and daughters as one of the main spheres of women's stifled expression. Luce Irigaray in her feminist manifesto declares:

> We also need to find, rediscover, invent the words, the sentences that speak of the most ancient and most current relationship we know — the relationship to the mother's body, to our body — sentences that translate the bond between our body, her body, the body of our daughter.[32]

In Yiddish folk songs, the mother is represented as the guardian of her daughter's virginity, and the dialogues between them refer to the daughter's failure to heed to the mother's warnings and the resulting consequences. In one of the songs, the daughter complains:

> Oy, vey, mame, ikh shpil a libe,
> Un s'tut mir vey mayn harts,
> Ver es shpilt a falshe libe,
> Der kon filn mayn biter harts.
>
> [Oy vey, mother, I'm playing love
> And pain has arrived in my heart,
> Whoever has engaged in the false game of love
> Can feel the grief of my heart.][33]

The girl then says that she saw her beloved with another girl, yet she still trusted him and slipped out of the house to secretly meet him at night:

> Tsvelf a zeyger bay der nakht
> In droysn iz geven kalt,
> Ikh hob aropgenumen dos zaydn tikhele
> Un ongeton im oyfn halts.
>
> Shpet bay nakht bin aheym gekumen,
> Fregt mikh mayn muter: vu bistu geven?
> Oy, vey, mame, dos zaydn tikhele,
> Dos zaydn tikhele vestu shoyn mer nisht zen!
>
> Vi di muter hot dos derhert
> Hot zi zikh bagosn mit trern.
>
> [It was midnight,
> It was cold outside,
> I took off my silk scarf
> And wrapped it around my neck.
>
> I returned home late
> And mother asks: Where have you been?
> Oy vey, mother, the silk scarf,
> The silk handkerchief won't again be seen!
>
> When this reached mother's ears,
> She burst into tears.][34]

The silk scarf becomes the symbol of lost virginity. But the despair of the mother and the girl does not end here. The song ends with the man abandoning her and getting engaged to another girl.

Interestingly, contemporary critics sometimes depicted Yiddish women's poetry in the very categories of heritage that mothers passed down to daughters. For instance, Yitskhok Sigal, writing about Berta Kling's poetry,[35] hears in her poems 'the melody of the "Got fun Avrom" prayer, taught by the mother to her daughter who is getting married'.[36] Undoubtedly, male critics wished to see women's Yiddish poetry as the continuation of *tkhines*, as can be demonstrated by the warm reception of poetry by Miriam Ulinover.[37] Kadia Molodowsky described Ulinover as a *shabesdiker mentsh* [Sabbath person], which emphasized her attachment to Jewish tradition. Ulinover, residing in Łódź, stayed clear of the literary milieu — the hotbed of modern Yiddish culture. She ran a religious home, devoting her time to raising children. She avoided evening literary meetings. Molodowsky characterized her poems as follows: 'quietness, piety, each word taken as if from a *tkhine*'. Even in the external form, her poems emanated Orthodoxy — 'dressed' in the cut of fonts and spelling used in religious literature. Paradoxically, it was Ulinover who received the greatest support and acclaim on the part of secular Yiddish critique, dominated by men. Why was this the case? Let us seek an answer in her poem, 'A brivele der boben' [A Letter to Grandma]. As in many other poems, Ulinover chooses a girl talking to her grandmother to be the speaker of the poem. The granddaughter, currently residing in a big city to which she came in order to study, writes a letter to her grandmother living in the girl's home shtetl. The girl reassures the grandmother that she is following the instructions the latter gave her before her departure for the city. The grandmother's wish was as follows:

> Neshome, mayne, — zogstu shtil,
> Mir gletendikg s'gezikht —
> Gedenk, vibald es lekhert zikh,
> Tu-oys dos kleyd, farrikht!
>
> Nisht zol keyn menshens hand oyf dir
> Farneyen, kind-leb, s'lokh:
> Der seykhl vert farneyt, farshpart,
> Farshtopt azoyernokh!
>
> [— My darling — you said quietly,
> Caressing my face,
> As soon as your robe has holes,
> Take it off and repair it immediately.
>
> No one's hand should ever
> Sew the holes in your robe,
> As then your brain
> Would be stitched up, closed up.][38]

A stranger's hand sewing up holes in a dress is a euphemism for the removal of physical distance and corporal intimacy. In ordering the daughter to take care of her dress, the grandmother is in fact talking about preserving her innocence and maintaining bodily purity. She warns the granddaughter of all the dangers lurking for a girl from the provinces in the big city, where it is so easy to cease being a *kosher kind* [kosher, i.e. pure, child]. According to the grandmother, transgressing the taboo of sexual exploration will lead to changes in her way of thinking. Sewing up holes in the robe will result in the mind's closure and imprisonment. Sewing the mind up here means closing it to moral lessons — altering the value system and departing from religious norms. But the granddaughter reassures the grandmother: 'No hand and no stranger sews up holes on me.' Yet loyalty to the grandmother's principles results above all from the indifference characterizing interpersonal relationships in the metropolis: 'Each man lives for himself | — Hoo-Ha! The savage turmoil of the city!' The poem ends with the lament 'Nobody, nobody cares | If my dress is torn! ...'. It is of no one's concern whether the girl's dress is without holes (that is, whether she remains a *kosher kind*) or whether her dress is torn (that is, whether she loses her virgin purity). This has no value in the modern world.

Through the voice of an innocent little girl whose closest relationship is with her grandmother, Ulinover's poetry becomes closer to moralistic poetry for children (it is very likely that this was her intention, since she was one of the very few women poets whose works appeared in *Beys Yakov*, a periodical published by the network of Orthodox schools for girls. The dress, carefully sewn up by her own hand, becomes the banner of the *tsnue*, the virtuous woman. Such was the women's voice subconsciously expected in Yiddish poetry by male critics, who themselves created modern and liberated literature but in women's poetry sought the familiar virtuosity of their mothers and grandmothers.

The legacy that mothers have passed onto their daughters for generations becomes problematic in modern Yiddish poetry, and the communication between generations breaks down. This happens in the poem sequence 'Froyen lider' by Kadia Molodowsky,[39] where mothers describe the heritage protected, guarded, and passed down to their daughters for centuries in the following way:

> Es veln di froyen fun undzer mishpokhe bay nakht in kholoymes mir kumen un zogn:
> Mir hobn in tsnies a loytere blut iber doyres getrogn,
> Tsu dir es gebrakht vi a vayn a gehitn in koshere kelers
> Fun undzere hertser.
>
> [The women of our family will come to me in dreams at night and say:
> Modestly we carried a pure blood across generations,
> Bringing it to you like well-guarded wine from the kosher
> Cellars of our hearts.][40]

Placing modesty, purity, and blood together in one verse inevitably introduces the interpretive context of the Jewish women's problem (keeping the laws of *niddah* that refer to the purity and impurity of the woman's body and regulate marital relations in regard to the cyclical menstrual state of women's exclusion). Thus, the question of preserving the mother's heritage applies mostly to her daughters' corporality and sexuality. The daughters — the citizens of modern society and the conscious participants in social revolution — reject the modesty of their mothers: Molodowsky refers to this as the 'escape from their kosher beds'.[41] Yet running away from the mothers' legacy causes a breach in one's own identity, a gap in the spiritual genealogical continuity, as Molodowsky says to her ancestors:

> Un ayere shtile farshtikte geveyen yogn nokh mir zikh vi harbstike vintn,
> Un ayere reyd zaynen zaydene fedim oyf mayn moekh farbundn.
> Un mayn lebn an oysgefliktn blat fun a seyfer
> Un di shure di ershte farrisn.
>
> [Your whimperings race like the autumn winds past me,
> And your words are the silken cord
> Still binding my thoughts,
> My life is a page ripped out of a holy book
> And part of the first line is missing.][42]

Bertha Kling puts it in a similar way in a poem that is a daughter's monologue addressed to her deceased mother, whose 'Sabbath candlesticks' the daughter rejected:

> On dayne bentshlaykhter,
> On dem tatns kidesh-bekher
> Hot mayn mazl mikh aher gebrakht.
> [...]
> Mame,
> In keyt fun di oves,
> Bin ikh
> Der ibergerisener ring
> Tsvishn dir
> Un mayn kind.
> [Without your Sabbath candlesticks,

> Without Father's kiddush cups,
> My fate plays out here.
> [...]
>
> Mother,
> In the chain of generations,
> I am
> The broken link
> Between you
> And my child.]⁴³

Nonetheless, the escape from the 'kosher beds' of the female ancestors turns out to be incomplete, if not illusory. These modern, 'liberated' women find a piece of their rejected mothers still lurking inside them. Molodowsky addresses this explicitly:

> In nekht ven ikh bin vakh,
> Un s'kumen tsu mir teg mayne fargangene
> Zikh far di oygn shteln,
> Kumt far mir mayn mames lebn.
> [...]
> Un s'hot der umglik fun mayn eygn lebn mikh deryogt
> Un vi a kro, oyf a kleyn hindele aroyfgefaln,
> Iz oft baloykhtn hel mayn tsimer in di nekht,
> Un kh'halt di hent iber mayn kop farvorfn
> Un s'zogn mayne lipn a shtiln eynfakhn
> Gebet tsu Got
> Un s'kumen trern, vi a karger-eyntsik-tropndiker regn.
>
> [Nights when I'm awake
> And one by one my past days come
> To place themselves before my eyes,
> My mother's life comes to me.
> [...]
> And now that my own life's misfortune has hunted me down
> Like a crow falling upon a chick,
> Often my room is lit up all night,
> And I hold my hands, reproaches, over my head,
> And my lips recite a quiet, simple
> Plea to God.
> And tears come drop by drop like a stingy drizzle.]⁴⁴

Earlier, the same poem features an image of the mother reciting the 'impatient words of the evening prayer, *Ha-mapil*',⁴⁵ and the daughter — like the mother — in moments of weakness recites a simple evening plea to God. An even more dramatic reference to the mother's gestures, subconsciously constantly present in the daughter's behaviour, can be found in the second poem of the 'Froyen lider' cycle, in which a woman grudgingly addresses her first lover, whom she once trusted:

> Tsu dem vel ikh kumen,
> Ver s'hot der ershter mir mayn froyen freyd gebrakht
> Un zogn: man,
> Kh'hob nor eynem mayn shtiln blik fartroyt

> Un in a nakht lem im mayn kop geleygt.
> Itst hob ikh mayn tsar vi binen ongeshtokhene
> Arum mayn harts gebrakht,
> Un hob keyn honik nit oyf lindern mayn vund.
>
> [I will come to the one
> Who first brought me woman's delight,
> And say: Husband,
> I trusted someone else with my quiet gaze,
> And one night laid my head down near him.
> Now I bring my sorrow
> Like bees stinging around my heart,
> And have no honey to soothe the hurt.][46]

Yet she does not expect that her 'quiet gaze' and 'broken heart' will evoke the man's tenderness. She predicts quite a different reaction:

> Un s'vet der man mir nemen farn tsop,
> Vel ikh aniderbrekhn zikh oyf beyde fis
> Un blaybn oyfn shvel vi di farshteynerung fun Sdom.
>
> [And when my husband takes me by the braid,
> I will drop to my knees,
> And will remain on the doorsill like the petrifaction of Sodom.][47]

What does 'takes me by the braid' mean? This gesture can be interpreted both in the sexual context, as an expression of lust and ruthless courtship, and also as a metaphorical rendition of brutality and possessiveness. Still, most significant for our consideration is the anticipated reaction of the woman depicted in the poem: she will drop to her knees and, kneeling at the doorsill, she will resemble the 'petrifaction of Sodom', that is, Lot's wife, punished for disobedience. We read on:

> Ikh vel di hent aroyfheybn tsum kop,
> Vi s'flegt mayn mame baym bentshn likht,
> Nor s'veln mayne finger shteyn vi tsen getseylte zind.
>
> [I will raise my hands to my head,
> As my mother used to, blessing the candles,
> But my fingers will stand up like ten numbered sins.][48]

The daughter then raises her hands, imitating the mother's gesture of blessing the candles (which at the same time constitutes the most common representation of the Jewish woman, a kind of female archetype of Judaism), but her hands — instead of being the intermediaries of the sacredness — become the symbol of her faults. These hands illustrate the distance between the mother's model of life and the way her daughter lives her life, unable to free herself from the guilt of sinning.

The departure from being a *kosher kind*[49] is also manifested in a change in the manner of dressing.[50] This motif often recurs in Yiddish poetry by women. The daughters take off the dresses tightly covering their bodies and cast off the long sleeves, exposing themselves to the sun and people's eyes. In the poem below, Molodowsky shows that the mother's womanhood was symbolized by:

> [...] ire oysgedarte hent
> In tsniesdike arbl fun nakhthemd ayngehilt,
> Vi a gotsforkhtike shrift in vayse goylim.
>
> [[...] her emaciated hands
> Wrapped in modest nightgown sleeves
> Are like a God-fearing script on white parchment.]⁵¹

Having stated that 'I myself am a woman', the daughter depicts this even more precisely through her attire:

> Un gey in broynem zayd gekleydt,
> Mit bloyzn kop
> Un naket haldz.
>
> [And walk, clad in brown silk
> With my head bare
> And my throat naked.]⁵²

The rebellion against the covering up, swathing, and binding of the Jewish woman's body in order to prevent its beauty from attracting the male gaze and tempting the male caress is expressed in the poetry of the Jewish feminist and communist Khana Levin. In her poem 'Kleyder' [Dresses], the generational conflict featuring the clash of the traditional Jewish shtetl woman's identity with the modern identity of a woman living the rhythm of the city and fighting for political and feminist ideas is presented through the contrast in the mother's and daughter's manners of dressing. The young woman's dresses alienate her from her mother's world — they do not embody identification with the Jewish world. Furthermore, their unfeminine cut blurs the clear divisions between the sexes:

> In mayne kurtse kleyder,
> On kolner un on arbl,
> Azoyne glate, prostinke, vi hemder,
> Mayn mamen ze ikh oys
> A vilde un a fremde,
> Un shemevdik zi kert fun mir ir blik,
> Tsum brik.
>
> [In my short dresses,
> With no collar and no sleeves,
> As smooth and simple as men's shirts,
> In my mother's eyes I look
> Wild and strange,
> Embarrassed, she looks away from me,
> And stares at the floor.]⁵³

Both women watch each other. The mother is embarrassed by her daughter's body. The roles are somehow reversed: the mother is less experienced in the corporeal sphere, less accustomed to female sexuality than her daughter. She is disconcerted and scandalized by looking at the body she herself gave birth to: 'Kukt mayn mame af mayn yinglish-shlankn kerper, | Kukt mit shemevdikn ekl un mit vey' [Mother glances at my boyish slender body, | Embarrassed she looks with aversion and pain].⁵⁴ The daughter in turn analyses the mother's dress, which becomes the signifier of the Jewish woman's sexual potential reduced to a procreative function. The thick creases hiding the contours of the body bring to mind babies' cradles. At the same time, they are 'filled with snow', symbolizing the cooled passions of the body, frozen by virtuousness:

> Zaynen breyte, lange,
> Un oysgeleygt in faldn in gedikhte —
> Yeder fald — a vigele farvorfene mit shney.
>
> [They are wide, long,
> Arranged into thick creases —
> Each crease — a cradle filled with snow.]⁵⁵

The young woman does not want to stifle the flame of her desires. She rejects modesty and shame, wishing to burn in the fire of lust without limits, without the boundaries of moderation and caution, even if it carries the risk of losing oneself and burning out:

> Mame mayne tayere,
> Mame mayne alte!
> Vos ton mit dayne kleyder,
> Zog shoyn du aleyn.
>
> Mit dayne lange kleyder
> Un mit di hent mit mayne zhedne,
> Vos tsit azoy tsu zun —
> Fun arbl nit farshpart.
> Ot azoy vel ikh zey lozn
> Hoyle,
> Broyne,
> Shvartse.
>
> [My dear mother,
> My old mother!
> What shall I do with your dresses,
> You tell me.
>
> With your long dresses
> And with my lustful hands,
> Which I'm stretching out towards the sun —
> Without the shackles of the sleeves.
> I will leave them on this way
> Naked,
> Brown,
> Black.]⁵⁶

Yet this does not mean that she eliminates the aspect of her body's fertility, since she says: 'Nobody ever fools the sun. | And I won't be fooled by the sun either!' (the sun symbolizes sexual desire in Levin's poetry). She takes into consideration the fact that she too might become a mother, but the child she will bear will be the fruit of her passion, burnt by the sun of the lust of its mother's body:

Un oyb a kind kh'vel hobn,
Oyb eyn kind ikh vel hobn —
A tokhter, tsi a zun —
Zol es zayn a shvartse
Mit lipn fule royte,
In der mames layb nokh
Ongezapt mit zun!

[If I have a child —
If I should have one child —
A daughter, or a son —
Let it be black
With lips full of red,
Still in its mother's body
Soaked with the sun!][57]

The mere introduction of the mother figure into the reflections on Jewish corporality and female sexuality transgresses the stereotype of the *yidishe mame*, who is conventionally deprived of her body.

Sometimes, however, Yiddish women poets take things a step further, showing that under virtuous modesty lies the turmoil of desires and longing, emanating onto the daughters who no longer need to stifle this heritage. The most famous poem touching upon this issue is an autobiographical poem by Celia Dropkin, 'Mayn mame' [My Mother], which still astonishes us with its courageous innovation in the representation of the mother, even though almost eighty years have passed since its publication. Dropkin depicts her mother, who became a widow with two children at the age of twenty-two years and chose not to marry again.[58] She remained faithful to this decision, but at night she burnt lonely in the fire of desire, instilling its sparks in her daughters:

Mayn mame iz tsu keynem a vayb nit gevorn,
Nor ale filtegike,
Filyorike, filnakhtike ziftsn
Fun ir yungn un libendn vezn,
Fun ir benkndik blut,
Hob ikh mit mayn kindershn harts farnumen,
Tif in zikh ayngezapt.

[My mother became wife to no one,
But all the daily,
Yearly, nightly sighs
Of her young and affectionate being
Of her longing blood,
Seeped deeply into me,
I knew them with my child's heart.][59]

The daughter's body becomes a vessel receiving the heat of the mother's blood, yet the heritage pulsating in her blood — called 'seething and holy lust'[60] — finds an outlet, freely exploding outside, unrestrained by the dams of modesty:

> Un mayn mames farborgene zudike benkshaft
> Hot zikh, vi fun an untererdishn kval,
> Fray in mir oysgegosn.
> Itst shpritst fun mir ofn,
> Mayn mames zudiker, heyliker,
> Tif-farbahaltener bager.
>
> [And like an underground spring,
> My mother's seething, concealed longing
> Flowed freely into me.
> Now out of me, into the open
> Spurts my mother's seething, holy,
> Deeply hidden lust.][61]

This groundbreaking poem separates female desire from the issues of fertility and childbirth, and, moreover, even from the figure of man, who does not appear in the poem. The female sexual desire exists as strength in itself — a drive not directed towards a concrete partner and not based on the foundation of love and affection uniting two people. The motherly heritage depicted in this way clearly deconstructs the myth of the *yidishe mame*.

The problem of female sexuality intertwined with motherhood is also a thematic axis of Rokhl Korn's poem 'Kloglid fun yunge mames' [The Young Mothers' Complaint].[62] Mothers — the collective speaker of the poem — are women whose bodies long for love, who at night, in their own beds, yearn in anguish for erotic satisfaction:

> Unzere kinder viln gornisht visn,
> Az unzere gufim lign oysgeshtrekte, vi in fiber heyse,
> Az di tsevorfene, nakhttseshmekte hor arum unzere kep
> Viklen zikh vi di hungerike shlangen arum zeyer korbn
> Un s'varfn zikh di kep un shrayen on a kol
> In tifer, heyser nakht:
> Kum shtarker man, kum un derleyz —
>
> [Our children do not want to know at all
> That our bodies lie stretched out, like in delirium,
> That night-scented hair scattered around our heads
> Is twisting like hungry snakes around their victim,
> And the heads are tossing about, silently screaming
> Into the deep, hot night:
> — Come, strong man, come and release us —][63]

They yearn for the man, but instead of male lips and hands, it is the children's little hands that wait for them and seek them out. Their nights are sleepless not because of love, although their young blood pulsates in their bodies. Nor are their nights the time of quietude and relaxation, as their rest is interrupted by breastfeeding and rocking crying babies to sleep. These nights 'quartered' by motherhood inflict true suffering on the young women. They are like bleeding wounds:

> Un unzere kinder viln gornisht visn,
> Az mir zenen tsvantsik, zeks-un-tsvantsik, draysik-yerike,

> Nor veynen azoy umetik un hoykh un on a sof
> In di ershte nekht fun kinderishn tser
> Un tserzegn unzere yunge nekht oyf shtiker blutike un fremde.
> Zeyere hentlekh tapn in der fintster
> Un di hungerike maylekhlekh zukhn nonte varemkayt bay unz.
>
> [And our children don't want to know at all,
> That we are twenty, twenty-six, thirty years old,
> They only keep crying so sadly so loud without an end
> In the first days of their children's sorrow,
> Cutting our young nights into pieces, bloody and strange.
> Their little hands seek us out in the darkness,
> And their hungry little mouths desire from us closeness and warmth.][64]

The night-time activity of the children is contrasted in Korn's poem with the passivity of the men who 'snore with their mouths open'. Unlike the nimble little hands of the children, the men's hands are passive, tired, and heavy like 'knotty logs':

> Khrapen mener mit ofene mayler,
> Opgehorevet fun shvere toggeng nokh parnose.
> S'kortshen zikh zeyere hent in midn shlof,
> Vi di senkate kletser.
>
> Zingen unzere dorshtike oygn baynakht
> Dos lid tsu di hent fun unzere mener:
> A shvartse, horepashne hent
> Kumt,
> Viklt aykh in veykhn flaks fun di tseshmekte hor,
> Hent fun unzere mener.
>
> [In the bed across the room,
> Men snore with their mouths open,
> Exhausted by the harsh pursuit of income.
> Their hands shrink in tired sleep,
> Like knotty logs.
>
> So our hungry eyes sing at night
> A song to the hands of our husbands:
> Oh, dark, work-worn hands
> Come,
> Submerge yourselves in the soft, scented flax of hair,
> The hands of our husbands.][65]

The body's sufferings during the nights of youth, during which one needs to be a mother, and not a passionate lover, are compared to crucifixion. This metaphor, culturally understood mainly in the Christian context, is an interesting motif in Yiddish poetry, although it is worth mentioning that both Jewish visual art in the 1910s and literature exploited Christian symbols and characters, bringing them into the Jewish context and reclaiming the Jewish roots of Christianity. However, in Korn's poem, the cross does not constitute the reclaiming of Jesus's Jewishness. The cross is evoked here as a symbol of corporal torture and sacrifice, an offering. The unsatisfied erotic desires symbolically crucify the woman's body, which must be sacrificed for maternal obligations:

> S'shlogt der hamer blut in oysgeshtrektn kreyts fun layb
> Di sharfe tshvekes fun di yorn:
> Tsvantsik,
> Zeks un tsvantsik,
> Draysik,
> Durkh a yedn eyver durkh,
> Durkh der mit fun yedn tsiterdikn brekl fun unzer fleysh.
>
> [The hammer of blood
> Strikes into the outstretched cross of the body
> Sharp nails of years:
> Twenty,
> Twenty-six,
> Thirty.
> Through each limb of the body,
> Through each trembling piece of our meat.][66]

The problem of loneliness in the experience of motherhood is a significant theme in Levin's poetry, where it recurs in various guises. One of the poems, with the characteristic title 'Kinder zaynen kleyn, vos konen kinder visn' [Children Are Small, What Can Children Know] is an account of parting — the woman and the daughter are abandoned by the man, who has found another partner. The child knows that this can happen from the lives of her friends, but now has to accept the fact that the same fate has befallen her. She realizes it when the father comes only in the evenings to visit his former house and his abandoned family. The tragedy of the situation is heightened by the child's naive questions and statements:

> Er voynt den af der arbet? Er shloft den in fabrik?
> S'hot Vites tate a mame zikh gekoyft.
> Gor a naye mame af an ander gas,
> Az tsu Vites mamen kumt er nor tsugast.
> Vi kon a tate voynen af an ander gas?
> Er iz dokh a tate, vi kon er zayn a gast?
>
> [Does daddy live at work now? Does he sleep in the factory?
> Vita's daddy bought a new mummy.
> A whole new mummy on another street.
> And now he just visits Vita's mummy.
> How can daddy live on a different street?
> He is my daddy, how can he be a guest?][67]

From the child's perspective, the change in her parents' relationship is an incomprehensible part of the games the adults play, an absurdity at odds with reason that shatters the order in the world. The tragedy of the child, and simultaneously of the mother, who is unable to do anything to change the course of events and to protect her child from unhappiness, is emphasized by the ironic verse recurring in the poem like a refrain: 'The years of childhood bliss, what can children understand.' The stereotype of carefree childhood is exposed as false, since the child, not yet protected by the shell of experience, is all the more vulnerable, becoming a victim of the affairs of the father, who has 'bought | A whole new mummy'.

The childish language exposes the brutal truth about the 'modern' relations between men and women based on free love. The poem ends with a moving image of the daughter and the mother, all the closer to each other, as they are united by shared tragedy:

> Tsu der mamen tulyet es dem vareminkn guf,
> Tsu der mames bakn, tsu der mames lip:
> — Ikh vel dikh shtendik, shtendik nokh merer hobn lib!
> — Vos plaplstu, du narele, shlof shoyn gikher ayn,
> Der tate vet dokh, narele, af dir broygez zayn.
> Nor di verter tayere hobn mer keyn makht,
> Un nokh hekher veynt dos kind, yomert in der nakht.
> Un in vey tsunoyfgemisht di blonde hor un groye,
> Veynen zey, vi glaykhe, tsvey farlozene froyen.
> Un ba der bet tsufusns kukt zikh shtilerheyt
> A hezele a militener mit eygelekh farshneyt,
> Mit a farneytn maylekhl zoygt zikh shtil zayn mer,
> Un s'rirt im nit keyn kleyninke, keyn tsiterdike trer.
>
> [She nestles her warm little body up to her mother,
> To mother's cheeks, to mother's mouth.
> — I will always, always love you more and more!
> — What twaddle, silly, go to sleep sooner,
> Because father will be angry,
> But the warm words have lost their power,
> And the child weeps ever louder, despairing in the night.
> Blonde and grey hairs are plaited.
> They weep, like two women abandoned just the same.
> And at the foot of the bed quietly looks on
> A little rabbit with stitched-on eyes,
> With its sewn mouth, it sucks on a carrot,
> And is not moved by any tiny, trembling tear.][68]

Other poems by Levin feature depictions of the struggles of the woman and mother in the reality of everyday life after separation, when she has to meet the challenge of fulfilling the roles of both a mother and a father, which eventually turns out to be not entirely possible:

> Keyner zol nit trakhtn, meynen,
> Az tsaytn baytn yeder zakh,
> Farlozte froyen shtendik veynen,
> Un ikh veyn oykhet yeder nakht.
> Nit derfar, vos ikh vel eyne nekht nit shlofn ba dayn vig,
> Kh'vel aleyn dikh konen vign,
> Treyst mayn eynzame, mayn glik.
> Darfst mayn libe nokh lesate,
> Mit mayn nomen ruf ikh dikh,
> Un zayn a mame un a tate
> Beyde zakhn kh'nem af zikh.

Nor dayn kindersh kol mikh matert,
Ven ikh her, ikh kuk zikh tsu —
Yedn fremdn rufstu — tate,
Tulyest zikh tsu fremde kni.

Tsi ikh tsertl dikh den veynik,
Tsertlen dikh ikh ver nit mid,
Alts ikh kon,
Eyn zakh ikh kon nit —
Dayn tate brengen kon ikh nit.
Un derfar ikh fil zikh shuldik
Far dayn umshuldikn blik,
Yedn fremdn rufstu — tate,
Tsu yeder kni gist zikh a drik.

Keyner zol nit trakhtn, denken,
Az tsaytn baytn yeder zakh,
Ven nokh tate kinder benken,
Veynen mames yeder nakht.

[Nobody should think
That time changes everything,
Abandoned women still weep,
And I, too, weep every night.
Not because sometimes
I cannot sleep at your cradle,
I always want to lull you,
Comfort my lonely fortune.
Meanwhile you need my love,
You bear my name,
Upon myself I take it
To be mother and father.
Only your childish voice torments me,
When I hear and see —
How you call every strange man — Daddy,
How you cuddle up to strangers' knees.

Do I caress you little,
In tenderness I do not cease,
I can do everything,
But one thing — not,
I cannot bring back your father.
This is why I feel guilty
Under your pure gaze,
When you call every strange man — daddy,
You cuddle up to strangers' knees.

Nobody should think,
That time changes everything,
When children miss their fathers,
Mothers weep at night.][69]

The child's presence prevents the mother from surrendering to the passage of time and forgetting about the man to whom she was once so close. The child is a continuous embodied manifestation of its father, and thus the woman's relationship with the latter cannot become a mere element of the past. The child's longing for the father constantly reopens the wounds of the break-up. What is worse, the woman's sense of guilt and remorse is evoked by the fact that she is unable to provide a father for her child. The woman's loneliness is intensified by the sense of the child's loneliness.

Levin's motherhood poems make a diagnosis about the great abyss dividing the male and female experiences of parenthood, from the bodily dimension of pregnancy when one body becomes a cradle for another — inaccessible to men — through the woman's inability to accept the tragedy of the loss of a child, to the consequences of broken relationships and the fate — assigned to the woman — of solitarily raising the 'fruit' of the man and woman's encounter.

Conclusion

The problem of motherhood and the relationships between mothers and daughters, perceived in the context of social revolution, constitutes a significant motif in modern women's Yiddish poetry. Yet the women's experience as expressed in the written word often met with patronization and rejection on the part of male editors and critics who did not consider it suitable for the accepted canons of discourse. The development and popularization of the Yiddish press, egalitarian in nature, was one of the crucial factors that contributed to the flourishing of women's poetry in print, although — it needs to be emphasized — the periodical editorial teams were male, and it was men who had the authority to decide what would be published and what would not. In their treatment of women's works, they often exhibited a tendency to impose on women's creations a literary *ezrat nashim*, or a women's section — a space separated from the main 'ceremony' of the construction of modern literature.

An excellent example of the difficulties faced by women poets in the patriarchal literary world is a commentary published in 1933 in regard to the publication of Ida Maze's *Mame* [Mama],[70] which is in its entirety a poetic lament on the grave of a deceased child. The poetry collection was sent for review to the prestigious literary periodical *Globus*, published in Warsaw. This was the editor's response: 'This little book was sent to the editorial office. Its title is too holy: Mama, and not incidentally. As seen in the poems, they were not written by a person with artistic weigh and measure in hand, but — indeed — simply by a mama. [...] Is it possible to review a mother's crying?'.[71] These few sentences reveal the 'demons' of male critique of women's literary works: the category of motherhood, often defining the discourse on women's poetry, is evoked here: on the one hand, it is seen in the context of exalted holiness, with the burden of glorification, and on the other hand, it is primitivized as a primeval experience. Nonetheless, the conclusion is unequivocal — the mother cannot be 'a person of artistic consideration and moderation'. Evading conventionally accepted aesthetic categories, women's poetry was often doomed to omission or silence; for how can one 'review a mother's crying?'. The 'person with artistic weight and measure in hand' — whose artistic creations can be evaluated using familiar criteria and models — had, in the domain of Yiddish critical discourse (and the vast majority of critics were also the editors of the literary periodicals), the face of a man.

Notes to Chapter 3

1. See Daniel Boyarin, *Unheroic Conduct: The Rise of Heterosexuality and the Invention of the Jewish Man* (Berkeley: University of California Press, 1997), pp. 151–85.
2. According to rabbinical law, a girl can get married after the age of twelve, a boy after the age of thirteen. Early marriage was seen in the traditional Jewish community as a religious ideal. As David Biale points out: 'In Eastern Europe, the age of marriage, especially among the elite, remained very young throughout the eighteenth century, and it became one of the marks that distinguished the *Ostjuden* (Eastern Jews) in the eyes of the German Jews' (*Eros and the Jew: From Biblical Israel to Contemporary America* (New York: Basic Books, 1992), p. 128). The state law regarding the age of marriage was bypassed by not reporting religious weddings.
3. See Iris Parush, *Reading Jewish Women: Marginality and Modernization in Nineteenth-Century Eastern European Jewish Society*, trans. by Saadya Strenberg (Waltham: Brandeis University Press, 2004), pp. 38–56.
4. See Paula E. Hyman, *Gender and Assimilation in Modern Jewish History: The Roles and Representation of Women* (Seattle and London: University of Washington Press, 1997).
5. See Joanna Lisek, 'Feminist Discourse in Women's Yiddish Press', *Pamiętnik Literacki*, 4 (2008), 61–77.
6. In 1888, Roza Goldshteyn made her debut in the *Judishes folks-blat*; currently, she is considered the first modern female Yiddish poet. See Kathryn Hellerstein, *A Question of Tradition: Women Poets in Yiddish, 1586–1987* (Stanford: Stanford University Press, 2014).
7. See Chava Weissler, *Voices of the Matriarchs: Listening to the Prayers of Early Modern Jewish Women* (Boston: Beacon Press, 1998); *The Merit of our Mothers: A Bilingual Anthology of Jewish Women's Prayers*, ed. and trans. by Tracy Guren Klirs, Ida Cohen Seavan, and Gella Schweid Fishman (Cincinnati: Hebrew Union College Press, 1992).
8. On Dropkin, see Sheva Zucker, 'The Red Flower: Rebellion and Guilt in the Poetry of Celia Dropkin', in *Women Writers of Yiddish Literature: Critical Essays*, ed. by Rosemary Horowitz (Jefferson: McFarland, 2015), pp. 51–69; Hellerstein, *Question of Tradition*, pp. 243–322; Janet Hadda, 'The Eyes Have It: Celia Dropkin's Love Poetry', in *Gender and Text in Modern Hebrew and Yiddish Literature*, ed. by Naomi B. Sokoloff, Anna Lapidus Lerner, and Anita Norich (Cambridge: Harvard University Press, 1992), pp. 93–112; Kathryn Hellerstein, 'From Ikh to Zikh: A Journey from "I" to "Self" in Yiddish Poems by Women', in *Gender and Text*, ed. by Sokoloff, Lerner, and Norich, pp. 113–43.
9. Celia Dropkin, *In heysn vint* (New York: Pozi-Shaulzon, 1935), p. 65.
10. Ibid.
11. Pessie Hershfeld, 'Oyfbli', *Der hamer*, December 1928, p. 9. Pessie Hershfeld (Pomerantz-Honigbaum; 1900–1978), born in Kamenbrod, Belarus, studied in a Russian school, had private tutoring in Yiddish and Russian, and also learned German and French. In 1913, she emigrated to America, where she became part of the young Jewish writers' circle affiliated with the periodical *Yung Shikago*. She made her debut in 1918. She also lived in Detroit and New York. She published her first volume of poetry, *Kareln*, in 1926. All in all, she published four poetry collections. She was married to the writer and cultural activist Chaim Pomerantz.
12. Hershfeld.
13. Ibid.
14. Ibid.
15. Ibid.
16. Ibid.

17. Rosa Yakubovitsh, 'Tsu zoyg-kind', in Rosa Yakubovitsh, *Mayne gezangen* (Warsaw: Sikora & Milner, 1924), p. 12. On Yakubovitsh, see Hellerstein, *Question of Tradition*, pp. 169–242.
18. Yakubovitsh, 'Tsu zoyg-kind'.
19. Ibid.
20. Rosa Yakubovitsh, 'Di shrek', in Yakubovitsh, *Mayne gezangen*, p. 13.
21. Ibid.
22. Kadya Molodowsky, *Paper Bridges: Selected Poems of Kadya Molodowsky*, ed. and trans. by Kathryn Hellerstein (Detroit: Wayne State University Press, 1999), p. 83. On Molodowsky, see e.g. Hellerstein, *Question of Tradition*, pp. 414–18.
23. Ibid.
24. Ibid.
25. Ibid.
26. On Levin, see Joanna Lisek, '"Of all the men I am the most manly": Aspects of Gender in the Poetry of Khane Levin', in *Women Writers*, ed. by Horowitz, pp. 126–56. See also Gennady Estraikh, 'Khana Levin's Verdict to Free Love', in *Yiddish Poets in the Soviet Union, 1917–1948*, ed. by Daniela Mantovan (Heidelberg: Winter, 2012), pp. 87–94.
27. Khana Levin, *Tsushtayer* (Kharkiv: State Publishing House of Ukraine, 1929), pp. 7–8.
28. Ibid., p. 8.
29. Ibid.
30. Ibid., pp. 8–9.
31. See Kathryn Hellerstein, 'The Metamorphosis of the Matriarchs in Modern Yiddish Poetry', in *Yiddish Language and Culture: Then and Now*, ed. by Leonard Jay Greenspoon (Omaha: Creighton University Press, 1998), pp. 201–64.
32. Luce Irigaray, 'Body against Body: In Relation to the Mother', in Luce Irigaray, *Sexes and Genealogies*, trans. by Gillian C. Gill (New York: Columbia University Press, 1987), pp. 18–19.
33. *Finf hundert yor yidishe poezye: Antologye*, ed. by Moshe Basin (New York: Dos bukh, 1917), p. 112.
34. Ibid., pp. 112–13.
35. Bertha Kling (1885–1978) was born in Novogrodek and present in America from 1899. She made her debut in 1916 in the New York newspaper *Varhayt* and later published three volumes of poetry.
36. Yakov Yitskhok Sigal, 'A vort', in Kling, pp. 3–4 (p. 3). 'Got fun Avrom' is a women's prayer/song which is read as the Sabbath concludes on Saturday night; see <http://yiddishsong.wordpress.com/2010/05/25/got-fun-avrom-performed-by-bella-bryks-klein/> [accessed 3 June 2016].
37. On Ulinover, see Natalia Krynicka, 'Araynfir', in Miriam Ulinover, *A grus fun der alter heym: Lider*, ed. by Natalia Krynicka, trans. by Batia Baum (Paris: Medem-bibliotek, 2003), pp. 23–27.
38. Ulinover, p. 83.
39. On Molodowsky's 'Froyen lider', see F. Peczenik, 'Encountering the Matriarchy: Kadye Molodowsky's Women Songs', *Yiddish*, 7.2–3 (1988), 170–73; Kathryn Hellerstein, 'Kadya Molodowsky's Froyen-lider: A Reading', *AJS Review*, 13.1–2 (1988), 47–79; Sheva Zucker, 'Kadye Molodowsky's "Froyen-lider"', *Yiddish*, 9.2 (1994), 44–51.
40. Molodowsky, p. 69 (trans. by Hellerstein).
41. Ezra Korman, *Yidishe dikhterins: Antologye* (Chicago: Stein, 1928), p. 191.
42. Molodowsky, p. 69 (trans. by Adrienne Rich, in *A Treasury of Yiddish Poetry*, ed. by Irving Howe and Eliezer Greenberg (New York, Chicago, and San Francisco: Holt, Rinehart and Winston, 1969), p. 284).
43. Kling, p. 41.
44. Molodowsky, p. 85 (trans. by Hellerstein).
45. Ibid.
46. Molodowsky, p. 71 (trans. by Hellerstein).
47. Ibid.
48. Ibid.

49. A *kosher kind* is a characteristic description of the speaker of the poem appearing in the Yiddish poems of the religious poet Miriam Ulinover (1890–1944); cf. e.g. her 'A brivele der boben', discussed above.
50. For more on this, see Joanna Lisek, 'Wigs, Clogs, and Silk: Poetic Dresses in the Yiddish Wardrobe', *RitaBaum*, 17 (November 2011), 18–23.
51. Molodowsky, p. 85 (trans. by Hellerstein).
52. Ibid.
53. Levin, *Tsushtayer*, p. 16.
54. Ibid.
55. Ibid., p. 17.
56. Ibid., p. 18.
57. Ibid.
58. Dropkin, p. 48.
59. Ibid. (trans. by Hellerstein, *Question of Tradition*, p. 246).
60. Ibid.
61. Ibid.
62. Rokhl Korn, *Dorf* (Vilna: Kletskin, 1928), p. 24. On Korn, see Heather Valencia, '"Yidishe dikhterins": The Emergence of Modern Women's Poetry in Yiddish and Rokhl Korn's Poetic Debut', *European Judaism*, 42.2 (2009), 80–93.
63. Korn, p. 24.
64. Ibid.
65. Ibid., p. 23.
66. Ibid.
67. Khana Levin, *Eygns* (Kiev: State Publishing House, 1941), pp. 58–59.
68. Ibid., pp. 60–61.
69. Levin, *Eygns*, pp. 64–65.
70. On Maze, see Adam Fuestenberg, 'Ida Maze (1893–1962)', in *Jewish Women's Archive* <https://jwa.org/encyclopedia/article/maze-ida> [accessed 7 January 2017].
71. 'A mame', *Globus*, 12 (1933), p. 84.

CHAPTER 4

Yidishe Dikhterins, Nice Jewish Girls: Creating Communities in Jewish Literary History*

Zohar Weiman-Kelman

1928 was a major year for women's writing in general and lesbian writing in particular.[1] That same year, *Yidishe dikhterins*, the first anthology of Yiddish women's writing, was published.[2] In 1982, between the feminist sex wars and the Lebanon War, *Nice Jewish Girls*, the first Jewish lesbian anthology, came out.[3] Looking at these anthologies, at poetry, essays, journalistic work, and literary criticism, this essay will trace some of the ways connections are drawn and communities are built within the particular moments (1928 and 1982), but also across time, generating what Christopher Nealon has termed queer sodality, a collectivity formed transhistorically.[4] Following Nealon, I embrace the idea that the generation of cross-temporal community is a queer act in and of itself, bringing writings based in non-heterosexual identities/desire (as in the case of lesbian literature) together with writers who cannot (and need not) be identified with non-heterosexual identities/ desires. Indeed, the act of connection across different identities and different times is what constitutes the queer historical impulse,[5] and what generates queer communities.

Collectivity in history and across history has largely been denied to women, whose history has been continually erased and rewritten. Giving voice to this rupture, Kadia Molodowsky turns to foremothers, writing:

> Un ayere shtile farshtikte geveyen yogn nokh mir zikh vi harbstike vintn,
> un ayere reyd zaynen zaydene fedim oyf mayn moekh farbundn.
> Um mayn lebn an oysgefliktn blat fun seyfer
> un di shure di ershte farrisn.

> [Your whimperings race like the autumn winds past me,
> and your words are the silken cord
> still binding my thoughts,
> My life is a page ripped out of a holy book
> and part of the first line is missing.][6]

---

* Some of this material has been published in my book, *Queer Expectations: A Genealogy of Jewish Women's Poetry* (Albany: SUNY Press, 2018).

These lines from Molodowsky's 'Froyen lider', which are perhaps the most famous lines of Yiddish women's poetry, were published in Korman's *Yidishe dikhterins* and translated by the Jewish lesbian poet Adrienne Rich, a leading voice in *Nice Jewish Girls*. They metaphorically bring together life and text as the poet/speaker negotiates her relationship with her foremothers and with Jewish history. Ripped out of the holy book, her line may be torn, but her lines of poetry give voice to the words and cries of the women who came before her, whose lives, like her own, 'have until so recently been forced out of history, ripped from our collective memory',[7] as Blanche Cook writes. Cook asserts that, 'like the historical denial of women's history generally, the historical denial of the vast range of women-loving women has not been an accident'.[8] It is in this denial that Adrienne Rich (the same author who translated Molodowsky's lines above) anchors her analysis in 'Compulsory Heterosexuality and Lesbian Existence', offering her own account of the consequences of erasure and its impact on women's collectivity:

> The destruction of records and memorabilia and letters documenting the realities of lesbian existence must be taken very seriously as a means of keeping heterosexuality compulsory for women, since what has been kept from our knowledge is joy, sensuality, courage, and community, as well as guilt, self-betrayal, and pain.[9]

Or, phrased poetically in 'Transcendental Etude', the final poem of Rich's 1978 *Dream of a Common Language*:

> Birth stripped our birthright from us,
> tore us from a woman, from women, from ourselves
> so early on
> and the whole chorus throbbing at our ears
> like midges, told us nothing, nothing
> of origins, nothing we needed
> to know, nothing that could re-member us.[10]

Both pieces connect the erasure of female and lesbian knowledge and/of history to the dominance of particular identities (enforcing heterosexuality) and to the foreclosure of community. Rich's poem ties this historical erasure to the fundamental psychoanalytic notion of female lack, only to discount the power of both. 'But in fact we were always like this,' writes Rich right before the lines quotes above, 'rootless, dismembered: knowing it makes the difference.' 'Like this' is a state of lack, being 'rootless, dismembered', echoing the psychoanalytic female condition. Teresa de Lauretis cites Rich's poem as a site 'where the fantasy of dispossession is most explicitly linked to the subject's loss of the female body in the mother, in herself and in the other woman'.[11] Over and against the fantasy of dispossession, I read the recognition that 'we were always like this' as a way of denying not the female body ('lack' of penis included) but castration itself; this didn't 'happen' to us, 'we were always like this'. Castration is then no threat, and Rich counters the phallocentric understanding of females as 'dismembered'. Rather than reading 'this' (lack) in relation to the biology or psychoanalytic models of an individual, Rich invites us to read her text as part of the very struggle against denial and erasure, a reclaiming of history, recasting the Oedipal drama as a collective call. Following this reading, the later wish to 're-member' (in the final line quoted) is not the near-literal repair of an original castration, focusing on a male 'member', but instead a way of connecting as members of a female collectivity, repairing the rupture created when birth 'tore us from women'. It is a return to a lost collectivity. The model of community that emerges is, therefore, one that exists both across time and within time, making memory and history necessarily communally based and community-generating projects.

Striving for such community, the feminist and lesbian movements of the late 1970s and early 1980s placed significant emphasis on women's history. In the Jewish case, this is particularly evident in projects like the 1986 *Tribe of Dina*, which 'revealed Jewish women's participation in Jewish life',[12] offering a diverse portrait of contemporary Jewish feminist reality, while placing significant weight on historical writing. While the *Tribe* was not titled a lesbian anthology, it was originally published as a special issue of *Sinister Wisdom: A Multicultural Lesbian Literary & Art Journal*. This is the oldest surviving lesbian literary journal, launched in 1976 and edited in the early 1980s by Adrienne Rich and her long-term partner, Michelle Cliff. Irena Klepfisz and Melanie Kaye/Kantrowitz, the editors of *The Tribe*, explicitly connect the beginning of their project to *Nice Jewish Girls*, the first Jewish lesbian anthology, published just a few years earlier. *Nice Jewish Girls* broke barriers of silence and erasure, and served as an important platform for articulating the challenges entailed in Jewish lesbian identities. In its footsteps, *The Tribe* was able to follow with more contemporary breadth while giving voice to women of the past, thus becoming one of the first resources for translations of primary texts by Yiddish women writers; it contained translations of Kadia Molodowsky, Anna Margolin, and Fradel Shtok.[13]

By the 1980s, there were certainly a number of other English-language anthologies of Yiddish writing, some of which included women, but as the scholar and translator Kathryn Hellerstein bemoans, the number of women included was by no means representative of their actual participation, leaving English-speaking readers unaware of how rich women's cultural production had been.[14] And although the treasures of women's writing were available to Yiddish readers in diverse publications, first and foremost Korman's *Yidishe dikhterins*, they were neither widely known nor accessible. In order to become 'found treasures', as the title of one relatively recent translation anthology puts it,[15] most women's texts had to wait many years. Many are still waiting.

Hellerstein describes having no knowledge of women's writing even when she was already a graduate student of Yiddish literature, and details her process of discovering this history.[16] Some twenty years later, my own experience was not dissimilar, illuminating the combination of hurdles facing projects such as my own: the challenges women faced when trying to enter Jewish history, the challenge of discovering women's history in the face of its discontinuous transmission, the challenge of identifying the lesbian over and against its historical erasure, the challenge of overcoming the persistent marginalization of both women and Yiddish

— alongside many others, such as Mizrahi writing and works by Mizrahi women writers — in Jewish and Israeli culture. This essay is an attempt to meet some of these challenges while viewing their persistence as another mode of cross-historical connection between women past and present.

Contrasting the trajectories of lesbian history and Jewish history, Rich writes that 'lesbian existence has been lived (unlike, say, Jewish or Catholic existence) without access to any knowledge of a tradition, a continuity, a social underpinning'.[17] True as Rich's qualifier may be for (some) Jewish men, Jewish women had to struggle for inclusion in Jewish tradition and history. Continuing this dynamic, Rich's turn to the Jewish past entailed a complex coming to terms with her own history and identity. As she reveals in her famous 1982 essay 'Split at the Root'[18] and in numerous other works, Rich's own access to Jewish tradition was more interrupted than continuous. What she inherited from both her father, whom she describes as an assimilated Jew, and her mother, a Protestant from the American South, was a sense of shame about her Jewishness. Her essay makes clear how fraught her path to Jewish identity was: writing it feels like a 'dangerous act filled with guilt and shame'.[19] Besides societal shame over being Jewish and/or gay, Rich and many of the women writing in *Nice Jewish Girls* describe not having access to all the resources of Jewish culture as a source of shame, frustration, and anger. Despite this frustration that Rich and other Jewish lesbians of the 1970s felt at being cut off from Jewish texts past and present, we might see the shared marginalization as an experience connecting them directly to their Jewish foremothers, who were in general equally or more directly marginalized from Jewish history and Jewish learning.

'The Yiddish cultural legacy, *di goldene keyt*, which had been passed on to me was strictly male', protests Irena Klepfisz, who then goes 'searching for *di bikher un sforim* from which Molodowsky's page might have been torn'. But Klepfisz desperately wanted to find out '*vos di froyen hobn getrakht un geshribn*, what the women had thought and written'.[20] Klepfisz explains that feminist identity politics 'with its implicit multiculturalism pushed many of us to strengthen our ties to our cultural origin and to search for our specific women's history, our cultural foremothers and role models'.[21] For Klepfisz, this is a meeting of feminism and a Jewish perspective, and is part of her 'beginning to think from a Jewish feminist perspective, helping make visible a woman's link in the chain of Jewish history'.[22] For 'it would be presumptuous of any of us to act as if nothing came before us',[23] writes Klepfisz, calling for Jewish writing in English that looks back to the Yiddish texts of the nineteenth and twentieth centuries, and makes Yiddish women writers a 'significant reference point in our writing',[24] as she herself does. Looking back, we see that even Molodowsky, one of the pioneers of Yiddish women's literature, who wrote contemporaneously with many other women, herself made women of the past 'a significant point of reference'.[25]

Molodowsky's turn to the past and her special interest in the notable women who came before her is manifested not only in her poetic turn to her foremother but also in the extensive series of women's biographies she wrote under the name 'Rivke Zilberg', published in the New York Yiddish newspaper *Forverts* in the

1950s.²⁶ She writes there about world-famous women such as Sappho and Harriet Beecher Stowe, Jewish women such as Glikl of Hameln and Henrietta Szold, as well as about wives and mothers of famous Jewish men. While researching this series in the YIVO Archives in New York, I was surprised to discover a strikingly similar series written by the Yiddish journalist Esther Luria in the women's pages of *Forverts* from 1914 to 1920. Luria, born in Warsaw in 1887, was far less successful than Molodowsky, and is said to have died 'alone and in poverty' in New York in the 1920s.²⁷ While Molodowsky's selection of women is very close to Luria's, the essays themselves bear little resemblance to each other, and Molodowsky likely had no knowledge of Luria's work. This unknowing repetition serves as an apt model for the perils of women's history and its many fissures and voids.

Before Molodowsky began dedicating her industrious efforts to women's history, one of her earliest essayistic publications, 'Bagegenishn' [Encounters],²⁸ rebels against the separate category of 'women's writing'. Molodowsky describes the challenges, possibly insurmountable, of building a contemporary community of Yiddish women writers. In contrast to Klepfisz's and Rich's desire and search for such a community, Molodowsky responds to disparaging literary critiques that categorically lump women's poetry into one category or even onto one page. Molodowsky insists that the poets themselves do not respect ('haltn nisht fun') such a grouping and nor do their poems. 'They', the poems, 'stand with their backs to one another and often don't even bump into each other, they want to avoid each other.' Molodowsky brilliantly continues by way of parody, bringing to life the encounters poets have when their poems share a single page ('eyn zaytl') and are quite literally confined together in various journals under the 'characterless rubric of women's poetry [*froyen dikhtung*]'. Weaving together images and quotations from their poems, she animates each poet, just to show how little they have in common with one another. While Miriam Ulinover (1890–1944) speaks of God and Jerusalem, Esther Shumiatcher (1899–1985) invokes Allah and crucifixes. Rokhl Korn (1898–1982) walks barefoot and Anna Margolin wears a mask. Molodowsky herself meets Khana Levin (1900–69), who is holding a 'Lenin in one hand and a revolver in the other', whereas Molodowsky stands surrounded by names from an old prayer book. When Levin notices this 'fayntlikhe relikvye' [enemy relic], as she terms the prayer book that Molodowsky is holding, she points the revolver at her, causing the cloud of names floating around her to disperse 'and a white paper trail' to stretch between them.²⁹

The target of Molodowsky's critique was actually one of her avid supporters, the Yiddish writer and literary critic Melech Ravitch (1893–1976). In his review of Korman's *Yidishe dikhterins*, Ravitch similarly animates women's poems, presenting them as a chorus of women, each speaking louder than the next, trying to 'iber-zing' [out-sing] the others.³⁰ Ravitch deems Molodowsky the actual 'firstin' [princess] of the entire anthology, saying that Korman could easily have tripled the space he gave her (which already consists of nine pages, whereas many writers only have one), letting her speak longer in this 'froyen-aseyfe' [women's gathering]. This inaugural 'gathering' of Yiddish women's writing holds poems by more than seventy Yiddish women poets ranging from 1586 to 1928.³¹

The sheer weight of the book is astounding, declaring defiantly *mir zaynen do*, 'we are here'. Indeed, my own initial surprise at the existence of Yiddish women's poetry seems especially misplaced when encountering the breadth of Korman's anthology. And yet, like so many other Yiddish books, like so much of women's history, it was not passed down to me as an integral part of my cultural legacy. Similarly, the history the anthology brings forth is itself a sort of rescue project; as Hellerstein writes, Korman himself 'claimed that this "*froyen literatur*" had been buried in the dust of archival libraries, inaccessible to the reading public and also even to literary researchers and historians'.[32] Like the case of the parallel works of Luria and Molodowsky, here too women's history is repeatedly lost and found. Moreover, Korman is not only excavating materials of the past but also making available a wide range of contemporary (or recently past) materials that Jewish dispersion made inaccessible, for example works separated by the geographical distance of South Africa or Australia, or by the political distance of the Soviet Union. Both aspects of the encounter offered by the anthology, the encounter across time and the encounter across space, create a community across discontinuity. This anthology, then, is in itself another version of a boundary-transgressing queer tribe.

Perhaps the most haunting aspect of the work is the inclusion of small photographic portraits of writers pasted into its hundreds of pages, which lends this large volume the feel of a handmade scrapbook or family album, making it all the more precious, fragile, and ultimately fleeting.[33] Echoing this personalized touch, *The Tribe of Dina* also includes portraits of its contributors, from Anna Margolin to Irena Klepfisz. Some are photographed in context, like a very young (by now famous and over fifty) Sarah Schulman, posing in front of the New York city skyscape, or the family-style portraits included under the rubric 'The Women in our Family' and ranging from Kadia Molodowsky to the Yiddish translator Ruth Whitman. These photographs serve, like those in Korman's anthology, to build a sense of familiarity and even familial kinship with the writers, while visually marking a temporal difference between the writers and today's reader. Even if the authors themselves were to return to the book, their own distance from the time in which they were portrayed would certainly be one of the first things they would encounter. For, of course, 1970s lesbians developed into 1980s and 1990s lesbians, and so on (even if adhering to many of the fashion markers and political dress codes they established back in the day!). The photos thus mark the passage of time as much as they bring the past closer to the reader in an unmediated visual presence.

Korman himself roots his anthologizing strategy in his historical time; since the new modernist *froyen dikhtung* (women's poetry) is only in its initial stages and not yet at its zenith, he explains, he will refrain from judgements and generalizations, though these will certainly come.[34] Realizing Korman's prediction for the future, Kathryn Hellerstein's long-awaited study, *A Question of Tradition: Women Poets in Yiddish, 1586–1987*, 'picks up where Korman left off. More than eighty years after his anthology appeared, with the benefit of subsequent scholarship in Yiddish and gender studies, we are now in a position to read these poets qualitatively and analytically'.[35] A central aspect of this work involves activating the wide historical span that Korman offers, by reading modern poems for their premodern, and specifically religious, resonance, while recognizing the unique strategies of both modern and premodern poets. This, indeed, was Korman's own stated intention; he explains that his juxtaposition of old and new enables us to see, in his words, both the *yerushedikayt*, the inheritance, of 'our modern women-poets' and 'the far journey' they have gone on the path divined and travelled by those before them.[36]

Rather than a simple line of lineage, however, Hellerstein claims that including premodern poets is part of Korman's attempt to

> resolve the contradiction between his desire to ground modern Yiddish poetry in premodern traditions and his stated belief in the *lack of a direct connection* between the two bodies of work. In other words, Korman was creating a tradition that he believed did not really exist.[37]

Similarly, Avraham Novershtern suggests that, rather than discovering a 'tradition' of Yiddish women's poetry, Korman creates the illusion of such a 'tradition'.[38] This is the anthology's most concrete influence ('hashpa'ot mukhashiyot') according to Novershtern, who deems the scope it declares as false ('prisa meduma'), for in practice only four of the seventy poets actually belong to the category of Old Yiddish literature (ending in the eighteenth century), and only two are from the nineteenth century.[39] He goes on to argue that there was no attempt on the part of Yiddish women poets to create their own literary tradition, for 'it is hard to point out a woman's poem in Yiddish that has an explicit dialogue with another woman's poem in Yiddish';[40] they generally turn to a male addressee (overturning the convention of Yiddish literature's female audience);[41] they do not refer to the tradition of the *tkhines*, but rather to the *taytsh-khumesh*, written for women but not by them (as he shows through the example of the unusually traditional poet Miriam Ulinover);[42] and they do not take up women's voices through Yiddish folklore (though here he invokes Ulinover as the exception to the rule).[43]

Novershtern is particularly concerned with Korman's focus on numbers of women writers, and suggests that his criteria for selection favoured quantity over quality, which not only skews the image of women's writing but also misleads later readers. It appears that the worst consequence of this 'illusion' is the feminist study of Yiddish it enables and against which Novershtern intervenes, naming among others, Norma Fain Pratt, Kathryn Hellerstein, and Anita Norich. Reducing the work of feminist scholarship to a focus on femininity, Novershtern binds this scholarship to the early ghettoizing of Yiddish women's writing, showing that the category of 'women's writing' is the product of a literary criticism controlled entirely by men. Speaking to the political and academic concerns of feminist scholars, who would most likely rather not be viewed as the heirs of a misogynistic tradition of literary criticism, Novershtern goes on to recruit Molodowsky's and other Yiddish women's own rejection of being grouped in this way. The analysis aims to expose feminist scholarship as a double betrayal of women's writing by aligning it retroactively with the women's critics and presenting it as against the women's wishes.

Ironically, these feminist scholars are not just the objects of Novershtern's critique but also, presumably, his target audience, since his study appeared in a special issue of the Israeli journal *Bikoret ufarshanut* [Criticism and Interpretation] dedicated to women's writing. Overall, it would seem that what Novershtern is most disturbed by is the very desire that there be a tradition of women's writing, be it expressed in the 1920s, in the 1970s, or today. Answering this critique in her stunning and already mentioned study, *A Question of Tradition*, Hellerstein undoes many of Novershtern's generalizations, armed with some thirty years of meticulous archival and literary scholarship. *A Question of Tradition* proves that a gendered lens does not limit our reading to one common denominator but rather reveals the many ways in which women had to vie with Jewish tradition, making it their own. As much as he riles against the idea of women's tradition, up until the publication of Hellerstein's book, Novershtern's essay was not only one of the most comprehensive pieces of scholarship on women's poetry; it was also one of the only works to offer an overview of literary criticism written about women's writing and of the feminist criticism done in the field. Therefore, Novershtern himself made an invaluable contribution to the legacy of Yiddish women writers and writing on them, inadvertently producing another version of this queer tribe's 'imagined tradition'[44] on the very basis of his difference from and conflict with it.

The desire for a cross-temporal community of women has certainly fuelled much of the work on Yiddish women's writing, and the investment in an 'imagined tradition' reflects both the desire for tradition and the fact that, at times, it can only be constituted by the imagination. Indeed, the limited availability of histories often led women to generate imaginary and fictional versions of the lives of both famous and anonymous women; as Bonnie Zimmerman notes specifically regarding lesbian authors, 'whether the image is created by Stephen Gordon, Beebo Brinker, or mythic Amazons, the reconstruction of past history is constant'.[45] Because even archival research and translation projects offered only partial access to the past, leaving many narratives lost and inaccessible, many women chose to imagine and recreate images of that past that had not been passed down to them. 'I looked around and saw that so many of my generation's activists were Jewish dykes, and I felt like we couldn't have sprung full-grown from our moment in time — we must have had some kind of origin', writes Elana Dykewomon, who went on to write *Beyond the Pale*, which recasts the classic Jewish tale of life in Eastern Europe and immigration to America as a lesbian *Bildungsroman*.[46]

I myself was seized by a similar impulse when first conducting research at the Żydowski Instytut Historyczny, the Jewish Historical Archives in Warsaw, an impulse to invent a lesbian Yiddish poet to stand in for the history I desired/the history of my desire. Imagine my surprise when I discovered that one already existed, when I first discovered the work of Irena Klepfisz, who is not only an editor and scholar (as evident from her previous appearances in this chapter) but also a Yiddish-writing lesbian poet. I encountered her work not in an archive but at a Jewish feminist conference at Mills College in California in 2006, where Klepfisz read the bilingual poem '*Der soyne*/The Enemy: An Interview in Gaza', in which a Palestinian child's encounter with an Israeli soldier is narrated in the first person in Yiddish and then in English. This poem offers a striking attempt to use Yiddish to 'enfold within this language our contemporary lives and cries'.[47] At the same time, other parts of Klepfisz's *oeuvre* use English and bilingual English–Yiddish poetics to imagine and create voices from the Jewish past.

But above all, Klepfisz seems driven by a desire for community, as she repeatedly wishes for a context within which her poems would grow 'tsuzamen mit di lider fun andere froyen' [together with the poems of other women].[48] Klepfisz's desire for contact and community offers an opposite vision to that of Molodowsky's 'Bagegenishn' as discussed above. Molodowsky has the 'context', on the page and to a certain extent in her life, and can thus resent it and rebel against it by depicting women's poems turning their backs on one another, even as they share a single page. For Klepfisz, it is the lack of actual community that generates the vision of community in her writing. In creating similar images that detach poems from their poets, Molodowsky and Klepfisz both position dialogue as impossible. In Molodowsky's case, we understand this as a product of actual differences between the poets, differences even more pronounced than their texts reveal, so that, while the poems may be printed on one page, the poets have good reason to resist being grouped together. In Klepfisz's case we are led to believe that there are no poets with whom she can share a context and the most that could even be desired is the company of other poems. For, as much as Klepfisz yearns to establish 'a dialogue *mit der yiddisher fargangenhayt*, with the Yiddish/Jewish past, a dialogue that would have to include women',[49] she consistently positions herself alone in the present, relegating Yiddish poets to the past. And while it is true that the heyday of Yiddish poetry passed long before she started writing, true that the *Khurbn* serves as an unbridgeable rupture on all counts, true that since then Yiddish has been on the decline — it is also a fact that there were women writing Yiddish contemporaneously with Klepfisz's beginnings as an English poet and even when she began writing bilingual Yiddish–English poetry in the 1980s.[50] Klepfisz bears no witness to any interaction with these poets, nor does she even make note of their existence, though many of them were living and working in the very same city as her; in effect, she turns her back on them as she looks back for them.[51]

The undeniable simultaneity of 70s lesbians and Yiddish writers is startlingly enacted in a photographic image included in an essay about Molodowsky (among others), by none other than Klepfisz herself.[52] The photograph, taken by Arnold Chekow, portrays what I believe to be a rare flesh-and-blood encounter between Adrienne Rich and Kadia Molodowsky, revealing 'the mutually disruptive energy of moments that are not yet past and yet are not entirely present either',[53] to quote Elizabeth Freeman. Indeed, it is not just energy that lingers and disrupts neat temporal divisions, but bodies and lives that continue to exist in time, showing the very division of women's writing in the 1920s, 1970s, and today to be wholly artificial, inevitably slipping from the historicist to the ahistorical.

The photograph was taken on 2 November 1969, and the occasion for the two writers sharing the stage is the publication of Rich's translations of Molodowsky's 'Froyen lider' in the anthology *A Treasury of Yiddish Poetry*. It tells a different story than the one Klepfisz tells about the gap between Yiddish and English poetry and its poets, between the past and the present. The two women mirror each other, both sitting cross-legged, both clasping their hands. Molodowsky's white hair radiates

Fig. 4.1. Adrienne Rich (left) and Kadia Molodowsky (center). Courtesy of Arnold Chekow.

around her face under her dark hat, and Rich's long dark hair (perhaps the most blatant mark of her then still heterosexual lifestyle, alongside the miniskirt) shines even in this black-and-white photograph as it runs down her shoulders, reaching below her chest. Molodowsky's light dress, finally, is *tsniesdik* in the manner her foremothers demanded, covering her elbows and knees, while Rich's dress, barely covering her thighs, marks the height of fashion of the moment. Both women are turned sideways, gazing at a source absent from the image, presumably the person reading at the front of the stage, while the third figure, John Hollander, stares blankly forward.[54] Hollander was also one of Molodowsky's translators for this anthology. Like Rich, Hollander was a recipient of the Yale Series of Younger Poets Award (he in 1958 and she in 1951). The award distinguished both of them as notable English-language poets, celebrating the beginning of their careers, and, though the photograph comes long after they received this recognition for their poetic promise, for the fleeting moment of this photograph, they both still represent the 'Younger Poets' in comparison with the aging Yiddish poetess. Neither of them spoke Yiddish fluently, and neither continued publishing Yiddish translations beyond that point.[55]

In the moment we glimpse here, Yiddish and English, as read by Molodowsky and Rich, coexisted, creating a community of Jewish women's poetry that transcends the rushing currents of history, even while, or precisely by, diving into them. The simultaneity exposed here does not open a dialogue; rather, it exposes the opposite trajectories of English and Yiddish poetry, embodied in the poets — Molodowsky's body tells the story of her impending death in 1975; a year later, in 1976, Rich came out as a lesbian, becoming a radical voice who would no longer be invited to share the spotlight of mainstream Jewish literature (at least not until much later, and then too with a set of strings attached, as she testified near the end of her life),[56] a marginalization Klepfisz has described experiencing as an out lesbian working in the field of Yiddish.

Indeed, once Klepfisz began publishing, just two years later, in 1971, she would not be invited to share such a prominent stage, despite her Yiddish expertise, which far exceeded that of Rich. This might also help explain why contemporary Yiddish poets are absent from Klepfisz's text, revealing how sexuality and politics shape the limits of community. Understanding the internal politics of their (past) present offers yet another explanation for the early Jewish lesbians' turn to the past, allowing them to identify with a foremother who could not reject them while avoiding their contemporaries, who might reject them given the chance. The 1970s lesbian ideal of 'sisterhood' also plays into this analysis as a site of contestation, as history has indeed shown it to be. The desire that 'all women' be grouped in a 'common cause' proved, not only rhetorically but also politically, to elide important differences between women, problematizing politics of collaboration and representation. Cross-temporal community is then a way to avoid challenges faced by the lesbian movement both internally and externally.

Despite sharing the position of Jewish lesbian writers and activists, and sharing many a page — in *Conditions*, *Nice Jewish Girls*, and, perhaps my favourite, as part of the group Di vilde chayes (The Wild Animals), the radical Jewish lesbian group that in 1982 spoke up simultaneously against Israel's actions in Lebanon and lesbian anti-Semitism[57] — Klepfisz and Rich still wound up in very different positions, certainly in terms of literary fame and the material security that can come with it. They each offer a very different story about Jewish lesbian life and literature in terms of their disparate Jewish backgrounds and the different roles they ultimately took in the women's movement and in the sphere of American poetry. Adrienne Rich published continually from the 1950s to her death,[58] and has long been a widely known and highly appreciated English-language poet. Irena Klepfisz is known in much narrower circles, and the focus has too often been on her *Khurbn* poetry and her role as the daughter of Michał Klepfisz, regarded as a hero of the Warsaw ghetto uprising who died protecting his better-known comrade, Marek Edelman.[59] Rich, on the other hand, had to struggle to access her Jewish heritage, alongside her struggle to reclaim the stories of women's history. Klepfisz studied Yiddish with Max Weinreich (one the most important figures of Yiddish studies in the twentieth century), and, though she was an active researcher and translator, the Yiddish institutions of the 1960s and 1970s were inhospitable to her lesbianism.[60] Rich gained literary fame in English and translated Yiddish poetry before coming out as a lesbian. Whereas working with Yiddish stands out as an exception in Rich's English-language career, Klepfisz's career drew closer and closer to Yiddish, culminating (for now) in a series of bilingual Yiddish–English poems after which her collected poetry is entitled, *Etlekhe verter oyf mame loshn/A Few Words in the Mother Tongue* (1990). Since then, she has fallen silent in the field of poetry, in effect joining the Yiddish women writers she translates and writes about. One can only hope this silence is temporary, for many of the issues Klepfisz has spoken out about are now more relevant than ever.[61]

The Jewish lesbian model of political engagement should continue to remind us how interconnected these liberation struggles are. Furthermore, in the context of my current reading, I want to suggest that it was the very frustration with the Zionist focus of American Jewish politics that led to the poets' backwards turn towards Yiddish, positioning it again over and against Hebrew (past or present).[62] Similarly, my own turn to the Yiddish past reflects a frustration with contemporary politics. In both cases, the past is recruited to rethink and indeed reconfigure the present. In this intervention, queer collectivity serves as 'an attempt to understand, through an identification with an ancestor, how history works, what it looks like, what possibilities it has offered in the past, and what those possibilities suggest about our ineffable present tense', as Nealon writes.[63] Aiming to intervene in my present, the writers and anthologies I turn to in this essay offer a cross-temporal political movement of sorts, which can be seen to answer the many challenges this essay has revealed for creating community in terms of both Yiddish women's writing and lesbian writing alike. As I have shown, these challenges are in fact sometimes part of what creates community, in time and across time, as in the case of Molodowsky's poetic negotiations with her contemporaries and her predecessors.

Retuning to Molodowsky's 'Froyen lider', Irena Klepfisz replaces the image of the missing line torn from the book with an 'illegible line',[64] and indeed *farrisn* also means 'smudged',[65] thereby implanting the possibility of reclamation that the missing line of the original poem forecloses. For what is illegible is nonetheless written and present, and what must change is our ability to read it. 'Having the resources and the evidence to name and analyze our world, feminists may begin to change its very contours',[66] wrote Cook in 1979; in bringing together Yiddish and Jewish lesbian writing, I want to offer such resources and evidence, across time and language, (re)creating communities past and stirring imagination for communities to come.

Notes to Chapter 4

1. 'In literary history, were all things equal, 1928 might be remembered as a banner year for lesbian publishing', writes Cook, who then goes on to explain how things are not equal at all; Blanche W. Cook, '"Women alone stir my imagination": Lesbianism and the Cultural Tradition', *Signs* 4.4 (summer 1979), 718–39 (p. 718). 1928 also stands at the centre of the entire first volume of Bonnie Kime Scott's four-part series *Refiguring Modernism*, as is revealed by its title, *The Women of 1928* (Bloomington: Indiana University Press, 1995).
2. *Yidishe dikhterins: Antologye*, ed. by Ezra Korman (Chicago: Shtayn, 1928). For extensive consideration of Korman's anthology, see Kathryn Hellerstein, *A Question of Tradition: Women Poets in Yiddish, 1586–1987* (Stanford: Stanford University Press, 2014).
3. *Nice Jewish Girls: A Lesbian Anthology*, ed. by Evelyn Torton Beck (Watertown: Persephone Press, 1982).
4. Christopher S. Nealon, *Foundlings: Lesbian and Gay Historical Emotion before Stonewall* (Durham: Duke University Press, 2001).
5. Carolyn Dinshaw, *Getting Medieval: Sexualities and Communities, Pre- and Postmodern* (Durham: Duke University Press, 1999), p. 1.
6. The Yiddish is from *Yidishe dikhterins*, p. 190; the translation is by Adrienne Rich, in *A Treasury of Yiddish Poetry*, ed. by Irving Howe and Eliezer Greenberg (New York, Chicago, and San Francisco: Holt, Rinehart and Winston, 1969), p. 284.

7. Cook, p. 735.
8. Ibid., p. 719.
9. Adrienne Rich, 'Compulsory Heterosexuality and Lesbian Existence', *Signs* 5.4 (summer 1980), 631–60 (p. 649).
10. Adrienne Rich, *Dream of a Common Language* (New York: Norton, 1978), p. 76.
11. Teresa de Lauretis, *The Practice of Love: Lesbian Sexuality and Perverse Desire* (Bloomington: Indiana University Press, 1994), p. 249.
12. Irena Klepfisz and Melanie Kaye/Kantrowitz, 'Introduction', *The Tribe of Dina*, ed. by Melaine Kaye/Kantrowitz and Irena Klepfisz (Boston: Beacon Press, 1986), pp. 9–13 (p. 9).
13. *The Tribe of Dina* was followed by the anthologies *Found Treasures: Stories by Yiddish Women Writers*, ed. by Frieda Forman and others (Toronto: Second Story Press, 1994) and *Beautiful as the Moon, Radiant as the Stars: Jewish Women in Yiddish Stories*, ed. by Sandra Bark (New York: Time Warner, 2003).
14. Kathryn Hellerstein, 'Canon and Gender: Women Poets in Two Modern Yiddish Anthologies', in *Women of the Word: Jewish Women and Jewish Writing*, ed. by Judith R. Baskin (Detroit: Wayne State University Press, 1994), pp. 136–52.
15. See n. 13 above.
16. Kathryn Hellerstein, 'Translating as a Feminist: Reconceiving Anna Margolin', *Prooftexts*, 20.1–2 (2000), 191–208 (p. 193).
17. Rich, 'Compulsory Heterosexuality', p. 649.
18. Originally published in *Nice Jewish Girls*, pp. 67–88.
19. Ibid., p. 67.
20. Irena Klepfisz, 'Forging a Woman's Link in *Di Goldene Keyt*: Some Possibilities for Jewish American Poetry', in Irena Klepfisz, *Dreams of an Insomniac: Jewish Feminist Essays, Speeches, and Diatribes* (Portland: Eighth Mountain Press, 1990), pp. 164–74 (p. 172).
21. Irena Klepfisz, '*Di feder fun harts*/The Pen of the Heart: *Tsveyshprakhikayt*/Bilingualism in Jewish American Poetry', in *Jewish American Poetry: Reflections, Poems, Commentary*, ed. by Jonathan Barron and Eric Murphy Selinger (New England: University Press of New England, 2000), pp. 320–47 (p. 322).
22. Ibid., p. 324.
23. Klepfisz, 'Forging a Woman's Link', p. 172.
24. Klepfisz, '*Di feder fun harts*/The Pen of the Heart', p. 335.
25. Ibid.
26. For a wider reading and contextualization of Molodowsky's essayistic work, see Allison Schachter, *Diasporic Modernisms: Hebrew and Yiddish Literature in the Twentieth Century* (Oxford: Oxford University Press, 2011).
27. Joyce Antler and Sari K. Biklen, *Changing Education: Women as Radicals and Conservators* (Albany: State University of New York Press, 1990), p. 108.
28. Kadia Molodowsky, 'Bagegenishn', *Literarishe bleter*, 7 (1930), 95.
29. The two had, in fact, recently (on 15 June 1928) shared a page in *Literarishe bleter*, 24 (1928), 465.
30. Melech Ravitch, '"Den mir hobn zunshtn keyn andri (mekhaye) in der velt": E. Korman — Yidishe dikhterins: antologye', *Literarishe bleter*, 42 (1928), 830–31.
31. Hellerstein's *Question of Tradition* deals extensively with the anthology, especially in Chapters 1 and 2.
32. Hellerstein, *Question of Tradition*, p. 50.
33. Korman's anthology is one of the thousands of titles available online through the National Yiddish Book Center — but the tactile experience lost in downloading it makes very clear the distance between the physical and digital versions of the same book. In this transitional moment I feel extremely lucky to have access to both.
34. Ezra Korman, 'Forvort', in *Yidishe dikhterins*, pp. vii–xii (p. lxv).
35. Hellerstein, *Question of Tradition*, p. 51.
36. Korman, p. vii.
37. Hellerstein, *Question of Tradition*, p. 45 (emphasis in original).

38. Avraham Novershtern, 'The Voices and the Choir: Yiddish Women's Poetry in the Interwar Period', *Criticism and Interpretation*, 40 (2008), 61–146. Novershtern himself places the word in quotation marks.
39. Ibid., p. 80.
40. Ibid., p. 82.
41. Ibid., p. 83.
42. Ibid., p. 85.
43. Ibid., p. 86.
44. Ibid.
45. Bonnie Zimmerman, 'The Politics of Transliteration: Lesbian Personal Narratives', *Signs*, 9.4 (summer 1984), 665–82 (p. 677).
46. Elana Dykewomon, *Beyond the Pale* (Vancouver: Press Gang, 1997). Although this novel was not published until 1997, it is very much a product of Dykewomon's participation in the early lesbian separatist movement. Her adherence to that particular political moment marks her difference from contemporary queer politics, as she herself expressed with Jyl Lynn Felman, 'Forward and Backward: Jewish Lesbian Writers', *Bridges*, 16.1 (spring 2011), 228–33.
47. Klepfisz, 'Di feder fun harts/The Pen of the Heart', p. 334.
48. Klepfisz, 'Forging a Woman's Link', p. 172.
49. Ibid.
50. Consider, for example, Malka Heifetz-Tussman (1893–1987), Rejzl Zychlinski (1910–2001), Chava Rozenfarb (1923–2011), and Rivka Bassman (b. 1923) — to name but a few.
51. We might compare this to Virginia Woolf's historical account of women's writing in *A Room of One's Own*, where none of her contemporary women writers are acknowledged, as Elizabeth Abel has pointed out to me in a private communication.
52. Irena Klepfisz, 'Di mames, dos loshn/The Mothers, the Language: Feminism, Yidishkayt, and the Politics of Memory', *Bridges*, 4.1 (winter/spring 1994), 12–47 (p. 36).
53. Elizabeth Freeman, 'Packing History, Count(er)ing Generations', *New Literary History*, 31.4 (autumn 2000), 727–44 (p. 729).
54. Hollander is absent from the version of the picture in Klepfisz's essay, which evidently underwent cropping to include only the women.
55. Hollander did make a significant contribution to the history of Jewish women's poetry as the editor of Emma Lazarus, *Selected Poems* (New York: Library of America, 2005).
56. Based on remarks made by Rich at the San Francisco Jewish Community Center (JCC) in 2006, right after the JCC cancelled an event connected to Jewish Voice for Peace, an organization on whose board Rich served.
57. Evelyn T. Beck, Nancy K. Bereano, Gloria Z. Greenfield, Melanie Kaye, Irena Klepfisz, Bernice Mennis, and Adrienne Rich, 'An Open Letter to the Women's Movement', signed 'in sisterhood and struggle', 22 April 1982 (New York, Lesbian Herstory Archives, folder: 'Jewish Lesbian').
58. I initially used the precarious marker 'to date' here, which became out of date just weeks after I originally wrote it, when Rich passed away. This brings to the fore the existence of poetry in time, for, as Rich wrote, 'poetry never stood a chance of standing outside history', and neither do its poets.
59. Klepfisz used this measure of acceptance to voice her own radical politics. For example, at a 2006 talk she gave at Mills College, she described how, invited to read poetry at the fiftieth anniversary of the uprising, she chose to read a poem about the Israeli occupation of Palestine, 'Der soyne/The Enemy'. She also described causing great discomfort at the National Yiddish Book Center by repeating the word lezbianke as she read her poem 'Etlekhe verter'. This, of course, was before the now-prevalent celebration of the intersections of 'queer' and Yiddish, which Jeffrey Shandler describes in 'Queer Yiddishkeit: Practice and Theory', *Shofar: An Interdisciplinary Journal of Jewish Studies*, 25.1 (2006), 90–113.
60. While homophobia has not disappeared from Jewish circles, we can certainly note a radical shift in the visibility and prominence of LGBT Jewish topics. A fascinating twist on this relatively recent shift is the role that LGBT rights in Israel play in American Jewish political discourse.

61. For example, both Klepfisz and Rich have been vocal on the topic of Israel/Palestine, and their poetic and political call for justice can continue to stand as a beacon for contemporary readers and liberation movements, especially as LGBT organizing must now contend with the issue of 'pinkwashing' the Israeli occupation (using the celebration of Israeli Jewish gay rights to mask and even justify the oppression of Palestinians, gay and straight alike). See Sarah Schulman, *Salt on Green Almonds: Israel/Palestine and the Queer International* (Durham: Duke University Press, 2012); Queer Politics and the Question of Palestine/Israel, ed. by Gil Hochberg (= GLQ: A Journal of Lesbian and Gay Studies, 16.4 (2010)).
62. The turn to Hebrew took place within the lesbian movement of the 1970s and 1980s not as a turn backwards but across, connecting with the story of the nascent lesbian movement in Israel rather than with historical Hebrew-speaking figures. The connection with the Israeli women's movement is based not only in lesbianism and Judaism, but also in a shared politics against the Occupation. Cf. *Lesbiyot: Israeli Lesbians Talk About Sexuality, Feminism, Judaism and their Lives*, ed. by Tracy Moore (London: Cassell, 1995). Even though this book was not published until the 1990s, its American and Israeli participants are the activists and writers of the 1970s and 1980s.
63. Nealon, p. 96.
64. Klepfisz, 'Forging a Woman's Link', p. 171.
65. Uriel Weinreich, *Modern Yiddish–English, English–Yiddish Dictionary* (New York: YIVO; McGraw-Hill, 1968), p. 468.
66. Cook, p. 736.

CHAPTER 5

The Best-Selling Shomer and his Fear of Emancipated Women

Gennady Estraikh

By ultimately becoming as obsolete as its itinerant peddlers, the Yiddish chapbook finally qualified for the status so long denied it: it became worthy of scholarly study.[1]

This article focuses on one of the scores of chapbooks that carry stories by Nokhem Meyer Shaykevitch (1849?–1905), better known under his literary pseudonym of Shomer, 'Watchman', which often became synonymous with trashy and even immoral novels. In 1887, Shomer faced a sharp critical attack from the literary critic Simon Dubnov, then a young reviewer and later a leading Jewish historian and political thinker. Dubnov accused the writer of flooding the book market with his adventure tales, populated by shtetl cobblers who, under Shomer's pen, turned easily into bankers and aristocrats, settled in various Western European countries, and then, in the style of Alexandre Dumas's Count of Monte Cristo, came back to their shtetl to punish its evil residents and make virtuous ones happy.[2] The next year, Sholem Aleichem joined the critical onslaught by publishing his pamphlet *Shomers mishpet* [The Judgement of Shomer], presented in numerous sources as a — or even *the* — signal event in the history of Yiddish literature, or, as Jeremy Dauber puts it, 'the beginning of a new chapter in the story of Yiddish: an emergent sense that Yiddish literature could and should be *literary*, with ideological and aesthetic dos and don'ts'.[3] A decade after the Dubnov/Sholem Aleichem broadside, the Harvard professor Leo Wiener, in his pioneering academic treatment of Yiddish literature, echoed Sholem Aleichem's characterization of Shomer's literary production as a harmful weed that should be mercilessly eradicated from the world of Yiddish letters. Wiener's book all but ignores Shomer, but mentions 'the ugliest production' of him and 'his tribe' of authors specializing in penning works of popular fiction.[4]

On the whole, despite a brisk demand for his books in his lifetime and for some years after his death, Shomer remained somewhere on the hard shoulder of, in Dan Miron's words, the perceived 'central highway of the development' of new Yiddish and Hebrew literatures. Miron adds, however, that the canonized Mendele Moykher-Sforim-centred model of literary history 'follows from conceptions and preconceptions — aesthetic, historical, and ideological — that condition the information we gather and determine the perspective from which we observe and evaluate it'.[5] As a result of a devastating reception, and/or for other reasons (scholarship is highly susceptible to trends and fashions), writings by Shomer and other authors of so-called *shund* (pulp) literature have been, with only a few exceptions, ignored by translators and scholars, and their books are widely perceived as lowbrow romances entirely devoid of aesthetic or even historically informative value.[6] The Jewish historian Saul Ginsburg, who also co-edited *Der fraynd* [Friend], launched in St Petersburg in 1903 as the first Yiddish daily in Russia, insisted that, strictly speaking, Shomer's prose had nothing to do with works of *shund* (or *Schund* in German, where this term originated) literature, notorious for its sexual content. His suggestion was to categorize this prose as an entertaining (*farvaylung*) one.[7] Ken Frieden, an attentive historian of classical Yiddish literature, observed that the venom of Sholem Aleichem's attack might have derived, at least in part, from his 'self-critical awareness that he had been guilty of similar offences'.[8] Dubnov also might have had 'personal scores to settle': as a twelve-year-old boy, he was overwhelmed by Eugène Sue's *Les Mystères de Paris* in its 1859 Hebrew translation, the first real novel with a convoluted plot he had read.[9]

The critical onslaught hardly affected Shomer's popularity among his readers in Europe and America. After his death in November 1905, *The New York Times* wrote:

> That he was the poet of his people, the dramatist of his people, the story teller beloved at the [New York] east side hearth, was evidenced by the 100,000 who turned out to honor his remains as they passed through the narrow streets for the last time.[10]

(Like other estimates of crowd size, 100,000 is, most probably, hyperbole rather than the actual number of mourners.) Not all Yiddish literary professionals agreed with an exclusively dismissive reading of Shomer's voluminous *oeuvre*. Shmuel Niger, one of the foremost Yiddish literary critics of the first half of the twentieth century, acknowledged the educational role of Shomerian literature for young people, who, after reading his capacious novels and short stories, did not think any more that behind their shtetl 'the sky dropped down on the earth and the "mountains of darkness rose"'.[11]

Abraham Reisen, himself a literary celebrity, saw Shomer as a legendary figure in Yiddish literary history and considered Sholem Aleichem's judgement to be undeservedly harsh. He even praised what David Roskies later called 'the artificial Deutschefied language' of Shomer[12] because this strongly Germanized, or *daytshmerish*, register, devoid of local idiomatic expressions, could be understood by Yiddish-speakers in different parts of the Russian Empire and beyond.[13] Some students of Yiddish letters, including Robert Peckerar, have asserted — with quite some degree of exaggeration — that the language of Shomer (which is, in fact, idiomatic in many of his works) was 'often fully mutually comprehensible between modern German and Yiddish'.[14] Wiener, on the other hand, noted that Shomer's language was 'nearer the spoken vernacular' than the language of Ayzik Meyer Dik (1807/14?–93), whose writings had previously dominated the market of popular

Yiddish fiction and, in contrast with Shomer's output, gained some respect among literary pundits.[15] Writing about Shomer, the Israeli historian of Yiddish literature Dov Sadan regretted that Sholem Aleichem's 'pamphlet not only sealed the fate of the marvellous storyteller in his own generation, but also blocked all subsequent revisionist attempts'.[16] One of those attempts was undertaken by Abraham Wieviorka in his 1931 book *Revision*, but failed to achieve the goal of giving Shomer a place of honour in the Soviet Yiddish literary canon.[17]

Shomer is usually presented in the history of Yiddish literature as a novelist who built his happy-ending narratives around romantic and at the same time didactic storylines, reflecting the author's commitment to the European-style Jewish Enlightenment, or Haskalah, aimed at transforming the shtetl populace by half-educating, half-coercing it, or at least its younger members, out of their backwardness. In reality, he also wrote numerous stories, published as chapbooks. One of them, *Halb-mentsh halb-affe; oder, Vu zukht man dem emes?* [Half-Human, Half-Ape; or, Where Can One Find Truth?], is the focus of this paper.

The plot of *Half-Human, Half-Ape* is anything but romantic. In addition, like some of Shomer's other short stories, it does not have what can be described as a perfectly happy ending (often a wedding) for positively portrayed protagonists.[18] Still, the story has a feature that places it squarely in the class of Shomerian fiction: the represented sequence of events is highly unbelievable. In Sholem Aleichem's words, the 'so-called novelist' Shomer did 'not provide a realistic, authentic picture of Jewish life' and his novels had 'no connection to the Jews whatsoever'.[19] On the other hand, exotic settings and improbable turns of plot were standard features of the popular literature of the time. Shomer was not shy to admit that exaggeration found a place in his writings. Moreover, he saw nothing wrong in that because, as he forcefully asserted, this literary device did not make his works unrealistic. He even categorized (on the cover page) many of his literary narratives, including *Half-Human, Half-Ape*, as 'real stories'. Introducing *Mayn vaybs spazmes: Eyne vare ertseylung* [My Wife's Spasms: A True Story] (1892), published in chapbook format, he wrote: 'Di kleyne geshikhte, obvol bay dem ershtn blik kon zayn az zi vet oyszen etvos iber[ge]tribn, nor az men vet zikh gut tsukukn vet men do derzen a rikhtik bild funem lebn [...]' [This short story may appear at first glance as somewhat exaggerated, but with a closer look one can find in it a real reflection of life [...]].

Half-Human, Half-Ape appeared in Vilna in 1888, around the same time as Sholem Aleichem's *Judgement* came out in Berdichev. In that year, 96,000 copies of Shomer's hardcovers and chapbooks saw the light of the day under various imprints.[20] This was an impressive success even for the contemporaneous Russian-language book market.[21] We know that on 10 May 1888 a Kiev censor gave permission to publish *Half-Human, Half-Ape*, and that the Widow and Brothers Romm, the largest Jewish publishing house of the day, produced three thousand copies of it, a rather significant print run for the time.[22] On 30 March 1888, the same Kiev censor made it legal to print Sholem Aleichem's *Judgement*.

Shomer stresses, in his preface 'On di lezer' [To the Readers], that the life of any person provides enough material for at least one book. Even a *staroveshtsnik*, 'junk peddler', can tell a story of his life-long struggle with 'thousands of misfortunes [*umglikn*]' (p. 4).[23] To emphasize that *Half-Human, Half-Ape* is ostensibly based on events in real life, Shomer cheekily invites anyone who desires to validate its reality to contact him — or, to be precise, the narrator — and thus get access to numerous verifying documents, which he ostensibly keeps safe in his private archive (p. 5). If we want to, we can hear in this introduction a motif of Sholem Aleichem's introduction to his autobiographical novel *From the Fair*: 'Why novel, if life is a novel?' and 'A carpenter lives and lives until he dies — and so does man.'[24]

Isaac Pintel, the protagonist of *Half-Human, Half-Ape*, is a thirty-five-year-old widower whose two children live with his parents. He is essentially a nice, well-mannered man, but this is clearly not enough for Shomer. A really positive man has to be a useful member of society, to which category his protagonist definitely does not belong. Rather, Pintel embodies negative traits widely associated with Jewish men brought up in a traditional way of life. Such characters — unable even to make use of capital, as a rule the wife's dowry — continued to appear in post-Shomer Yiddish literature, notably in Sholem Aleichem's feuilletons (*Menachem Mendel*; 1892–1909) and in David Bergelson's debut novella, *At the Depot* (1909).

By Shomer's own admission, Pintel — meaning a 'dot' — is an insignificant 'kleyn mentshele [...] drayerl nit vert' [little man [...] not worth three rubles] and a 'groyser shlimazl' [inept person] who himself sees his own spinelessness and credulity as the reason for all his business problems. He has given loans to many people who 'hobn aza rakhmones gehat oyf mayn gelt az zey hobn zikh fun zey gor nit gevolt sheydn' [had such pity on my money that they were very reluctant to part with it]. Still, he has at his disposal one thousand roubles in cash, which he seeks, but fails, to invest in the best way possible, travelling from one place to another (pp. 21–22). Similarly, Benish Rubinstein, the protagonist of Bergelson's *At the Depot*, is a maladroit businessman who is unable to reclaim his money, part of which he had acquired as his wife's dowry, from an arrogant borrower. Sholem Aleichem's Menachem Mendel became a moniker for an incompetent entrepreneur who unsuccessfully tried his hands at many things,[25] never mind the fact that Sholem Aleichem himself squandered in a few years the inheritance left by his rich father-in-law.

In one of the story's numerous dialogues, Pintel explains that a Christian man of his social status and age either runs a business or has a job, and does not hurry to get married, whereas a Jewish man by his mid-thirties has no profession in hand and is already a worn-out paterfamilias ('oysgehoreveter familye-foter'; p. 25). Although it remains unknown to the reader if Pintel had any systematic schooling, Shomer portrays him as an educated person, linguistically equipped with Yiddish, Hebrew, Russian, and, apparently, German. He also interjects French words in his speech. In general, he cuts the figure of a maskil, or an adherent of the Haskalah, the Jewish Enlightenment. Shomer makes Pintel's knowledge of Talmudic and Midrashic literature evident, but there is no mention of him or any other characters doing religious practices. Jewish holidays come up in the story, but with the sole purpose of creating the chronotope of the narrative. The traditional time axis of Jewish fast days and holidays also appears in other Yiddish works, including modernist ones. Three decades later, Bergelson employed it in *At the Depot*, otherwise populated by religiously non-practising characters.

The events of Shomer's story take place mainly in East Prussia, at the western borders of the Russian Empire, in towns with fictional names. To a regular Yiddish speaker, a resident of Russia's Pale of Jewish Settlement, it was an outlandish place. Yet, Shomer and his readers — whom the Yiddish writer Rokhl Faygenberg described as essentially naive people — preferred stories set somewhere in a 'fremder velt fun unnatirlekhe lebns-gesheenishn' [unfamiliar world of extraordinary life occurrences].[26] Significantly, this setting provided some justification, if the reader really needed it, for the characters' Germanized language and non-traditional lifestyle.

Like Shomer, a native of Nezvizh (now in Belarus), Pintel is a Litvak, that is a 'Lithuanian Jew', and his origin makes him a second-rate person among local Jewish residents. In fact, Shomer describes the social climate that was characteristic of Polish Jews, who dubbed as Litvaks any Jews whose Yiddish sounded different from the local dialect of Yiddish, though usually people from 'Jewish Lithuania', or Lite (roughly the territory of contemporary Lithuania and Belarus, and some areas of Poland and Latvia) bore the brunt of ridicule and even hatred. The Warsaw-born Yiddish journalist A. Almi (Elias Chaim Sheps) contended that Warsaw Jews' stigmatization of Litvaks, people of the same confession, was similar to Catholic Poles' attitude to Jews.[27] A Jewish resident of Warsaw could say, for instance, that 'a litvak iz a halber goy' [a Litvak is a half-gentile] or 'ot geyen tsvey yidn un a litvak' [two Jews and a Litvak are walking here].[28] According to the journalist and historian Azriel Natan Frenk, around 1907 the term 'Litwak' appeared in the Polish press as a euphemism for a 'bad Jewish migrant'.[29] Shomer's story, however, can be seen as a piece of evidence that Litvaks, who in the 1860s started to migrate in significant numbers — notably to the Russian-controlled Kingdom of Poland, informally known as Congress Poland — had been unpopular more or less since the time of their arrival:[30]

> Di litvakes hobn shoyn aza finstern mazl az iberal rekhnt men zey far shlekhte fardorbene mentshn. Tomer tut eyn litvak a falsh, vern derfar ale litvakes farhast. Dos bisl yidn fun der Lite hobn dos zelbe mazl fun di yidn in algemeyn. Mir veysn dokh az iberal bashuldikt men ale yidn tsulib eyn fardorbenem mentshn. In Poyl, Besarabye, Volinyen iz der litvak shreklekh farhast, derfar vos in di letste yorn hobn zikh zeyer fil oreme litvishe yidn bazetst tsvishn zey, [...] zaynen ahin gekumen naket un borves [un] zaynen dort raykh gevorn un shpiln groyse rolyes. Un dos hot dervekt a shtarke kine bay di bashtendike aynvoyner fun di kantn, un zey zukhn darum feler in ale litvakes. (p. 39)

> [The Litvaks are extremely unlucky to suffer the reputation of bad corrupt people. Every time one Litvak does something wrong, it results in generating hatred towards all Litvaks. The trickle of Jews from Lite has the same good fortune as that of Jews in general. We know that people tend to accuse all Jews because of one corrupt person. The Litvak is terribly hated [by Jews] in Poland, Bessarabia, and Volhinya, because in recent years many poor Lithuanian Jews

settled among them, [...] they came there hungry and naked, [but] have become rich and are playing important roles. This provoked the jealousy of the local permanent residents, and they try to find faults with all Litvaks.]

In Shomer's story, Litvaks also have a reputation of being weak-willed (*kharakterloze*) and perverted people (p. 50). Later, when Pintel faces an accusation of bigamy, a local Jew comments: 'Di litvakes zaynen gor keyn naronim nit, zey farshteyen az tsvey vayber iz beser als eyne' [The Litvaks are no fools, they understand that it's better to have two wives than one] (p. 45). And his father-in-law does not even try to protect him from ostracism, or at least to give him the benefit of the doubt. Instead, he simply throws him out of the house, calling him a 'farflukhter litvak' [damn Litvak] (p. 48).

All this will happen later, when the happy phase in Pintel's life comes to a dramatic end, and all because he has the bad luck of meeting an emancipated woman, who — by the role assigned to her in the story — ruins the protagonist's life. *Fräulein*, or mademoiselle, Rachel Plefen is hardly an embodiment of seductive femininity, a femme fatale. She is over forty years old and makes the greatest impression on Pintel by her striking features (*plefn* means 'to dumbfound' in Yiddish):

> Ir hot gikher gepast der nomen urang-utang (eyne affe) als der nomen froy. Nye in maynem lebn hob ikh aza heslekhkayt gezen. Shtelt aykh for a perzon hoykh un dar vi eyne altmodishe kotshere, shvarts vi eyne negerin mit groye katsn-oygn. A noz (azelkhe nez zol men nit zen in keyn yidish shtub) az in yedn fun zayne tsvey lekher kon araynforn an ekipazh mit fir ferd na shpits. Dos breyte ponem iz geshtuplt ful mit gribelekh, zo dos in yedn grub kon arayn a veleshener nus. Kurts geredt ven yemand volt di karikature arumgefirt in der velt, un volt zi gevizn far gelt, bin ikh nit mesupek az er volt zikh a raykhtum farshafn. Den aza meshunedike brie iz vayt tsu gefinen. (p. 6)

> [The name of orang-utan (an ape) would suit her better than that of a woman. Never in my life have I seen such a minger. Imagine a person who is tall and thin like an old-fashioned poker, black like a Negress with wide cat-like eyes. A nose (may any Jewish house be protected from seeing noses of this kind) such that a couch drawn by four horses in tandem could enter each of its two nostrils. Her broad face riddled with pockmarks, each of them the size of a walnut. In short, should someone have taken this caricature out in public and paraded her around, he would, without doubt, have made a fortune of it. Indeed, it is difficult to find another creature of such oddity.]

To make the picture even worse, her smile reveals 'tsvey reyen shvartse foyle tseyn' [two rows of black rotten teeth] (p. 7). The Russian philosopher Nikolai Berdyaev wrote, in 1916, that an emancipated woman, 'by mechanical imitation, out of envy and enmity, appropriates masculine characteristics to herself and becomes a spiritual and physical caricature',[31] while Eliyana Adler, a historian of Jewish women's education in imperial Russia, points out that even those maskilim 'who espoused a more egalitarian vision had trouble imagining woman with the same intellectual needs and abilities as themselves. At times this ambivalence played out in overtly misogynist rhetoric.'[32] Shomer had dehumanized his character by giving her caricatural animalistic traits.

At the time he wrote *Half-Human, Half-Ape*, Shomer most probably had not seen any dark-skinned person (he emigrated to America a year after the story's publication). His description of Plefen as 'black like a Negress' simply reflects the stereotypes of his time and milieu — for instance the Midrashic view that only a white woman could be 'beautiful', whereas black skin meant 'ugliness'.[33] The eleventh-century Jewish philosopher and poet Judah Halevi also portrayed a terribly unattractive woman as 'ugly and black, like smoke in the stormwind'.[34] Even more meaningful, however, could be the influence of the general understanding of beauty in the nineteenth century.[35]

Plefen, a product of Shomer's imagination, is not a nihilist woman. She does not fully reject conventions of Jewish traditions and, significantly, pays attention to her appearance.[36] In his turn, by paying attention to his female character's appearance (not only in this story), Shomer breaks the conventions of Jewish writings.[37] Having done this, he places her in the category of those self-confident people who misread the reflection they see in the mirror and consider themselves as pretty. Shomer comments: 'Mir bagegenen kimat oyf yedn trit heslekhe mentshn farputst vi di pupn. Zeyer puts makht zey nokh shreklekher, nokh mieser, un zey aleyn meynen bay zikh az zey zaynen anttsiknd sheyn' [At almost every turn we meet ugly people dressed like dolls. Their attire makes them even ghastlier, more hideous, but they are sure that they are exceptionally pretty] (p. 11). Plefen appears 'farputst vi di kenigin Vashti in a shpogl nayem shtrohut' [flashily dressed like Queen Vashti in a brand-new straw hat] (p. 12). A similar motif is present in Mendele Moykher-Sforim's 1894 Hebrew story 'In the Days of the Noise'. He wrote about 'ugly women who are convinced, as they adorn themselves before the mirror, that they're great beauties without any equal'.[38]

Plefen has literary flair. She recently published, in Russian, a book with the title *Di koshere libe; oder, Di kats iber der smetene* [The Kosher Love; or, The Cat over Cream]. Interestingly, in 1891, a novel by Shomer would be published with a similar-sounding title: *Der kosherer yid; oder, Tsvey kets in eyn zak* [The Kosher Love; or, Two Cats in a Sack]. Pintel is amazed that his new acquaintance uses in her language numerous Hebrew and Aramaic ('Talmudic') words and is ready to discuss tough philosophical issues (p. 7). Later, we learn that she can write letters in Hebrew (p. 29). She tells Pintel that she has been corresponding with the Russian writer Ivan Turgenev (1818–83), who was widely read by maskilic literati.[39] The mention of correspondence with Turgenev provides some time reference for the events and, generally, makes the story sound 'more real'. It also serves as an allusion to Turgenev's female characters, the so-called Turgenev girls, known for rejecting a traditional idea about the role of a woman in society.[40] Plefen claims that the France-based author of *Father and Sons*, a landmark novel in Russian literature, admires her work and wants to translate it into French (p. 12). We know that Turgenev befriended a Jewish woman writer, Rachel (or Rashel) Khin, who dedicated to him several of her works.[41] It is highly possible that Shomer knew and alluded to this particular fact.

Tova Cohen, who constructed a portrait of a typical maskilah or maskilot, a female maskil, maintains that 'the only way a nineteenth-century Jewish woman could obtain the key to the locked gates of the Hebrew language was by having it consciously and intentionally given to her by her father'.⁴² Indeed, we learn that Plefen was the only child of a *melamed*, a Jewish religious teacher, which was an occupation that carried little respect among Russia's Jews. Indeed, her father — her only parent mentioned in the story — did not even have a home of his own and '[hot] zikh glat arumgeshlept in di hayzer' [simply roved from one household to another] (p. 8). It is known that educated fathers tended to encourage their daughters' secular education, 'along with the Eastern European tradition of learning and the desire to pass on canonical texts and a knowledge of Hebrew, especially when there were no sons'.⁴³

Pintel happens to read Plefen's novel. His judgement of it is overtly and unapologetically gender-biased:

> Far a mansperzon volt er geven shlekht. Nor koym hot im a froy gemakht muzn mir ir oyf ale feler fartseyen. Yo, oyf di gramatishe feler kon men ir fartseyen vayl zi iz a froy. Ober di moralishe feler zaynen umfartseylekh. Fun a froys feder hobn nit badarft aroysgeyn azelkhe khtsufishe verter. Ir heldin fun dem roman kumt for vi eyne fun di gasnmeydlekh vos loyfn arum durkh di nekht [...]. (p. 8)

> [For a male author it would have been a failure. But we have to condescend to all its weaknesses, because the author is a woman. Yes, we can close our eyes to the problems with the storyline written by a woman. However, there are unforgivable moral faults. It was wrong for a woman to write such immodest words. The heroine of the novel appears as a whore that walks the street [...].]

When Plefen out of the blue asks Pintel to marry her, he realizes that his new acquaintance is a brave and determined person. Initially, he does not realize that she is also manipulative and, considering her new acquaintance as a target of opportunity, is luring him into a dangerous legal trap (p. 17). As it turns out, her unconventional marriage proposal does not mean that she has fallen in love with him. Rather, it has a clear rationale: she desperately seeks a way of securing for herself the status of a married woman and thereby saving her reputation in the eyes of society. Plefen is pregnant from someone unknown to the reader; it is therefore vital to have a nominal father for her child, and she will stop at nothing to achieve her end. It is not clear if she singles Pintel out as a gullible target or as a progressive man. In the latter case, he would have been supposed to be open to using fictitious marriage as a device for liberation of a woman. This was advocated by Nikolai Chernyshevsky in his 1863 novel *What Is To Be Done?*, the bible of young people unhappy with present societal realities.⁴⁴ Significantly, traditional marriage had little value or meaning to the rebellious youth of the time. For instance, Dubnov and his would-be wife planned to go to France to register a civil marriage, but had no choice but to follow the tradition because they were penniless and therefore dependent on their parents.⁴⁵

Pintel, however, is not as entirely naive as he looks, and he certainly does not belong to the admirers of Chernyshevsky. Like Shomer and other authors of popular Yiddish novels,⁴⁶ he adheres to contemporary Western European middle-class ideals and perceives Plefen as a morally degenerate woman. Also, it does not occur to him that he is getting into trouble by making clear his aversion to the idea of getting married with Plefen. Instead of letting him get away with his rebuff of her request, she starts spreading rumours that Pintel is her lawful husband, as a result of which his half-arranged and half-romantic marriage with Anna, the eighteen-year-old daughter of a respected man, renders him bigamous.

Plefen knows that Jews like rumours better than facts. They are more than ready to dismiss even solid evidence of his innocence and stamp Pintel, a helpless victim of her outrageous slander, with an indelible stain on his reputation (p. 51). She also knows the power of Jewish religious obscurantism. Even when it becomes undeniable that her assertions are patently false, Plefen comes out as the winning party because the Talmudic tractate Kiddushin, which discusses the law of betrothal and marriage, and a Rashi commentary stipulate that a divorce is the only way out from a situation in which a woman claims to be married to a man who dismisses this claim as a lie (p. 63). As a result of the decision taken by the local Jewish religious court, or *beys-din*, Plefen gets the respectable status of a divorcee, while Pintel's marriage with Anna is annulled. The story ends tragically: Anna, her grandmother, and Pintel's father die, all from nervous breakdowns. Pintel's fortune and reputation are in ruins, while the outcome is a happy one for Plefen: she finds a 'proper' husband and is well regarded as a decent woman victimized by her unscrupulous first husband (p. 66).

What did Shomer want his readers to learn from *Half-Human, Half-Ape*? We can find one of the answers in David Pinsky's 1896 story 'Men vart' [People Are Waiting], describing a labour dispute at a printing shop owned by a man called Bergshuld:

> Es iz arayn Bergshuld, a hoykher diker yid fun a yor fuftsik mit a breytn shivlekhn bord. Mit dem gebloyztn hemd un mit dem kapelyush oyfn kop iz er shoyn a hayntveltiker, nor mit di dine peyelekh, vos lign fardreyt nebn di oyern, mitn langn rok un mit di hoyzn in di shtivl iz er nokh a khosid. Eyn arbeter, velkher iz bakant mit di nemen fun Shomers mayses, hot im a nomen gegebn 'halb-mentsh, halb affe'.[47]
>
> [Bergshuld came in, a tall fat Jewish man of about forty, with a wide slanting beard. With his shirt out on his trousers and a hat on his head, he already looked like a modernized man. However, with thin side-locks curled at his ears, with a long coat, and with trousers tucked into his boots, he still remained a Hasid. A worker, who knew the titles of Shomer's stories, gave him a name: Half-Human, Half-Ape.]

In other words, the 'half-human/half-ape' stage is a Darwinian-inspired metaphor for a transitional phase — between the Jewish tradition and modernity. Some of Shomer's other characters also appeared as half-something/half-something-else. Thus, a character in the story *My Wife's Spasms* was 'a halber aristokrat, zayn kleydung var halb daytsh halb yidish, zayn shprakh halb yidish halb rusish, ikh hob afile oykh gekont zogn az er iz geven halb sheyn halb mies' [a half-aristocrat, his dress was half-German and half-Jewish, his language was half-Yiddish and half-Russian; I could even say that he was half-handsome and half-ugly].[48]

At the same time, there is one more important moral to this story: wariness/ fear of educated women. Shomer sends the same message in his bilingual Yiddish–English *brivnshteler*, or letter manual, published in the US. In a sample of a letter, Bella, a married woman, writes to her unmarried friend Liza:

> Just like you, as you know, I once fantasized that a woman must know and be erudite about everything. [...]
> But since I became a married woman, I've often been very angry at myself. Instead of mathematics, geography, and history, it would have been better if I had thoroughly learned cooking and sewing.
> Ach, dear friend, how unacceptable is the woman who doesn't know how to do both of these things.
> My husband does not care about all my academic expertise. A good lunch makes him much happier than any mathematics problem and I think he's right. [...]
> I have told you all this, dear friend, so that you will knock out the idée fixe of higher education right out of your head.
> Better to learn how to be good housewife.[49]

Plefen, the 'exceedingly educated', emancipated woman, was an alarming warning from Shomer, a conservative maskil writer, that a new — intellectual, aggressive, and self-sufficient — type of a woman, later called the New Jewish Woman, had appeared in Jewish society. Indeed, such 'dangerous' women were already present in Russian Jewish society. Thus, the cosmopolitan, knowledgeable, and intelligent mother of one of the first Russian Jewish revolutionaries, Grigory Gurevich (1852–1929) 'embodied the emancipated Jewish woman *par excellence*'. A native of Vilna, she received there an excellent education, knew several European languages, and was well read in German and Russian literature. Her son, known as Gershon-Badanes, adopted her name, Badane — the Yiddish version of the Slavic 'Bogdana' — as his revolutionary and literary pseudonym.[50]

It is instructive to examine the ways in which emancipated women were depicted in Yiddish writings from a masculine point of view, especially as men fully dominated Yiddish prose literary production of the nineteenth century. To all appearances, Shomer's ideal of a Jewish woman essentially coincided with Sholem Aleichem's ideal: a Jewish woman who supressed her ambitions and fantasies if they were in conflict with her loyalty to God (or, in secular circles, to Jewish traditions), then with her loyalty to her parents, and then with her loyalty to her husband and children.[51] Shomer, Sholem Aleichem, and, generally, Jewish writers of the time would usually 'allow' women (and men) to practice 'free love' by rejecting arranged marriages. Otherwise, however, they continued to attach high importance to traditional marriage with gender-based role divisions.

In all, Shomer's criticism was threefold. First, in his view, too much education could deprive women of their femininity, make them 'half-ape' or, to be precise, 'half-masculine', independent, and dangerous, particularly in dealing with an infantile man such as Pintel, whose secular erudition had failed to make him a mature and enterprising breadwinner. In the maskilic understanding, men were 'assigned a greater weakness and helplessness in their confrontation with the near-demonic forces attributed to women'.⁵² As a matter of fact, Pintel, the 'victim', was the secondary — or, given the fact that the story ends well (with a wedding) for Plefen, perhaps even the primary — target of sharp ridicule. Tellingly, his fate is sad, revealing Shomer's derision of a secular version of the 'zaydener yungerman[tshik]' [silken young man]. Whereas the latter was engrossed in lifelong learning with Talmudic, Midrashic, and Kabbalistic commentaries, the former did more or less the same with his impractical knowledge of secular subjects. Finally, Shomer derided the society which idealized its 'silken' denizens. The denouement of the story clearly aimed to show that this society's retrograde institutions and ossified moral dogmas could be manipulated and misused too easily, leading to immoral and unjust judgements.

More generally, scholars of Jewish history and culture may find it worthwhile to pay more attention to Yiddish entertainment literature, which remains a largely neglected source of information about the zeitgeist of the age, traditions, social life, language, and perhaps much more. Research focused on such works may well show that the sky did not drop down on the earth and the mountains of darkness did not rise outside the perceived central highway of the development of Yiddish literature and that, importantly, Shomer's and Shomerian fiction gives us insights into the realities of Jewish life in the nineteenth century.

Notes to Chapter 5

1. David G. Roskies, 'The Medium and Message of the Maskilic Chapbook', *Jewish Social Studies* 41.3/4 (1979), 275–90 (p. 286).
2. Semen M. Dubnov, *Kniga zhizni: Materialy dlia istorii moego vremeni, vospominaniia i razmyshleniia* (Moscow and Jerusalem: Mosty kul'tury/Gesharim, 2004), p. 148.
3. Jeremy Dauber, *The Worlds of Sholem Aleichem* (New York: Schocken, 2013), p. 58 (emphasis in original).
4. Leo Wiener, *The History of Yiddish Literature in the Nineteenth Century* (New York: C. Scribner's Sons, 1899), p. 134.
5. Dan Miron, *The Image of the Shtetl and Other Studies of Modern Jewish Literary Imagination* (Syracuse: Syracuse University Press, 2000), p. 355.
6. For a notable exception, see Justin Cammy, 'Judging the Judgment of Shomer: Jewish Literature versus Jewish Reading', in *Arguing the Modern Jewish Canon: Essays on Literature and Culture in Honor of Ruth R. Wisse*, ed. by Justin Cammy and others (Cambridge: Harvard University Press, 2008), pp. 85–127.
7. Rose Shomer-Bachelis, *Undzer foter Shomer* (New York: IKUF, 1950), p. 79.
8. Ken Frieden, *Classic Yiddish Fiction: Abramovitsh, Sholem Aleichem, and Peretz* (Albany: State University of New York Press, 1995), p. 139.
9. Sofia Dubnova-Erlich, *The Life and Work of S. M. Dubnov: Diaspora Nationalism and Jewish History* (Bloomington: Indiana University Press, 1991), p. 47.
10. '100,000 Honor Remains of East Side Poet', *The New York Times*, 27 November 1905, p. 9.
11. Shmuel Niger, *Lezer, dikhter, kritiker*, 2 vols (New York: Yidisher kultur farlag, 1928), I, 22.
12. David Roskies, 'Call It Jewspeak: On the Evolution of Speech in Modern Yiddish Writing', *Poetics Today*, 35.3 (2014), 225–301 (p. 278).
13. Abraham Reisen, 'Shomers romanen — far vos zey hobn in zeyer tsayt azoy batsoybert di lezer fun yidishe mayse-bikhlekh', *Forverts*, 14 November 1940, section 2, p. 5. On *daytshmerish*, see, in particular, Steffen Krogh, '*Dos iz eyne vahre geshikhte ...*: On the Germanization of Eastern Yiddish in the Nineteenth Century', in *Jews and Germans in Eastern Europe: Shared and Comparative Histories*, ed. by Tobias Grill (Berlin and Boston: De Gruyter, 2018), pp. 88–114.

14. Robert James Adler Peckerar, 'The Allure of Germanness in Modern Ashkenazi Literature: 1833–1933' (unpublished doctoral dissertation, University of California, 2009), pp. 92–93. Idiomatic Yiddish is used to write, for instance, the story *A Groom for a Minute*, published as a chapbook: *A khosn oyf a vayle* (Vilna: Mats, 1889).
15. Wiener, p. 174.
16. Dov Sadan, 'Three Foundations', *Prooftexts*, 6.1 (1986), 55–63 (p. 56).
17. Abraham Wieviorka, *Revizye* (Kharkov and Kiev: Literatur un kunst, 1931).
18. See ibid., p. 91.
19. 'The Judgement of Shomer; or, The Jury Trial of All of Shomer's Novels, Transcribed Word for Word by Sholem Aleichem', trans. and annotated by Justin Cammy, in *Arguing the Modern Jewish Canon*, ed. by Cammy and others, pp. 129–85 (p. 135).
20. Alyssa Quint, '"Yiddish Literature for the Masses?": A Reconstruction of Who Read What in Jewish Eastern Europe', *AJS Review*, 29.1 (2005), 61–89 (p. 81).
21. See Richard Ware, 'Some Aspects of the Russian Reading Public in the 1880s', *Renaissance and Modern Studies*, 24.1 (1980), 18–37.
22. Zalmen Reisen, 'Tsu der statistik fun yidishn bukh', *YIVO Bleter*, 1.2 (1931), 180–95 (p. 185).
23. Shomer, *Halb-mentsh halb-affe; oder, Vu zukht man dem emes? Eyne vare ertseylung* (Vilna: Widow and Brothers Romm, 1888). This will be cited by page number in parentheses in the text.
24. Sholem Aleichem, *Ale verk*, 28 vols (New York: Sholem-Aleykhem folksfond, 1917–23), XXVI (1923), 15.
25. See e.g. Valery Dymshits, 'The Return of Menachem Mendel: Sholem Aleichem as a Political Commentator', *East European Jewish Affairs*, 43.1 (2013), 31–42.
26. Rokhl Faygenberg, 'Briv tsu der yidisher tokhter in Poyln', *Moment*, 18 November 1927, p. 5.
27. A. Almi, *Momentn fun a lebn: Zikhroynes, bilder un epizodn* (Buenos Aires: Tsentral-farband fun Poylishe Yidn in Argentine, 1948), pp. 182–83.
28. A gevezener rusisher professor [A former Russian professor], 'Di litvishe yidn', in *Di mizrekh-yidn* (Berlin and Warsaw: Misrach, 1916), pp. 112–13; Max Weinreich, 'Galitsianer lakhn fun litvakes, litvakes fun galitsianer', *Forverts*, 11 January 1930, p. 6.
29. Azriel Natan Frenk, 'Litvakes', *Dos yidishe folk*, 7 February 1918, pp. 7–8.
30. See Joanna Nalewajko-Kulikov, 'Missionaries of the Jewish Nation: Meeting Points between Russian and Polish Jewry before the First World War', in *Three Cities of Yiddish: St Petersburg, Warsaw, and Moscow*, ed. by Gennady Estraikh and Mikhail Krutikov (Oxford: Legenda, 2017), pp. 22–32 (23–29).
31. Quoted by Eric Naiman, *Sex in Public: The Incarnation of Early Soviet Ideology* (Princeton: Princeton University Press, 1997), p. 41.
32. Eliyana R. Adler, *In her Hands: The Education of Jewish Girls in Tsarist Russia* (Detroit: Wayne State University Press, 2011), p. 26. See also ChaeRan Y. Freeze, *Jewish Marriage and Divorce in Imperial Russia* (Hanover: Brandeis University Press, 2001), p. 70.
33. Abraham Melamed, *The Image of the Black in Jewish Culture* (London: Routledge, 2010), p. 92.
34. Quoted in Israel Zinberg, *A History of Jewish Literature*, 12 vols (Cincinnati: Hebrew Union College Press, 1972–78), V: *The Jewish Center of Culture in the Ottoman Empire* (1974), p. 13
35. See, in particular, Sander L. Gilman, 'Black Bodies, White Bodies: Toward an Iconography of Female Sexuality in Late Nineteenth-Century Art, Medicine, and Literature', *Critical Inquiry*, 12.1 (1985), 204–42.
36. Cf. Erich Haberer, 'Emancipation and Revolution: Jewish Women in the Nihilist and Populist Intelligentsia of Nineteenth-Century Russia', in *Ethnic and National Issues in Russia and East European History*, ed. by John Morison (New York: St. Martin's Press, 2000), pp. 146–73 (p. 150).
37. Shomer-Bachelis, pp. 78–79. In contemporary Hasidic novels, too, women appear as 'functions', for example, 'a nice wife', rather than full-blooded images — see Gennady Estraikh, 'Hasidic Authors Offer Readers a Thrill', *Forward*, 2 March 2007 <http://forward.com/articles/10214/hasidic-authors-offer-readers-a-thrill> [accessed 13 June 2019].
38. Quoted in Naomi Seidman, *A Marriage Made in Heaven: The Sexual Politics of Hebrew and Yiddish* (Berkeley: University of California Press, 1997), p. 55.

39. See e.g. Ben Ami Feingold, 'Feminism in Hebrew Nineteenth Century Fiction', *Jewish Social Studies*, 47.3–4 (1987), 235–50 (p. 236).
40. See e.g. Christine Johanson, 'Turgenev's Heroines: A Historical Assessment', *Canadian Slavonic Papers/Revue Canadienne des Slavistes*, 26.1 (1984), 15–23; Vladimir K. Vasilyev, 'On the Semantics of the "Turgenev's Girl" Psychotype', *Journal of Siberian Federal University: Humanities and Social Sciences*, 5 (2014), 757–67.
41. Elena Katz, 'Turgenev and the "Jewish Question"', in *Turgenev: Art, Ideology and Legacy*, ed. by Robert Reid and Joe Andrew (Amsterdam: Rodopi, 2010), pp. 169–88 (p. 175).
42. Tova Cohen, 'Portrait of the Maskilah as a Young Woman', *Noshim: A Journal of Jewish Women's Studies and Gender Issues*, 15 (2008), 9–29 (p. 13). According to Alicia Ramos Gonzalez, 'the term "maskil" has never been applied to women, nor is there a feminine equivalent' ('The First Hebrew Writers Writing on the Margins', in *Jewish Studies at the Turn of the Twentieth Century*, ed. by Judit Targarona Borrás and Angel Sáenz-Badilos, 2 vols (Leiden: Brill, 1999), II: *Judaism from the Renaissance to Modern Times*, pp. 215–24 (p. 215)). In this case, 'maskilah' or 'maskilot' are retrospective coinages.
43. Beverly Bailis, 'Fantasies of Modernity: Representations of the Jewish Female Body in Turn-of-the-20th-Century Hebrew Fiction' (unpublished doctoral dissertation, Jewish Theological Seminary, 2012), p. 95.
44. See e.g. Richard Stites, *The Women's Liberation Movement in Russia: Feminism, Nihilism, and Bolshevism* (Princeton: Princeton University Press, 1978), p. 105.
45. Dubnov, pp. 95, 101, 109–10.
46. Iris Parush, *Reading Jewish Women: Marginality and Modernization in Nineteenth-Century Eastern European Jewish Society* (Waltham: Brandeis University Press, 2004), p. 42.
47. David Pinsky, *Ertseylungen*, 2 vols (New York: Di internatsyonale bibliotek farlag, 1906), II, p. 202.
48. Shomer, *Mayn vaybs spazmes* (Vilna: The Widow and Brothers Romm, 1892), p. 10.
49. Alice Stone Nakhimovsky and Roberta Newman, *Dear Mendl, Dear Reyzl: Yiddish Letter Manuals from Russia and America* (Bloomington: Indiana University Press, 2014), pp. 132–33.
50. Erich Haberer, *Jews and Revolution in Nineteenth-Century Russia* (Cambridge: Cambridge University Press, 1995), p. 64.
51. Wieviorka, p. 58.
52. Parush, p. 196.

CHAPTER 6

❖

Dreams of a Jewish Queen: A Literary Itinerary of National-Sexual Desires, from the Book of Esther to Aaron Zeitlin's *Esterke*

Roni Masel

It is some distant time in history. The Jews are in danger. A young and beautiful Jewish woman faces an extraordinary opportunity: to influence a powerful, gentile ruler in favour of her people by using her beauty and feminine wisdom. Will she agree? Will she succeed in turning the king's heart? Will such rescue be worth the intimacy with a gentile? Such questions and others have informed the retellings and reiterations of what we might characterize as Esther-like narratives that appeared repeatedly in Hebrew and Yiddish literature from the late nineteenth century up to World War II.

What follows seeks to sketch out a general mapping of this literary trope, the dream of a Jewish queen, and to follow its itinerary, the different locations and temporalities in which the historical fiction takes place and in which these texts were produced. But before turning to survey these narratives, it seems necessary to explain the appeal and fascination of this trope by suggesting an initial conceptual framework which would assist in approaching the texts. As the following analysis demonstrates, contemplating the image of the Jewish queen seems worthwhile since it stands at a dramatic crossroads of nationalism and notions of gender and sexuality. The young Jewish woman who rises to power through her relationship with a gentile ruler, as a cultural trope, enables a discussion regarding national ideology and identity and a construction of gender and of sexual norms. In the figure of the Jewish queen, as a merger of the two, no separation between notions of gender and nation is possible: its sexuality is nationalized, its national ideology gendered and sexualized.

More specifically, the trope of a Jewish queen lends itself readily to a national-symbolic interpretation. Royalty, in general, can serve as a compelling literary device. A king, for example, might stand for ideas of power and agency; or, in the Jewish diasporic setting, the king might represent the surrounding gentile nationalism and sovereignty. Female figures have also been used for allegorical personifications, usually representing the entirety of the country or the empire, such as Britannia, Columbia, Marianne, or Mother Russia. However, as opposed to the king, the inclusive quality of these female figures lies in their anonymity, in their being 'the ordinary woman', not queens: since they are no one specific, they can be anyone; since they do not have any known children, they could be the mothers of the entire nation. The king is part of the nation, but through his image one can tell the story of the collective, as is the case in a metonymy. The anonymous woman, however, is not a significant member of the national collective; rather, her image substitutes the collective in its entirety, as in the rhetorical structure of allegory. What, then, activates the image of the Jewish queen? Does she, *like* the king and through her relationship *with* a ruler, represent the political circumstances of the people and enable a discussion of them? Or perhaps, like the anonymous plebian woman, her story overlaps and replaces that of the nation? The works presented in this study move between these two modes of representation, between metonymic depiction and allegorical substitution. In doing so, these works present varying configurations of national-sexual imagery and sexuality. This trope's aesthetic and thematic flexibility, as we will see, turns it into an evocative literary apparatus.

Let us begin by considering the first possibility, in which the narrative of the particular Jewish woman who encounters the gentile ruler is metonymic to the narrative of the nation and allows for an examination of the nation's burning issues. As Chone Shmeruk argued, the representation of young Jewish girls who immerse themselves in their surrounding culture had become a widespread theme in Yiddish literature by the late nineteenth century as an emblem of the fear of assimilation.[1] This is comparable to other nationalist discourses, in which discussions regarding the collective, its borders, its unity, and its future focus their attention on women's symbolic and concrete body and on what nationalist ideology often terms its 'sexual purity' which parallels the idea of 'national honour'.[2] Against this background, the trope of the Jewish queen stands out as exceptional, for it considers the possibility of physical-sexual contact between a Jewish woman and a 'foreign' man in positive terms. In this narrative, rescuing the Jewish people might render the in principle forbidden sexual 'contamination' — kosher. Nevertheless, this conflict of interest between benefitting the people and guarding the collective's purity and sexual honour continues to stand at the very core of all the Esther-like retellings considered in this study. Will the political benefit be worth the sexual contamination? Will the forbidden contact achieve political power and thereby justify itself?

In 1884, Shomer (Nahum Meyer Shaykevich), the writer and mass-producer of popular Yiddish literature, published a novella entitled *Di yidishe kenigin* [The Jewish Queen], which draws on the Polish Jewish folk tale of King Casimir the Great and his Jewish mistress/wife.[3] In Shomer's version, Esterke, the beautiful Jewish woman and daughter of a poor tailor, is saved by King Casimir from a Christian mob outraged by a blood libel. The king takes her with him to his castle, where he falls in love with her after they have a long intellectual conversation on the origins of anti-Semitism and bigotry. Esterke realizes that she loves Casimir as well, but her loyalty to her people and religion torments her. After a night of tossing and turning, she comes to the conclusion that, if she succeeds in influencing the king in favour of the Jews, it would justify her love for a gentile. The two marry, and the king, who had already perceived himself as an enlightened ruler who favoured the rule of law over knightly ethos or religious fanaticism, listens to Esterke's words of reason and tolerance. Following her requests, he issues a decree that brings the surge of violence to an end, and the Polish Jews are relieved. Esterke does not want her identity to be revealed, for she worries it would harm her honour in the eyes of the Jewish community. The novella comes to its dramatic end after her parents arrive at the palace, seeking the new queen's help in finding their lost daughter. They arrive accompanied by their town's rabbi, who was previously in love with Esterke but forced to separate from her by his uncle, who arranged his marriage. The three meet the queen and are shocked to discover she is none other than their own Esterke. The unified family is thrilled, and the rabbi exclaims that he is happy for Esterke and for the Jewish people, thereby approving her marriage and resolving the love triangle.

On first impression, Shomer's Esterke is the most perfect and optimistic enunciation of her biblical prefiguration, Esther: she is beautiful and clever, and her influential deeds in support of her people soothe the pain of her sexual detachment from it in an exceptional manner that allows for an enlightened critique against Jewish separatism while simultaneously reaffirming the borders of the Jewish nation, defining Esterke as the exception that proves the rule.[4] However, when considering the structure of Shomer's narrative, the potential for another reading appears. The harmonious ending appeases the collective sentiment while simultaneously shifting the reader's eye from the national plot line to the romantic one, focusing on the resolution of the love triangle and thus transforming the story from one devoted to the national collective to one preoccupied with the romantic paradigm. This structural transformation emphasizes not a collectivist message but rather a distinctively maskilic programme of contradictory nationalist humanism or conservative universalism, promoting ideas of enlightened tolerance, rejecting parochial practices of arranged marriages that confine love to fanatic religious borders and economic circumstances, and championing a romantic ethos.[5]

Another interesting structural interplay between romantic love-triangle narratives and national-didactic ones can be found in adaptations of the apocryphal story of Judith and Holofernes. This story received many visual and textual representations during the centuries following its canonization in the Christian Bible. Since the nineteenth century, Jewish interest in this narrative has grown. One expression of this interest can be found in the translation of Friedrich Hebbel's play *Judith* (1841) into Hebrew by Shmuel-Leib Gordon in 1900.[6] Hebbel's play deviates considerably from the apocryphal original, most notably with regards to its end. After five days in Holofernes's camp, Judith faces the moment of truth. She has already captured his heart but now has to fulfil her task. Yet is precisely then that Holofernes loses patience with Judith's sexual modesty, or what she calls her 'honour'; he takes her into his tent, rapes her, and falls asleep. Judith feels violated, and begs her servant to help her in killing Holofernes. The only way she would be able to do so, she says, is if her servant constantly reminded her of the way Holofernes had stolen her virginity and purity. Utilizing the rage over her violated sexuality, she gathers the required strength and decapitates him. Judith returns to her city with his head, but while her people celebrate the victory, she pleads to her fellow Jews to swear that if and when she asks them to kill her, they will do so. She dreadfully explains her will to her servant: if she conceived as a result of being raped by Holofernes, she would rather die and spare herself the pain of her impurity than give birth to Holofernes's bastard child. From a heroic deed of collective salvation, as in the original apocryphal narrative, the killing of Holofernes in this play becomes a tragedy of non-liberating revenge for sexual violation of the national purity.

Another important deviation of the play from the apocryphal original lies in a love triangle that Hebbel created. Before leaving her besieged town and going to Holofernes's camp in order to kill him, Judith dares her long-time rejected suitor, Ephraim, to go and kill him. Ephraim, the cowardly opportunist, is reluctant to do so, and therefore Judith decides to go there herself in order to prove Ephraim's cowardice to him, saying 'every woman has the right to demand of the man seeking her affection that he be brave and fearless'.[7] Ephraim, the effeminate Jewish man, wishing to save face, arrives at the military camp with a sword after Judith has already been there for a few days. He tries to stab Holofernes, but the guards block his way. He then tries to kill himself in utter despair, but Holofernes, full of contempt for this unmanly creature, does not even grant him the dignity of being executed by his enemy; instead, he incarcerates Ephraim in the same cage as his monkey, for entertainment.

Of the two men seeking Judith's grace, it is clear that, despite her resentment of his cruelty, Holofernes nevertheless attracts her far more than Ephraim, towards whom she feels nothing but disdain. As Hannan Hever elucidates regarding the motif, perhaps even the *idée fixe*, of retaliation in modern Hebrew literature, its significance lies in the structure and mechanism of revenge as a violent act.[8] As an empty action, as an action that could not fulfil any goals exterior to the act itself, it is a form of violence for the sake of violence, the exertion of power for its own sake and within an idiosyncratic, cyclical, and hollow structure that, precisely due to this sealed cyclicality, enables the use of power from a position of utter powerlessness. The year 1900, the year when Gordon's translation was published, might symbolize for us in this context a moment of powerlessness and an intensifying Zionist struggle to rehabilitate Jewish masculinity and Jewish national honour,[9] to make the great leap from a position of utter powerlessness to possessing and exerting power.[10] In order to perform such a leap, radical action must be taken. Ephraim is unable to rehabilitate his own injured masculinity, and therefore the play ends in tragedy. However, Judith, utilizing the violence turned against her, can channel the strength needed in order to spring from the position of the victim to that of the murderer, to attain power where it does not exist, even at the expense of dignity and national honour.

Twelve years before the Hebrew translation, the playwright and promoter of Yiddish theatre Yosef Yehuda Lerner published a drama under the same title, *Judith*

(1888).[11] While large parts of the play are in fact a plagiarized translation of Hebbel's play, its end transforms the original completely by adhering more closely to the paradigm of the Jewish queen. In Lerner's version, Holofernes does not rape Judith but rather admires her, claims she ought to be his queen, and plans to marry her. Eventually, however, she kills him for the original, national-strategic reason of saving her besieged town, and not as an act of retaliation, for she has successfully avoided sexual contact with Holofernes prior to his death. After she returns victorious to the town with her sexual honour intact, she marries Ephraim, whom she grows to love. As Hebbel's tragedy is turned into a comedy, ending in a wedding rather than an implied suicide, it seems that the structural focus of the play centres even more intensely on the question of national-sexual purity. While Hebbel's love triangle is shattered (both Judith and Holofernes die), in Lerner's version, Judith replaces the romantic possibility of marrying Holofernes with her true and worthy love for Ephraim. While the original play realizes the sexual potential of the encounter between the Jewish woman and the gentile ruler, the fantasy of a Jewish queen comes crashing down in a tragic ending. The Yiddish adaptation, by contrast, refrains from materializing the sexual potential in the first place, and ends in the celebratory union of intranational love and the rehabilitation of proper gender roles and characteristics. If we compare the political effect of the two versions, it seems that the act of retaliation in Hebrew literature aims at creating a tragedy, a cathartic crisis violently breaking with the past in order to build anew; whereas Lerner, in using similar materials, allows for a political rehabilitation of the Jewish national image by drawing the narrative closer to a more respectful and tolerated framework of contact between a Jewish woman and a gentile — by drawing Judith's story closer to the paradigmatic narrative of a Jewish queen.

In Lerner's *Judith*, we find a potential rehabilitation of Jewish masculinity through the image of the Jewish queen, but the divide between the Yiddish and Hebrew literary-political imaginations cannot be paradigmatically portrayed as the supposed opposition between Hebraist Zionism and Yiddishist diasporic nationalism. As a case in point, we might turn to David Pinsky's short story 'Zerubovel', which tells the story of the Book of Esther from the point of view of a young Jewish man in Shushan, Zerubovel, and his fiancée, Shoshana.[12] The Jews of Shushan entrust Esther with their fate, and they prepare for three days of fasting and praying. Zerubovel refuses to cooperate with the community elders' plan, arguing that a nation cannot be saved by a woman and demanding that the Jews join him in armed resistance and fight their persecutors in self-defence, that they 'not be lead easily like sheep to slaughter, rather be like lions, who come forward and fight their hunters'.[13] Mordechai explains that, while Zerubovel wishes to employ his arms and muscles for self-defence, the community knows how to navigate other resources for defence, such as money and the Jewish feminine body, just as Jacob in his day used his wealth in his meeting with Esau and just as Judith in her turn used her body and beauty to defeat Holofernes. 'Since when', Zerubovel further reproaches Mordechai and the crowd, 'is the meaning of self-defence — the pretty face of a young woman? Is Esther's body our self-defence?'.[14] The crowd dismisses him, and he looks for Shoshana for comfort. However, when he finds her covered like the rest of the community in sackcloth and ashes, he finally understands that he is alone in his position, that the rest of the community feels comfortable in 'hiding behind a skirt', and that the rest of the Jewish men have no 'sense of honour'.[15] The story ends with the tragic separation of the lovers after the furious Zerubovel tells Shoshana she is not worthy of being the mother of his children. Thus, we might say that responses in Yiddish literature to the question of and need for rehabilitating Jewish masculinity with regards to the trope of the Jewish queen range from Lerner's celebratory embrace of the use of women for national relief to Pinsky's utter rejection of the trope and his demand for androcentric narratives and masculinist nationalism.

An opportunity for a different sort of negotiation of Jewish identity opens up through the use of the paradigm of the Jewish woman as a national saviour in another historical context: Sepharad, Spain, which was, in general, a prime locus of fascination for modern Jewish intellectuals.[16] Narratives that engage the cultural trope of the Jewish queen appeared in works that focus on the image of crypto-Jews — the Marranos or conversos — and their return to Judaism. The crypto-Jew serves as a very powerful token through which to discuss questions of identity.[17] As an image, it stirs a great deal of anxiety in both Jewish and non-Jewish political imagination. On the one hand, there is the anxiety of being exposed, of failing to pass; on the other hand, the fact that the stranger cannot necessarily be identified as such demands constant suspicion, since essentially anyone could be the enemy. This idea of a double-layered existence, composed of elements of exposure and concealment, resonates well with various articulations of modern Jewish identity, most famously in the maskilic Hebrew poet Yehudah Leib Gordon's construct: 'Be a man in the streets and a Jew at home'.[18] This duality of modern Jewish experience might explain its fascination with the image of the conversos.

A drama by Sholem Asch, entitled *Maronen* [Marranos], tells the story of the converso Jacob Tirado, who fled Portugal in order to establish a community of ex-conversos in Amsterdam.[19] The story is based originally on the folklore of Amsterdam's Sephardic community;[20] Asch had likely encountered it through its literary adaptation by the German Jewish writer Ludwig Philippson, which, by the time Asch wrote his drama, had already been translated twice into Hebrew and once into Yiddish and widely disseminated.[21] While Philippson focused on the figure of Jacob Tirado, Asch took pains to dramatize extensively one scene of the story. According to communal lore, Tirado left Portugal with four other conversos, among them one woman. The group's ship was captured by an English one and brought to London; their possessions were taken away, and they were imprisoned. An English duke saw the young and beautiful woman, Maria Nunes, and fell in love with her. As the fascination with her grew among the guards, Queen Elizabeth herself asked to meet her. As a result of the meeting, the queen gave them permission to settle in her land, but they insisted on continuing their journey to Amsterdam. Asch's drama begins after their arrival in the Netherlands, while the English duke tries, for the very last time, to convince Maria Nunes to marry him and become his duchess. He presents her with enlightened ideas of transcending religious boundaries. The offer is tempting, but Maria decides in favour of her faith, claiming that leaving her ancestors' religion, about which she knows very little, would render worthless their holy sufferings at the hands of the Inquisition.

If the converso can indeed serve as an emblem of modern Jewish identity, as a Janus-faced being torn between political loyalties and cultures, it seems that, when the risk of assimilation and utter loss of identity is at stake, the literary fantasy of a Jewish woman rising to power weakens. Such duality might be tolerated in certain circumstances, but when faced with a threat to the painfully sought-after identity, power gives way to the opportunity of authentically expressing one's Jewish self. The rejection of the ideas of enlightenment and universalist tolerance advocated by the English duke in Asch's play perhaps parallels a rejection of the maskilic demand for a double gesture of integration into the surrounding society while preserving a sense of Jewish particularism.[22] Maria Nunes wishes to do away with the duality that dictated her life as a conversa, even at the cost of missing the opportunity to gain power for the sake of the nation. She therefore vows to keep her body within the borders of the collective and refrain from contaminating it. A fantasy of national power gives way to that of national purity and honour; Jewish identity is restored.

Such is the case in a novella by Sholem Asch, *Di kishef-makherin fun Kastilien* [The Witch of Castile],[23] built around the paradigmatic character of a beautiful Jewish woman who is capable of helping her people through her beauty, in which a family of ex-conversos arrive in Rome in their struggle to return to their original faith. In this novella, too, the young woman refuses to form any sort of connection with a gentile through which she could deliver her people, and the story ends tragically with her execution in an auto-da-fé. Shomer also dedicated one of his novellas to the character of a young Jewish woman, *Di sheyne Rokhele* [The Beautiful Rachel],[24] who lived in Portugal as a crypto-Jew. The narrative touches upon themes of sexual violence and purity, romance disturbed by national borders, the aspiration to political power, and finally the restoration of authentic Jewish identity (when Rachel's ostensibly gentile lover discovers his hidden Jewish roots, which allows for the couple's happy reunification).

For the last location and temporality of the Jewish queen's itinerary to be examined here, we return to the historical setting of Shomer's novella that opened this study: fourteenth-century Poland and the legend of Esterke. As mentioned earlier, Chone Shmeruk surveyed and analysed this theme, and the relationship between Polish and Yiddish literature, as it evolved around the characters of Esterke and Casimir. Shmeruk outlined two general trends. In Polish literature, he traced a shift in the course of the nineteenth century from Esterke's negative depiction as the source of the Jews' unjustifiable rights and privileges in Poland, to a more positive portrayal, perhaps even a celebratory one, at a time when the Polish intelligentsia was looking for symbols of Polish–Jewish coexistence and brotherhood. In reading Yiddish and Hebrew sources, Shmeruk pointed to perhaps an opposite move: one from a positive and naive characterization of Esterke as the perfect materialization of her biblical prefiguration to the more complex use of this motif as an emblem of the difficulties, advantages, and disadvantages of Jewish integration or assimilation into Polish society. Natan Cohen continued Shmeruk's work by adding five sources, two in Hebrew and three in Yiddish, previously not accessible and therefore absent from Shmeruk's survey, which further support Shmeruk's observations regarding the shift in the Jewish sources from a naive embrace of Esterke's story as re-enacting the Book of Esther to a growing discomfort and ambiguity regarding the possibility of a young Jewish woman fraternizing with gentiles and flirting with the idea of assimilation. Cohen's survey ends with a serialized novel published in 1934 and 1935, about three years after the drama written by Aaron Zeitlin between 1929 and 1932 with which Shmeruk's study ends. By the mid-1930s, Cohen argues, the fantasy of a Polish–Jewish brotherhood was already crumbling, and the legend of Esterke, as a pre-text of that fantasy, with it. However, it seems that we can draw the end of this itinerant narrative out a bit further, since Zeitlin rewrote his drama in 1967, essentially creating a new Esterke story, an afterlife of the dream of a Jewish queen. Thus, although Chone Shmeruk and Yehiel Szeintuch have already attended to Zeitlin's drama,[25] it seems worthwhile to revisit his two versions of the story, the first written in pre-war Warsaw, the second in post-war New York.

Aaron Zeitlin's drama *Esterke un Kazimir der groyser: Ahaswer in Poilin* [Esterke and Casimir the Great: Ahaswer in Poland],[26] first published in 1932, resembles other narratives of a Jewish queen: here too, her image stirs up a fear of assimilation just as much as national pride or a feeling of relief. In the opening act, King Casimir sits in his palace surrounded by his ministers when a group of Jews enter and ask the king for his permission to settle in the land as God's angel had ordered them to do, saying: 'Po lin!' [Here dwell!]. When, soon afterwards, Esterke enters the scene, searching for the king's protection, Casimir falls in love with her immediately. Everyone present tries to prevent him from marrying her: his knights, his clergy, and the rabbi and the Jews who accompanied him all believe it to be a bad idea. Only his loyal finance minister, the Jew Levko, fantasizes over the potential of having a Jewish queen: 'Esther is her name, why not a second Esther?'.[27] Throughout the play, Levko remains the chief mediator and articulator of the dream of a Jewish queen, and he reveals the assumption that encourages him to pursue this dream at the very beginning. When the Jews ask Casimir for his patronage, Levko tries to convince him to agree to the request thus:

> If two peoples chance on one land — surely a mystery lies therein, as in the encounter of a woman and man. A man's existence is no simple fact — great deeds he must accomplish. Nations too must complete great tasks. If two peoples come together, and they breath the same air — it is no mere coincidence, my king — .[28]

In this quotation, Levko positions Esterke as a placeholder of the nation; he offers a shift from the metonymic presentation of Esterke or of her counterparts, and transforms Esterke into an allegory. For Levko, her story does not simply allow for an engagement with questions of assimilation and national identity through the narrative of sexual encounter and its costs or benefits. Rather, her figure substitutes that of the national collective; her story becomes that of the nation in the same way that Casimir here stands for the entire Polish people. The encounter of Casimir and Esterke in the royal palace is the same as two nations coming together in one land.

What then is this secret, or mystery, that Levko suggests exists in the encounter of two nations or in that of a man and a woman? Perhaps harmony, strong attraction, physical union? By using the structural symbol of the heterosexual family, the fantasy of a Jewish queen suggests that the two collectives live together peacefully, not threatening each other's selfhood. If the Polish nation is the man and the Jewish nation is a woman, then the two national identities do not come at the expense of each other and do not dispute or challenge the distribution of power and control. Jewish nationalism imagined as a woman, as opposed to the local nationalism imagined as a man, creates space for a non-territorial nationalism, searching for individual expression yet at the same time aspiring to integration into the local society. In other words, imagining the Jewish queen marrying the Polish king configures the ideal national-political existence for Jewish diasporic nationalism.

This understanding of the figure of Esterke as an allegory corresponds to the genre with which Zeitlin categorized his play: *misterie*, 'mystery-play', and with the appearance of other symbolic figures which Zeitlin called *gayster*, 'spirits', such as Christ; Ahasver the Eternal Jew; the Shepherd who is described as 'the Good Dream'; and the Elder, described as 'the Bad Dream'. Adam Mickiewicz and Y. L. Peretz also appear in the last act, discussing the possibility of a Polish–Jewish symbiosis. This anachronistic anti-realism, or existential irrationalism, as Yehiel Szeintuch termed it, goes hand-in-hand with the universalist agenda that marks Zeitlin's Warsaw period.[29]

And indeed, it is precisely the narrative's resentment of rationalism and its embrace of fantastic and spiritual qualities that creates the universalistic vision that concludes the play: King Casimir's ministers force him to separate from Esterke, and he agrees. However, on the night they part, Casimir says to Esterke: 'We will die. But as long as the descendants of my race and yours sit together in this land — our story has no end, Esterke of Opoczno.'[30] While the two are sitting outside the castle, spending their last night together, two of the spirits observe them — the Shepherd, the Good Dream, and the Elder, the Bad Dream. The pessimist Elder complains about the end of their story, but the Shepherd comforts him: 'Their dream isn't "caput". Dreams always remain. The two might separate, but something still remains. There is a pillar of light between them, you cannot see it.'[31] The Elder insists: 'Only one thing has the power to remain — blood.'[32] His reference to blood echoes one of Levko's articulations of his dream of a Jewish queen. In one of his meetings with Esterke, Levko tries to educate Esterke on what he thinks of as her national role, and attempts to convince her that the only way she could keep Casimir with her is if she gave birth to his heir. Then he begins speaking more abstractly: 'Do you know what that means? A king, a Jewish king, Esterke ... A king who rules over us and them, whose blood — ours and theirs ...'.[33] As opposed to Levko's fantasy of a blood-tie, of a physical-sexual synthesis, groups of Christians and Jews who argue over well-poisoning and the accusation that the Jews are responsible for it, eventually come to agree on their mutual goals: 'Our waters — yours; our blood

— separate from yours.'[34] While the Polish soil and resources can be shared by the two groups, physical-sexual separation must be preserved.

In other words, two concepts of national existence compete in this play: spiritual and abstract connection through shared life on the same land on the one hand, or, on the other hand, a physical-sexual symbiosis which is a source either of wonderful fantasy (for Levko) or of great anxiety (for the rest of the general public). The end of the play, however, rules in favour of the spiritual connection and rejects Levko's allegorical-yet-physical understanding of Esterke and Casimir's encounter as that of two nations. The Shepherd wins the argument with the pessimist Elder. Peretz poetically claims that he can hear the world speaking to him in Yiddish from the depths of the Polish soil. Adam Mickiewicz muses over the elements composing his name — *dam*, 'blood', and *Adam*, 'human': 'There is a solution! "Dam" becomes "Adam"!'[35] — meaning that the logic of blood gives way to a humanistic and universalist philosophy. Ahaswer, the Eternal Jew, concludes the play with a long monologue which celebrates 'the kiss of the two races', regardless of the termination of a concrete physical union between the two nations and between Casimir and Esterke, and he encourages everyone to come out in dance, in a universalist utopia, 'until through dance we find our way to the one and only mother!'.[36]

In this play, Zeitlin endorses the Esterke motif in its entirety, asserting its legitimacy. The inter-ethnic sexual contact is freed from the binary judgement of assimilation versus segregation through a unique formula that Zeitlin creates. The drama maintains physical separation while at the same time holding on to the spiritual symbiosis between Esterke and Casimir and between Jews and Poles. Thus it avoids the national-sexual anxiety fundamental to a nationalist discourse. This unique formula is indebted to the play's genre — Zeitlin's choice of symbolistic plot lines, and his rejection of realist or allegorical representation, allows for equivocal yet powerful configurations, creating space for Jewish particularism through a symbolic, non-physical symbiosis with the local non-Jewish nationalism.

However, Zeitlin, who had by chance left Warsaw for a visit to New York in 1939 and who had lost his family in the war, rewrote the play in 1967, thereby creating an afterlife for the dream of a Jewish queen in Yiddish literature.[37] The revisited version realizes all the elements that in the first, open-ended version remained merely an abstract potential. Esterke gives birth to Casimir's son, Pelko, who is kidnapped by the king's ministers and raised in a monastery. Once he is separated from his national and religious collective, his 'mixed blood' loses meaning. Esterke's love for Casimir also becomes more concrete when she argues against Levko that, in fact, she was never interested in Casimir's love because of his royalty and the potential to help her people through him, and that she has always loved him as an individual instead.[38] By de-allegorizing herself and de-nationalizing their love, turning the story into a paradigmatic romantic narrative, the sexual contamination loses its legitimacy — if Esterke never meant to act in favour of her people through her marriage, then no justification can be found for her violation of the collective boundaries. In turn, the story becomes nationalized and allegorized again when, towards the end, Esterke, persecuted by the Christian masses, understands for the first time the meaning of national oppression. As a result, Esterke, together with Levko, Peretz, Mickiewicz, and a new symbolic figure, Meshigener, apparently a Holocaust survivor, decide to leave Poland. Ahaswer, who in this version is called Nitshiel, 'Eternal', or 'Eternal God', changes his celebratory concluding monologue to a shorter one, replacing the initial divine order of 'Po lin!' [Here dwell!] with 'oys po lin' [here dwell no more]:

> Po lin! Po lin!
> Such was the verdict.
> You must spend your night here,
> you must.
> Why?
> Somewhere in the unknowns the answer lies.
> But once, when the night
> will nightly fall
> with a demonic force
> unforeseeable,
> then, consequently, will it be
> *oys po lin.*
> And in Jerusalem
> will a new dawn rise
> and to Jerusalem will we go;
> to Jerusalem will we go.[39]

In the second version of the play, the dream of salvation, of national empowerment through Jewish femininity and sexuality, falls apart. Zeitlin's fantasy of a universalistic, Jewish–Polish symbiosis fails with it. The Jewish queen refuses her role as an allegorical substitute for the collective and concretizes the romantic narrative, thereby rendering the Jewish–Polish relationship illegitimate. Consequently, the collapse of the allegory ends the hope that the heterosexual family, as a metaphor of a political *modus vivendi*, would enable two competing national identities to live peacefully in the same territory. The utopic articulation of diasporic nationalism through the image of the Jewish queen has given way to a notion of national introversion, an ingathering of the exiles in Jerusalem, and the creation of a separatist identity. *Oys po lin*; *oys* Jewish queen.

To conclude the discussion of Zeitlin's work, the key to understanding the shift between the pre-war and the post-war versions lies in two fundamental elements of this drama: its genre and mode of representation, and the way in which it uses the historical material. First, while the pre-war version uses symbolistic figures, language, and plot lines, the second version witnesses the destruction of representation through the materialization of all elements of the drama that previously had a symbolic potential. Further, in the second version we witness the shattering of Esterke as an allegorical figure. The drama shifts from a symbolistic mystery play to a realist allegory. The difference between symbol and allegory in Walter Benjamin's theory of the *Trauerspiel* might help us make sense of this generic shift.[40] While the symbol is based on deep intimacy and kinship between the signifier and the signified (as is the case, for example, in the River of Time,

Mother Earth, or the Horn of Plenty), in the allegory an arbitrary figure is chosen (say, a woman) in order to convey an unrelated idea (e.g. Grace, Christianity, Music, or War). This arbitrariness postpones the derivation of meaning; it leaves traces of the process of representation, and by doing so is thus always embedded in its historical context, in its singular historical moment. The allegory thus gains its meaning only through what Benjamin calls the 'stations of destruction',[41] where the allegory stands as a monument to the failure of representation and meaning. The textual affect that is therefore tied to the allegory is melancholy. Like melancholy, the allegory forms arbitrary attachments between linguistic objects as a transference of the unmourned loss of language and expression.

If we return to Zeitlin's drama, his rewritten play intentionally fails at enacting figurative mechanisms of narrative and representation. All of the abstract ideas of the pre-war version become concrete, material, embodied, and 'fleshed out' — the sexual desire, the physical union, and the shared blood. In the language of the text, we might say that '*Adam* becomes *Dam*'. The text cannot hold figures of speech, just as the melancholic cannot: metaphors collapse and the system of signification is shattered. On the face of it, the play ends with a Zionist message — the protagonists decide to leave Poland and go to Jerusalem, where a redemptive new dawn is ostensibly rising. However, the text's affect runs against any narrative of redemption. Whereas the past in the first version served as a source for utopian fantasy, in the second version history appears as a continuum of ruins, as an allegorical monument to the failure of representation. In this way, Zeitlin's drama reveals the affective melancholic logic underlying many post-war representations of Jewish history. This is particularly true of those representations which build on such historical ruins in order to argue in favour of national introversion and pseudo-redemptive narratives of an ingathering of the exiles. The past appears there repeatedly as a haunted gravestone, melancholically chained to the unmourned loss of language, exilic homes, and diasporic dreams.

In conclusion, the trope of a young Jewish woman who, by using her body and beauty, attains the ear of a powerful ruler, dubbed here as the 'dream of a Jewish queen', emerges as a strong and evocative literary apparatus. Whether as a figure through which one could probe questions of assimilation, national identity, and Jewish masculinity and potency, or as an allegorical substitute for the nation that enables a political message regarding diaspora, territory, and sovereignty, the Jewish queen is a discursive token in which piercing national-sexual anxieties as well as avid fantasies converge. Moreover, the literary appeal of the dream of a Jewish queen is an illuminating intersection of nationalist and sexual ideas not only in the sense that the two are interrelated in this particular fictional figure, but also in the sense that notions of nationalism, gender, and sexuality ought to be read and analysed in conjunction with one another. This analytical sensibility seems of particular importance with regards to modern Yiddish and Hebrew literatures and Jewish nationalism. As literatures indebted to and in constant correspondence with nationalist movements of the nineteenth and twentieth centuries, and as cultural systems imbued by their very linguistic choices in a sexualized discourse,[42] their representations, formulations, and narratives ought to be read with a multifocal perspective for a finer understanding of sexualized nationalism, nationalized gender identity, or racialized Jewish physiology.

Lastly, the dream of a Jewish queen directs our attention to the encounter between history and fantasy. While imagining a historical reality, in its legendary elements and its saturation with sexual anxieties and fantasies, this trope draws the genre of historical fiction towards that of fantasy and thereby hints at the profound affinities between the two. Further, as a dream of national-sexual salvation, it proposes an understanding of the role of historical charm and fascination in the nationalist imagination: desiring history and the historical can be seen as a source for national redemption and deliverance.[43] Further still, in moments of the disintegration of the dream of a Jewish queen, we find instances of history and historicity as a haunting force, as a non-liberating and compulsive matter, a textual site where unmourned ghosts of political fantasies converge.

Notes to Chapter 6

1. Chone Shmeruk, *The Esterke Story in Yiddish and Polish Literature* (Jerusalem: Zalman Shazar Center, 1985), pp. 71–74. See also Avraham Novershtern, 'Ha-kolot veha-maqhela: Shirat nashim be-yidish bein shtei milhemot ha-olam', in *Nashim be-tarbut yidish*, ed. by Tova Cohen and Aviva Tal (= *Bikoret u-farshanut*, 40 (spring 2008)), pp. 61–145 (pp. 76–77).
2. Joane Nagel, *Race, Ethnicity, and Sexuality: Intimate Intersections, Forbidden Frontiers* (New York: Oxford University Press, 2003).
3. Shomer [Nahum Meyer Shaykevich], *Di yidishe kenigin* (Warsaw: [n. pub.], 1884). The literary adaptations of the Esterke story and its various reincarnations were comprehensively discussed by Shmeruk and later by Natan Cohen, who added to Shmeruk's work an analysis of materials previously not at hand; Natan Cohen, 'The Love Story of Esterke and Kazimierz, King of Poland — New Perspectives', *European Journal of Jewish Studies*, 9.2 (2015), 176–209. The present study, therefore, will not focus on the works already analysed in detail by Shmeruk and Cohen unless they are of critical significance for our more general understanding of the trope of the Jewish queen.
4. This is Shmeruk's reading of Shomer's version — he explains this optimistic ending as a result of Shomer's traditional adaptation, which naively follows the biblical narrative.
5. See Olga Litvak's reassessment of the Haskalah not as a form of Jewish Enlightenment but rather as a distinctively Eastern European brand of Romanticism, interested in universalist ideas of the Enlightenment yet also sceptical of them: *Haskalah: The Romantic Movement in Judaism* (New Brunswick and London: Rutgers University Press, 2012).
6. Friedrich Hebbel, *Yehudit*, trans. by Shmuel-Leib Gordon (Warsaw: Tushiya, 1900).
7. Ibid., p. 27.
8. See the chapter 'Mavo: Uma be-ikvot ha-shevet, veha-shevet be-ikvot ha-uma' in Hannan Hever's forthcoming *Ha-uma veha-shevet ba-sifrut ha-ivrit ha-modernit*.
9. For a broader discussion of the ties between Hebrew literature and the attempt to rehabilitate Jewish masculinity, see Michael Gluzman, *Ha-guf ha-tsiyoni: Le'umiyut, migdar u-miniyut ba-sifrut ha-ivrit ha-hadasha* (Tel Aviv: Hakibbutz Hameuchad, 2007); see p. 27 specifically on Gordon's own participation in this discourse.
10. Dan Miron, *Bodedim be-mo'adam* (Tel Aviv: Am Oved, 1988), pp. 23–111, described extensively the expression in the world of letters of this feeling of utter powerlessness, of weakness, of a 'literary republic' struggling with scarce resources and dwindling readership around the year 1900.
11. Yosef Yehuda Lerner, *Yehudis* (Warsaw: Alapin, 1888).
12. David Pinsky, 'Zerubovel', in David Pinsky, *Naye ertseylungen* (Berlin: Funken, 1923), pp.

79–100. Although there is a considerable chronological gap between Lerner's publication and Pinsky's, I believe this serves to further stress the need to refrain from paradigmatic distinctions that attribute, as a rule, diasporic nationalist ideology to Yiddish literary texts — if, as late as the 1920s, we find narratives in Yiddish that follow Gordon's extreme more closely than Lerner's, the same situation can be observed in earlier texts that were published in an ideological atmosphere less sharply divided.
13. Pinsky, p. 90.
14. Ibid., p. 93.
15. Ibid., p. 98.
16. For a collection of studies dealing with this fascination in various contexts, see *Sephardism: Spanish Jewish History and the Modern Literary Imagination*, ed. by Yael Halevi-Wise (Stanford: Stanford University Press, 2012).
17. For a more general mapping of the imaginative connection between the conversos and questions of identity, see Ban-Ami Feingold, 'Historical Dramas on the Inquisition and Expulsion', *JTD: Journal of Theater and Drama*, 1.1 (1995), 9–30.
18. From the poem 'Hakitsah 'ami' [Awake, my People!], translated in Michael Stanislawski, *For Whom Do I Toil? Judah Leib Gordon and the Crisis of Russian Jewry* (New York and Oxford: Oxford University Press, 1988), pp. 49–50 (p. 50).
19. Sholem Asch, 'Maronen' (signed 1919), in Sholem Asch, *Dramatishe shriftn*, 4 vols (Vilna and New York: Sholem Asch Committee, 1922), IV, 199–230.
20. For an elaborate description and analysis of this tradition, see Miriam Bodian, *Hebrews of the Portuguese Nation: Conversos and Community in Early Modern Amsterdam* (Bloomington: Indiana University Press, 1997), pp. 22–24.
21. Ludwig Philippson, *Jakob Tirado: Geschichtlicher Roman aus der zweiten Hälfte des sechszehnten Jahrhunderts* (Leipzig: Leiner, 1867). Translations prior to 1922: *Ya'akov Tirado: Sipur korot yesud hama'alah le-yishuv ha-yehudim ha-sefaradim be-holandiya*, trans. by Shmuel Yosef Fünn (Vilna: Fünn, Rosenkranz, Schriftsetzer, 1881); *Di blutike nekome; oder, Yakov Tirado*, trans. by Yitzhak Yoel Linetsky (Warsaw: [n. pub.], 1893); *Ya'akov Tirado: Sipur histori*, trans. by Aleksander Ziskind Rabinovitz (Warsaw: Tushiya, 1907). All these translations were reprinted at least once.
22. For a discussion regarding a similar process in German Jewish literature, particularly with regards to later adaptations of Philippson's work, see Jonathan Skolnik, 'Dissimilation and the Historical Novel: Hermann Sinsheimer's *Maria Nunnez*', *Leo Baeck Institute Yearbook*, 43.1 (1998), 225–37.
23. Sholem Asch, 'Di kishef-makherin fun Kastilien', in Sholem Asch, *Gezamelte shriftn*, 12 vols (New York: Sholem Asch Committee, 1921–24), XII (1923), 1–144.
24. Shomer [Nahum Meyer Shaykevich], *Di sheyne Rokhele* (Vilna: Mats, 1884).
25. Shmeruk; Yehiel Szeintuch, 'Al shnei mahazot historyim mi-toldot yehudei Polin bi-ytsirato shel Aaron Zeitlin', in *Bein shtei milhemot olam*, ed. by Chone Shmeruk and Shmuel Werses (Jerusalem: Magnes, 1997), pp. 182–207.
26. Aaron Zeitlin, 'Esterke un Kazimir der groyser: Ahaswer in Poilin', *Golbus*, 5 (November 1932), 5–38; 6 (December 1932), 12–46.
27. Zeitlin, 'Esterke', *Golbus*, 5, p. 22.
28. Ibid., p. 20.
29. Szeintuch, pp. 184–85.
30. Zeitlin, 'Esterke', *Golbus*, 6, p. 37.
31. Ibid., p. 39.
32. Ibid.
33. Ibid., p. 14.
34. Ibid., p. 21.
35. Ibid., p. 45.
36. Ibid., p. 46.
37. Aaron Zeitlin, 'Esterke' (signed 1967), in Aaron Zeitlin, *Drames*, 2 vols (Tel Aviv: Peretz, 1974–80), II (1980), 80–150.
38. Ibid., pp. 129–30.

39. Ibid., p. 150.
40. Walter Benjamin, 'Ursprung des deutschen Trauerspiels', in Walter Benjamin, *Gesammelte Schriften*, 5 vols in 11 parts, ed. by Theodor W. Adorno and Gershom Scholem (Frankfurt a.M.: Suhrkamp, 1971–82), I. 1 (1978), 203–409.
41. Ibid., p. 343.
42. Naomi Seidman, *A Marriage Made in Heaven: The Sexual Politics of Hebrew and Yiddish* (Berkeley: University of California Press, 1997). See also Seidman's recent work on the intertwined processes of Jewish secularization and adoption of the romantic paradigm as an organizing social and cultural principle: *The Marriage Plot; or, How Jews Fell in Love with Love, and with Literature* (Stanford: Stanford University Press, 2016).
43. On the interplay of nationalism and the ideas of history and of salvation in a closely related context, see Amnon Raz-Krakotzkin, 'Exile, History and the Nationalization of Jewish Memory: Some Reflections on the Zionist Notion of History and Return', *Journal of Levantine Studies*, 3.2 (winter 2013), 37–70.

CHAPTER 7

Between Talmud and Feminism: Bashevis Singer's Playful Jugglery in his Bilingual Corpus*

Valentina Fedchenko

Introduction

Yitskhok Bashevis Singer, or Isaac Singer, has produced a double corpus of literary texts, aimed at fitting into two different literary traditions and at appealing to both Yiddish and general readers. Most of his writings have been translated from Yiddish into English by professional translators, but he revised their final versions himself.[1] Overall, he played a pivotal role adapting his works for non-Yiddish audiences. Singer's works in English have entered worldwide circulation, whereas most Yiddish texts remain in the serialized form in which they were published in the New York daily Yiddish newspaper *Forverts*. According to some critics, Singer even discouraged translation of his works from Yiddish into other languages, thus considering the English versions final.[2]

World literature knows other examples of writers who created in two languages, such as Samuel Beckett or Vladimir Nabokov. The latter, after he switched to English, never fully returned to the Russian language. Nabokov did not have to face the challenge of introducing his culture to an American readership, since Russian literature was sufficiently familiar to the latter through translation. With Singer the situation was quite different. Having decided to translate his novels into English, he assumed, in some way, the role of an indigenous ethnographer of a minor literary tradition[3] who set himself the task of presenting his own exotic culture to a foreign audience. Although ancient Jewish culture can be considered as one of the essential bases of world culture, the Yiddish tradition has remained marginal in the constitution of the modern Western literary canon. The secularization of society and its general modernization during the nineteenth century slightly improved the low reputation of the language, but did not reverse the situation significantly.

---

* This research was supported by the Russian Foundation of Science, project 15-18-00062, 'Formation of Culture in Diaspora', St Petersburg State University. I would also like to express my gratitude to Mikhail Krutikov for his idea that the title *Neshome-ekspeditsyes* might be related to Fishl Shneerson's term *psikhologishe ekspeditsyes*, and to Borukh Gorin for revealing the connection between the name 'Isbel' and the biblical figure of Jezebel.

The idea of translation, or even self-translation, into major languages, such as Russian and English, was not new for Yiddish writers, who elaborated different strategies of overcoming cultural exoticism on the levels of content and expression. Sholem Aleichem's Russian stories were deprived of many Jewish elements: ethnic or religious details, terms, and even proper names.[4] The first writer who made a great attempt to reach a wider American audience through English translations, Sholem Asch, gained popularity with historical and biblical plots common to Jewish and Christian worlds. By the 1960s, some Yiddish narratives were already known to an American public, like *Fiddler on the Roof* that had been embedded in popular American culture in its English-language adaptation. Comparing the Yiddish and English versions of Singer's novels, we can observe how his attitude to the very translation process changed, becoming more conscious, how he progressed in identifying his *oeuvre* as a diasporic or emigrant literary production. Perhaps spontaneously,[5] he devised a specific strategy to convert his own literary material from Yiddish into English, and furthermore filled his English texts with Jewish cultural realia and Yiddish-specific terms without any English translation.

The term 'diasporic literature' was used by Singer himself to designate his works. When he describes the specificity of Yiddish literature as pertaining to the diasporic experience, he argues that this literature will never be able to get out of the ghetto, with all the advantages and disadvantages that move entails:

> The idea that Yiddish literature and culture as a whole could be cosmopolitan, an equal among equals, was from the very beginning built on an illusion. Jews who desired to become full blown cosmopolitans, switched to other languages and assimilated into other cultures. And those who stuck to the Yiddish word and letters, unavoidably remained encumbered by a centuries-old spiritual experience of diaspora. Yiddish literature cannot make do without writing about *shoykhets*, *lamdens*, shopkeepers [...] and the latter determine the content and form of this literature.[6]

Singer states that the best Yiddish writers in America do not write about America, but about past life.[7] The Yiddish language prevents them from writing about America in Yiddish. Their 'noble' words remain too loaded with tradition, and new words are alien and awkward. It means that social changes, and then linguistic ones, imply a form of conservatism and limit the topics of Yiddish literature in America. Immigration tends to isolate the community or to accelerate the assimilation of its members. Translation into English is — on the one hand — an attempt to overcome this isolation, but supposes — on the other hand — a will to create an image of this very culture for an external readership.

If we compare the Yiddish and English versions of Singer's later novels, we do not find essential differences in the topics of the novels. Differences are to be observed not only at the level of content but also at the level of its expression. When discussing the literature of the Jewish Diaspora in other languages, not Yiddish and Hebrew but English or Russian, we often talk about cleaved identities and about strategies of double writing when a text is written both for a narrow circle of initiates and for a wider audience.[8] Singer adheres to this dual strategy, but in two different languages, and thus creates two, distinct, corpora.

The transfer of Singer's long novels from the Yiddish literary world to a wider cultural context entailed significant changes, which also concern the representation of women and their structural role within the narration. Much attention has already been devoted to the topics of women, androgynies, and the queering of sexual identities in his works. In my paper, I would like to focus on the gender-influenced changes that occurred in Singer's late prose when it was translated into English.

Changing Readership, Changing Gender Boundaries

Reading Singer's early novels in English, we notice that, even when women appear as their main characters, they are somewhat deprived of any psychological acuteness. For example, Singer does not show any interest in the interior life of Reykhele, the main character of *Satan in Goray*, a young woman haunted by a dybbuk. She is cut off from the society of the shtetl Goray, which is overcome by the Sabbatean heresy, and experiences ecstatic messianic visions which become a public affair. The secretiveness of the character is justified by the specific narrative mode Singer has chosen. The story is told by a traditional-minded narrator who explains the contradictory personality of Reykhele, her manic-depressive condition, through typical categories from the traditional, deeply religious world, that is, through the intervention of dybbuks. Singer has privileged a literary convention which makes it impossible for the narrator to look into the interior world of this woman. Published as a serialized novel in *Globus* in 1933 and then two years later by the Library of the Yiddish PEN Club in Warsaw, the novel happened to have undergone in its English translation[9] (1955) by Jacob Sloan a very few slight changes which did not affect the main female character and representation of the gender question. The critical perception of both versions appeared to be spectacularly diverse. Whereas Yiddish commentators admired the authentic depiction of seventeenth-century Poland and a precise stylistic elaboration, American critics interpreted the novel in a symbolic dehistoricized way and underlined instead its metaphysical significance. In this case, the long formal and substantial distance between the Yiddish and American English literary worlds somehow facilitated translation and presentation of the novel for a foreign readership. This process became more complicated in Singer's later realistic novels, where the intercultural distance was reduced. The novel *Sonim: Geshikhte fun a libe*, where the action takes place in the New World, presents an interesting example of this evolution.

In the 1960s, women's rights became a key issue in public discourse in the US.[10] The novel *Sonim: Geshikhte fun a libe* was published twice a week in *Forverts* from 11 February to 13 August 1966, when second-wave feminism had already called for new discussions about gender-related questions. In the following eight years, when the English version of the novel was prepared for publication, the impact of different minority movements and the counterculture of the 1960s grew significantly. A certain influence of those heated discussions can be traced in the novel.

In both the Yiddish and English versions of the novel, women are presented as active participants in World War II events: the protagonist Herman Broder spent the whole war period lying in a barn where the Polish servant Yadwiga, later his second wife, hid him; his first wife, Tamara, was wounded during a shooting and imprisoned in a Soviet camp; his mistress Masha had a concentration camp experience. All the female protagonists were active during a period of major disaster when history deprived the individual of its independence and freedom.

Moreover, the woman is depicted as subject to assimilation.[11] While Herman Broder does not manage to adapt to changes in the post-war world, two of the three women between whom he lives, tormented by his hesitations, succeed much better in adapting to the new American reality. The Polish peasant girl Yadwiga converts to Judaism and finds her place in a Jewish community by eliminating the traditional interconfessional and interethnic borders and contributing to the emergence of a new, open American Jewish society. Herman's first wife, Tamara, who has miraculously escaped death in Nazi-occupied Poland, starts a business at the end of the novel when she runs a bookstore, a traditionally masculine occupation in old Jewish society.

Women's modernity, liberation, and active social life are, at best, embodied by the fourth female figure, a typical incarnation of the American modern woman: Nancy Isbel, who has disappeared from the English version of the novel. Her name can be deciphered as an anagram for 'lesbi'. She is described as a human being of indefinite gender with short hair, a huge bag, shoes with low heels. When Herman sees Nancy, he reacts in the following way: ' "Avade a lezbyanerin", — hot German a trakht geton. Di froy hot gehat a kol vos hot geklungen nit vayberish un nit mansbilsh' [She is, of course, a lesbian, — thought Herman. The woman had a voice which sounded neither feminine, nor masculine].[12]

In general, the part of the story related to Nancy Isbel is imbued with mysticism. Beginning with the appearance of Nancy, a series of strange events occur. Nancy surprises Herman with her knowledge of ancient Hebrew when she reads a series of Kabbalistic book titles without any fault. On the next day, after Herman has told Nancy about his desire to hide himself in an isolated farm, Nancy reveals that she has an aunt in Vermont. At first sight, Nancy Isbel is a very positive character, but a Jewish reader, experienced in reading the Tanakh, can easily guess her symbolic role in the text: her name, 'Isbel', alludes to her connection with the Gentile Princess Jezebel who incited her husband King Ahab to abandon the worship of Yahweh and encouraged the worship of pagan deities such as Baal and Asherah. She persecuted the Jewish religion, turned Jews to idolatry, and destroyed her house with her own hands. Singer gives some details about Nancy Isbel's biography which reinforce her connection with the biblical character of Jezebel: Nancy's husband was a Christian and a professor of astronomy; in traditional Yiddish literature, astronomy is associated with *avode zore* (idolatry). In the Yiddish Bible interpretation *Tseena Ureena*, Ahasia, the son of Ahab and Jezebel, was punished with a shortening of his days because of *avodes kokhavim* (worship of stars), another Yiddish term for pagan worship.[13] It is also worth noting that the Midrashic tradition reinforces the positive side of Jezebel's personality and lists the acts of kindness that she performed. According to Midrash Yalkut Shimoni II Kings 232, Jezebel has merits: 'Whenever a funeral cortège passed the royal palace, Jezebel would descend and join the ranks of the mourners, and, also, when a marriage procession went by, she took part in the merry-making in honor of the bridal couple.'[14] Therefore, the duality of this character has its roots in rabbinic literature.

For the Jewish traditional world, the inversion of genders and of their roles seems exotic and strange, while modernization transforms both male and female identities. In the Yiddish version of *Enemies: A Love Story*, Bashevis accentuates the confusion of female and male roles in the community and introduces a surprising innovation — a lesbian Jewish girl who is not one of the transgender heroes from his earlier stories such as 'Yentl der yeshive-bokher' [Yentl the Yeshiva Boy] or 'Androginus' [Androgyne], but a potential mistress of the protagonist, one of the women he encounters in America. His precursor Sholem Asch had not named 'lesbian' a sexual relationship that he presented in *Got fun nekome* (1907) and *God of Vengeance* (1923); Singer introduces this topic only linguistically,[15] by applying the word *lezbyanerin*, which is related to Nancy Isbel's modernity in general, but without discussing the phenomenon of crossing gender boundaries. The character of the modern young American woman has a different function in the novel. According to several scholars and critics, 'to Singer, the most serious betrayal of all [...] is the blurring of masculine and feminine clarity'.[16] I would not be so categorical, but in the particular example of Nance Isbel, the apocalyptic dimension of the character is obvious in the Yiddish novel. Herman Broder disappears from the pages of the novel, accompanied by Nancy Isbel: he retires to the farm of her aunt in Vermont. In the epilogue, it is Nancy who announces to Herman's wife, Tamara, his disappearance. A Jew from Eastern Europe cannot find their place outside of it, in a foreign country. Nancy Isbel serves to describe the catastrophe which the Jewish traditional world is facing and its dissolution in contact with the American way of life.

The depiction of America in the Yiddish version of the novel has an evident apocalyptic connotation. In Yiddish, New York receives some characteristics of concentration camps, of hell. It is a world where nothing can be repaired, where sirens of fire trucks howl like the mourning of Hadadrimmon in the valley of Megiddon (Zachariah 12. 11).[17] All these allusions are removed from the English version. The discarding of the character of Nancy Isbel might be linked to this will to subdue the apocalyptic note, but this is probably not the only reason.

For an American reader, such a character does not seem particularly exotic or shocking. When the obvious link of the name 'Isbel' to the biblical text is lost, when the allusions to the Scriptures are not anymore easily recognizable outside the Jewish context, the symbolic role of the character in the novel is no longer visible. Yet the character of Jezebel could have been familiar to an American readership in the 1960s because of several popular representations of this biblical plot: a soap-opera-like novel by Frank G. Slaughter, *The Curse of Jezebel: A Novel of the Biblical Queen of Evil* (1961); a movie by Reginald Le Borg, *Sins of Jezebel* (1953); a hit recorded by Frankie Laine in 1951; or the historical personality of Anne Hutchison, called the 'American Jezebel'.[18] In the American context, the figure of Jezebel was more related to its Judaeo-Christian interpretations or to a controversial personality in American historiography. It could have brought into the novel contemporary feminist and gay rights discussions. These associations would have blurred the apocalyptic perspective of the end of the novel. Nevertheless, it seems to me even more relevant to explain the exclusion of Nancy Isbel from the English text by the fact that Singer tends to create, for an external readership, a very conservative, traditional depiction of an exotic Ashkenazic society where gender boundaries remain untouched. At the end of the English novel, when the protagonist leaves all his women and disappears, his first wife, Tamara, remains faithful to her missing husband, although his departure makes her an *aguna*, the most difficult status for a Jewish woman in the traditional world — a woman who has no husband but is not divorced, so she cannot marry for a second time. Tamara prefers to remain an *aguna* and rejects every offer of marriage, retaining her loyalty to her missing husband and to the Ashkenazi family traditions. She obeys the rules of the traditional world instead of turning to the modern solution that would allow her to get rid of this painful social status. The English version ends with Tamara's words: having been asked by Rabbi Lempert, if she plans to get married in future, she answers: 'Perhaps, in the next world — to Herman.'[19]

These slight changes of the plot shift the accent from some problems close to the hearts of Yiddish-speakers (assimilation and the decadence of Yiddish culture in America) to universal human questions about relationships between men and women. The fact that the translator of the English novel, *Enemies: A Love Story*,[20] into French decided to render the word 'Enemies' in the feminine gender (with an -*e*) is an additional testimony about how an external English-speaking readership perceives the gender problem as the most important in the novel.[21] According to this translator's decision, only the female characters can qualify for the role of 'enemies' in the novel, but not the post-Holocaust syndrome or the threat of assimilation, as might be the case in its Yiddish version. Moreover, the observed changes allow Singer to substitute a modern challenging discussion about free gender identity and its expression with an idealized image of a traditional — as far as it can be such in America — Ashkenazi society with persistent family values, as Tamara reveals them at the end of the novel. They push American critics to an optimistic interpretation of the novel's end, for example, about Tamara and Yadwiga:

> Through female bounding, the Jewish wife and the gentile wife are not the enemies Broder feared they would become. Sharing a common destiny of abandonment, they have, through mutual concern, created a home in the alien world. [...] As women who survive with dignity and purpose, they not only provide a sanctuary for an errant husband, but they reflect Singer's hope that a meaningful existence is still possible after the Holocaust.[22]

It is obvious that such a reading would be impossible with knowledge of the Yiddish novel.

Genderless Shosha as a Metaphor for the In-Betweenness of Jewish Culture

The novel *Neshome-ekspeditsyes* (known in its English version as *Shosha*) was published, in its serialized version, only eight years after the publication of *Sonim: Geshikhte fun a libe* in Yiddish, and four years after the publication of the English version, but Singer had seriously changed his strategy in presenting his work to a foreign audience, the American readership. He was apparently gaining a greater influence on his publisher in controlling English translations of his works. We can also observe a significant evolution on the formal level. Singer's experience was growing. By reading American critics, he gained a better understanding of his new readership. He more clearly expects readers to adapt their cultural competence and interests to the Jewish culture he presents, and, at the same time, he plays with the somewhat stereotyped representation of Yiddish culture in a broader context. The author's cultural identity becomes an object of literary play.

The English novel *Shosha*[23] begins with an exposition which is absent from the Yiddish version. Singer, from the very first sentence, presents Yiddish as a dead language and recalls that there is some doubt as to whether it is even a language at all. The first paragraph of the novel lists a series of clichés about the absurd conservatism of Jewish education and its past-oriented cultural strategies, as well as its disconnection from the surrounding reality in practical life and in social communication. Although his ancestors have lived in Poland for seven centuries, the protagonist speaks only a few words of Polish. In this bizarre anti-modern world, the strange friendship between the protagonist, Arn Graydinger, and Shosha, and even his later choosing her as his spouse, do not really surprise the reader. It looks exotic, but the reader has been warned from the beginning about the abnormality of Eastern European Yiddish culture. Moreover, Shosha became one of the most famous and most memorable female characters in the whole corpus of Singer's work; the novel is named after her. An English reader may have the impression that Shosha and her psychology are described with much more conscientiousness than the female protagonists of earlier novels. This is, in part, due to the fact that Singer's later novels are less experimental from a formal point of view. The diversity of styles and genres which we can observe in *Satan in Goray* (it includes a part written in the form of a medieval martyrological chronicle about the Khmelnytsky massacres, and another in the form of a *mayse-noyre* — a horror story about the exorcism of dybbuks),[24] has been replaced by a more straightforward and stylistically less unsettling mode of narration, a narration imbued with nostalgia. This is, in particular, the case with Shosha. The educated, nostalgic narrator, no more bound by strict literary techniques, seems to fathom without difficulty the psychological condition of women. But this impression is contradicted by the original Yiddish version of the same novel. The editor of the Russian publishing house who asked me to translate *Shosha* from the original Yiddish into Russian was bitterly disappointed by the radically different representation of the female character of Shosha he discovered.

The Yiddish version of this novel bears a different title, *Neshome ekspeditsyes* [Soul Expeditions]. It is under this quite mysterious and intriguing name that it was serialized in *Forverts* in 1974. The title was partly borrowed by Singer from a collection of lectures on psychology, *Der veg tsum mentsh* [The Way to the Human Being], published by psychiatrist Dr Fishl Schneerson in Vilno in 1927.[25] The term *psikhologishe ekspeditsyes* (psychological expeditions) was invented by Schneerson, as was the idea of therapeutic psychoanalytic sessions with a Hasidic spiritual background (he belonged to a Hasidic line). The very Yiddish title *Neshome-*

ekspeditsyes might remind a competent reader of these therapeutic practices, which are reflected inside the novel. Singer describes the Jewish Bohemians living in prewar Warsaw who got their entertainment from collective psychoanalytic sessions to which they added ingredients of Hasidic mysticism.

It is worth noting that the character of Shosha does not appear in Singer's work for the first time here. She appears for the first time under the guise of the little girl to which Itshele tells an invented story in the children's book *The Day of the Fulfillment of Wishes: Stories about a Young Boy Growing Up in Warsaw*, which received the American National Book Prize in 1970.[26] There, the author writes: 'with time, Shosha became for me an incarnation of the past'. In *Neshome-ekspeditsyes*, the character is significantly paler than in the English version, and the love story of the protagonist with her is devoid of psychological verisimilitude. She does not really get involved in the plot. By neglecting to give any realistic details, Singer forces his reader to understand the character on a symbolic level, removed from the corporality, the emotionality, and even sentimentality with which the English version later endowed Shosha.

In the Yiddish version of the novel, Shosha belongs, like Reykhele in *Satan in Goray* or Nancy Isbel in *Sonim: Geshikhte fun a libe*, to the group of mysterious, secretive female characters in Singer's novels: these characters have a symbolic value and assume in some way a mystical function. She is a genderless and nearly dumb creature. The Yiddish version of the novel, contrary to the English one, does not present the scene of the night after the wedding. Shosha does not mention, at any time, that she wants to have a child (a recurrent object of discussion on her part in the English version): as a whole, she is deprived of any specifically feminine physical features and of a reproductive function.

Shosha cannot play her role as a woman in society. After the wedding, when Shosha and Arn Graydinger move to live together with the Khentshiners (Khayml and Tsiliya), Shosha spends all her time sitting in the kitchen with the cat. In the traditional Ashkenazic community, as it is reflected in Yiddish literature and memoirs, the woman tends to establish connections with the outside world, being more integrated than the man in the multi-ethnic environment of her place of living: she is granted instruction in foreign languages and often runs some kind of business.[27] Shosha, on the contrary, cannot exist either outside the community or within it, but only in her original environment of the frozen past.

Having left her home on Krokhmalnaya Street, she is confronted with a modern emancipated world that provides greater freedom of choice. In one episode of the novel, Shosha hesitates while choosing one of the little chocolates brought to her by Arn Graydinger as a gift. The author explains this reaction as a psychological disorder — a pathological indecisiveness, an inability to make any choice. This scene has been included in both the English and the Yiddish versions, but it elicits further interpretation in the latter. The ambivalence of Shosha, in terms of gender, makes her a kind of *tumtum*,[28] a genderless creature which symbolizes an insurmountable state of doubt. Shosha's irresolution is mirrored in the novel by Arn Graydinger's unclear personal desires in his relations with women. One great choice seems to reflect his personal history: on one side, the American actress Betty; on the other side, the devoted communist Dora. Beyond this alternative, he is supposed to give preference to one of two possible diasporic life strategies and to select the destination of his emigration: America or the Soviet Union. When Arn Graydinger chooses Shosha among all his potential brides, he makes a pseudo-choice which illustrates the general frustration and fear of an individual faced with complicated historical events which force him to leave his place of birth. The protagonist prefers not to assume responsibility for this decision about his future. Both versions of the novel end with a scene in which two characters, Arn Graydinger and Khayml, are sitting in the darkness and, when asked 'What are you waiting for?' by Genya, who enters the room, they answer: 'We are waiting for an answer.'[29] There is an evident messianic implication to this epilogue: the frustration of endless waiting that, in the Yiddish version, is not attenuated by nostalgia for the charming little girl Shosha.

The character of Shosha, in the Yiddish novel, appears voluntarily unnatural and mysterious. She does not fear death (whereas everyone around her lives with the premonition of death), or maybe she does not even understand the danger. Arn Graydinger, describing his bride, tells Moris Faytlzon that Shosha has been, from her birth, a prophetess (this is absent from the English version). Tsilya, in a conversation with Arn, invites Shosha to her circle of Warsaw intellectuals and says: 'Oyb du host di shoshen af an emes lib, muz zi vern eyne fun undz. Ober teylmol bin ikh khoyshed az zi ekzistirt iberhoypt nisht' [If you really love Shosha, she has to become one of us, but sometimes I suspect that she doesn't exist at all].[30]

Shosha gains humanity and naturalness in the English version of the novel. This metamorphosis of the character is achieved mostly by clarifying its gender: in the introduction, the friendship between two children is endowed with features of naive sexuality and allusions to the Song of Songs, a universal point of reference of Jewish origin for a love story. Shosha is obviously feminine: she wants to give birth to children. This touching little girl fascinates the reader with her nostalgic charm, which contrasts with the complexity of the character and of its message in the Yiddish version.

American English-language critics sometimes blamed Singer for his tendency to dwell upon difficult and superfluous philosophical discussions in which the same thought repeats itself over long paragraphs. As a consequence, with his understanding for readers' expectations, and sometimes also following the suggestions of his editors, Singer shortened his last novels and put the accent no more on mystical-philosophical considerations but on the action and the mutual relations of his characters. This is precisely the way in which *Neshome-ekspeditsyes* has been reworked to become *Shosha*. The change of title is not fortuitous. *Shosha* begins with an evocation of the childhood of Arn Graydinger, the protagonist, in which Shosha plays an important role, whereas *Neshome-ekspeditsyes* presents, first of all, the doctor Moris Faytlzon, whose role is notably greater in the original version than in the translation.

Mixing Gender and Ethnic Stereotypes

The Yiddish versions of both novels present a number of theoretical passages about gender and the role of women that were later eliminated from the English adaptations. One of the main characters of the Yiddish version of *Neshome-ekspeditsyes*, Moris Faytlzon, who conceived the idea of psychoanalytic sessions called *neshome-ekspeditsyes*, is misogynistic and, he expresses his own theories about gender and the differences between men and women. It is worth quoting some examples of such reflections about women's nature and the future of the world. Faytlzon asks Arn who Shosha is, and he answers: 'A geboyrene tsadeykes!' [A real pious woman!].[31] And Faytlzon starts presenting his conception:

> Di tayve tsu shpiln iz do in ale vayber, on oysnam. Tsvey moyres hobn gehaltn in der tsoym dos vayberishe min: moyre far shvangershaft un moyre farn man-broyt-geber. Es halt derbay az di beyde moyres zoln ufhern un demolt vet di gezelshaft farvandelt vern in eyn groyser orgye. Di manslayt veln bald mid vern un di vayber veln zikh porn eyne mit der anderer vi es iz alts do in khumesh breyshes, in der gemore, in medresh.
>
> [All the women without exception have a passion for games. Two fears held back the feminine gender: the fear of becoming pregnant and the fear of a male breadwinner. Now both fears will disappear, and the society will plunge into a huge orgy. Men will soon get tired, and the females will mate with each other, as it is written in the book of Genesis, the Talmud, and Midrash.][32]

The gender question receives an unexpected interpretation in Faytlzon's philosophical presentation of the world's modernization. It is viewed from an apocalyptic perspective, rooted in Jewish authoritative sources. Gender stereotypes are mixed with ethnic ones. Faytlzon's monologue continues:

> Der meshugener Oto Vayninger iz geven gerekht. Der yiddisher mansbil hot in zikh a gresern protsent vayblekhkayt vi der azoygerufener aryer. Di natsis haltn im in eyn tsitirn, a tog geyt nit ariber me zol im nisht dermonen in 'Felkisher beobakhter', ober er iz geven a goen say vi say. Di tsukunft gehert tsu vayber un tsu yidn.
>
> [The crazy Otto Weininger was right. The Jewish male has a bigger percentage of femininity than the so-called Aryan. The Nazis constantly quote him, and the *Völkischer Beobachter* mentions him every day. He was a genius, of course. The future belongs to women and to Jews.][33]

Singer alludes here to the ideas of the Austrian philosopher Otto Weininger as they were exposed in his book *Sex and Character*. It was translated into Yiddish in 1929 and published by Yatshkovski's (or Iaczkowski's) Popular-Scientific Library (Populer Visnshaftlekhe Biblyotek) as *Geshlekht un kharakter*. Singer was fascinated by this personality and wrote, in collaboration with Aaron Zeitlin, a novel entitled *Der toyt fun Oto Vayninger: Filosofisher shund-roman* [The Death of Otto Weininger: A Philosophical Novelette]. Zeitlin underlined, in his exchange with the Buenos Aires-based Yiddish writer Jacob Botoshansky, Bashevis's sympathy for the Austrian philosopher, a feeling that lasted until the later period of his life.[34] The novel has never been published in a book form and was considered as lost. Ofer Dynes has found one fragment in the monthly journal *Shriftn* (November–December 1938) in the National Library of Poland.[35]

On the one hand, Singer presents a specific nationalist discourse that existed in some Warsaw intellectual circles, and also in Jewish ones, on the eve of World War II. On the other hand, he obviously aims at provoking his Yiddish readership, which was waiting for some piquant stuff when reading Singer's novels in *Forverts*. Singer puts before the eyes of his readers these unclear and paradoxical declarations, which compare misogyny and anti-Semitism. The same character also ascribes to Jews a passion for playing ('di tayve tsu shpiln'). In another of Faytlzon's monologues, we read: 'Di letste milkhome vet zayn tsvishn di humoristn un ernste mentshn. Umkumen veln farshteyt zikh di humoristn. Un der mentsh vet tsurik vern a malpe' [The last war will be between humorists and serious people. The humorists will obviously loose. And man will become a monkey again].[36]

Singer uses these philosophical discussions of the 1930s as a background for his representation of the Holocaust and as a way to question the Jewish future as a whole. Some references to them can be found earlier in the Yiddish version of the novel *Sonim: Geshikhte fun a libe*, in the dialogue between the protagonist, Herman Broder, and the feminist Nancy Isbel, who studies Kabbalah at university:

— Loyt der kabole iz di dozike velt di ergste fun ale veltn. Zey rufn zi: nukvo de-thomo rabo — di froy fun dem grestn thom.
— Farvos grod di nekeyve?
— Vayl zi zet nit dem thom.
— Zi zet, zi zet. Me hot geharget in eyrope punkt azoyfil froyen vifl mener.

[— According to Kabbalah, this world is the worst of all the worlds, they call it *nukvo de-thomo rabo* — the woman of the biggest abyss.
— Why necessarily a woman?
— Because she doesn't see the abyss.
— Yes, she does. In Europe they killed as many women as men.][37]

Herman deliberately confuses the words *nukvo*, 'cave, tunnel', and *nekeyve*, 'woman', which have the same root, and translates the former into Yiddish by the word *froy* — 'woman'. Nancy reacts to this wordplay with feminist fervour, insisting on the equality of men and women who died in the Holocaust. It is worth noting that the field of women's history and the phenomenon of biblical feminism underwent a momentous development in the 1960s,[38] when the Yiddish version of the novel was published and the biblical Jezebel, whose story challenges 'fundamental patriarchal assumptions about what personality traits and behaviors constitute bad women',[39] became one of the most frequent references in feminist scholarship. The quoted scene is highly ironic; it reveals the clash between Jewish (Yiddish) and American culture, and the absurdity of the latter: the demon of Jezebel (in the person of Nancy Isbel), resurrected and exculpated by American feminists, fights for the equality of murdered Jewish men and women.

It is very probable that Singer's American editors could not accept these unclear, strange, and misogynistic passages being presented to an American readership. As a result, the novels have undergone significant changes: the allusions to concrete philosophies and to their gender- and ethnic-related theories were eliminated. The female characters became more realistic and less conceptual.

Conclusion

As a conclusion, I would like to analyse the mechanisms in the evolution of gender-related questions as they are presented for Yiddish and English readerships in the two novels I have studied. As he wrote these works, in the 1960s and -70s, Singer was surrounded, in America, by intense debates on the political and social level. As a consequence, he borrows some actual interrogations of gender from the wider American discourse, but adjusts them to his own European cultural experience and to the philosophical theories of his youth. In the Yiddish versions, he exploits the gender question (through the presentation of extremities and anomalies in particular) in order to speak about more general problems. The depiction of gender anomalies serves as a vehicle for other messages, which are relevant for Jewish society and Yiddish literature in America: the slow extinction of the Yiddish language and of its cultural specificity in the face of modernization and the dominant American environment, the perplexity of the Eastern European Jew caught in a whirlwind of dramatic historical changes, the search for a superior entity which could assume responsibility for tragic events and difficult personal decisions. The gender ambivalence of Shosha becomes a metaphor for the intermediate position of diasporic Jewish culture, which is jammed between tradition and modernity, closeness and isolation, or openness and assimilation, but it also reflects the passivity of Polish Jews in front of the impending catastrophe they were conscious of. The masculinity of Nancy Isbel provokes a discussion about the destiny of Yiddish culture in America.[40]

The English versions present a society with more traditional gender relationships. Singer does not raise the same gender-related problems with his 'external' American readership as he does in the Yiddish texts, probably because of his lack of cultural background and experience in the dominant culture. In America, this is the period of second feminism, but Singer remains on the periphery of American intellectual and social life and realizes his lack of cultural competence when it comes to American gender discussions. A certain form of discomfort towards the established literary traditions is inevitable when a writer loses his national cultural autonomy by switching into the dominant language and facing a relatively unfamiliar cultural and literary background.

Singer chose different strategies to deal with the notion of exoticism depending on his implied reader. For the traditional Yiddish world, deviations in gender behaviours and strategies seem exotic. The figure of the genderless Shosha in the Yiddish version is a product of cultural hybridization because it is inspired at the same time by Talmudic discussions and by the general American cultural trends of the postmodernist turn, as this period was named by David Hoeveler Jr: 'The recurrent motif in 1970s culture is the dismantling of inherited forms, descriptive norms, sharp and inclusive modes of categorization; instead, we have the blurring of distinctions, the mixing of forms, a discomfort with preciseness in signification and representation.'[41] The character of Nancy Isbel is also a cultural hybrid of American and Jewish traditional interpretations of the Bible. In the English versions, on the other hand, Singer proposes a society with a conservative distribution of male and female roles and with traditional gender-related values that were already perceived as an old-fashioned cultural model in the 1970s.

Published in a newspaper, the Yiddish corpus of Singer's works treated contemporary issues of the Jewish community in America and invited, or better provoked, the reader to think about and discuss the word they lived in. In his English-language corpus, on the other hand, when he takes upon himself the role of representative of his 'minor' Yiddish culture, Bashevis Singer reverses the perspective and accepts narrating about an exotic past, which induces him to idealize or simplify the image of Eastern European Ashkenazic culture for future generations.

Notes to Chapter 7

1. A number of errors and corruptions prove that Bashevis was not always involved in the process of translation, as is illustrated with text examples from the novel *Meshuga* in Chone Shmeruk, 'The Perils of Translation: Isaac Bashevis Singer in English and Hebrew', in *Literary Strategies: Jewish Texts and Contexts*, ed. by Ezra Mendelsohn (New York: Oxford University Press, 1997), pp. 228–34 (pp. 232–33). The plot of the novel *Farloyrene neshomes* (or in English *Meshuga*) is directly related to the novel *Sonim: Geshikhte fun a libe*, which is discussed here.
2. The priority of the English versions is underlined by one of Bashevis's translators: Nili Wachtel, 'Translator's Postscript', in Isaac Bashevis Singer, *Meshugah*, trans. by Isaac Bashevis Singer and Nili Wachtel (New York: Farrar, Straus, Giroux, 1994), pp. 229–32 (p. 231).
3. The concept of world literature was thoroughly elaborated in Pascale Casanova, *La République mondiale des Lettres* (Paris: Éditions du Seuil, 1999), while the term 'minor literature' was introduced and first applied to Kafka's writings in Gilles Deleuze and Félix Guattari, 'What is a Minor Literature?', trans. by Robert Brinkley, *Mississippi Review*, 11.3 (1983), 13–33.
4. A detailed discussion of Sholem Aleichem's prose in Russian can be found in Alexander Frenkel, 'Sholem Aleichem as a Self-Translator', in *Translating Shlolem Aleichem: History, Politics, and Art*, ed. by Gennady Estraikh and others (New York: Modern Humanities Research Association; Routledge, 2012), pp. 25–46 (p. 33).
5. Bashevis mentioned several times in his interviews that he never thought about his readership while writing (Joel Blocker and Richard Elman, 'An Interview with Isaac Bashevis Singer', in *Critical Views of Isaac Bashevis Singer*, ed. by Irving Malin (New York: New York University Press, 1969), pp. 3–26 (pp. 3, 6)), but I fully agree with Anita Norich, who calls this claim 'disingenuous at best' in 'Translation and Transgression: Isaac Bashevis Singer in America', in *Isaac Bashevis Singer: His Work and his World*, ed. by Hugh Denman (Boston: Brill, 2002), pp. 81–94 (p. 86).
6. Isaac Bashevis Singer, 'Problems of Yiddish Prose in America', trans. by Robert H. Wolf, *A Journal for Jewish Literary History*, 9 (1989), 5–12 (p. 7).
7. This generalization, even if applied only to immigrant Jewish writers, is obviously arrogant and concerns, first of all, Bashevis's own strategy as a writer. See also the discussion in Monika Adamczyk-Garbowska, 'The Place of Isaac Bashevis Singer in World Literature', *Studia Judaica*, 13 (2005), 219–27.
8. An interesting discussion about Jewish literature as a diasporic phenomenon is proposed in the section 'Diaspora i literatura', ed. by Mikhail Krutikov, *Novoe literaturnoe obozrenie*, 127.3 (2014), 95–147.
9. As a recent study (Faith Jones, 'The Real First Translation of Bashevis into English!', *In geveb*, 20

September 2015 <https://ingeveb.org/blog/the-real-first-translation-of-bashevis-into-english> [accessed 27 September 2017]) demonstrates, a section from *Sotn in Goray* [Satan in Goray] appears to be the earliest English translation of Singer's work. It was published in 1938 in a British anthology by his nephew Morris Kreitman.

10. The 1960s are the period of the second wave of feminism, increasing visibility of homosexuality, and gay liberation; see e.g. Neeru Tandon, *Feminism: A Paradigm Shift* (Delphi: Nice Printing Press, 2008).
11. Bashevis declared this thesis later in a public lecture in the New York City Hall, criticizing Judaism for not teaching women Tora and saying that 'the denial of equal religious rights to women has contributed to assimilation' (quoted in David Friedman, 'Singer: Yiddish Needs No Defense', *Jewish Telegraphic Agency*, 8 November 1978, pp. 2–3 (p. 2)). The thesis was considered a favourable response to the 'feminist challenge' (Evelyne Torton Beck, 'I. B. Singer's Misogyny', *Lilith*, 6 (1979), 34–36 (p. 36)).
12. Itskhok Bashevis, 'Sonim: Geshikhte fun a libe', *Forverts*, 22 July 1966, p. 3 (my translation).
13. Yaakov ben Yitskhak Ashkenazi, *Sefer Tseena Ureena: Al hamisha humshe tora im haftarot ve-hamesh megilot ve-targum le-megilot be-lashon Ashkenaz, ivri taytsh* (Vilno: Dfus Rozenkrants ve-Shriftzetser, 1895), p. 248.
14. Louis Ginzberg and others, *The Legends of Jews*, 7 vols (Philadelphia: Jewish Publication Society of America, 1909–38), IV (1913), p. 189.
15. An interesting remark about the development of spontaneous censorship in the American Yiddish literature of the 1960s can be found in Josh Lambert, *Unclean Lips: Obscenity, Jews, and American Culture* (New York: New York University Press, 2014), p. 151: 'Isaac Goldberg, a Harvard PhD in modern languages who energetically promoted American Yiddish literature in the first three decades of the 20th century, observed in 1918 that "the theme of sex ... is treated by Yiddish writers with far greater freedom than would be permitted to their American confrères." By contrast, in 1964 the preeminent modernist poet and critic Yankev Glatshteyn called Yiddish "one of the most modest languages in world literature." In a sense, though, both of these knowledgeable critics were correct: limits and restraints were imposed on the representations of sex in American Yiddish literature [...].'
16. Irving H. Buchen, *Isaac Bashevis Singer and the Eternal Past* (New York: New York University Press, 1968), p. 118.
17. On the contrary, American critics call Bashevis's descriptions in the English version of the novel an 'American Edenic landscape' (Dorothy S. Bilik, 'Singer's Diasporan Novel: *Enemies: A Love Story*', in *Studies in American Jewish Literature*, ed. by D. Walden (Albany: State University of New York Press, 1981), pp. 90–100 (p. 92)).
18. The biographer of Anne Hutchison, Eve LaPlante, describes the historical significance of her personality: 'In a world without religious freedom, civil rights, or free speech — the colonial world of the 1630s that was the seed of the modern United States — Anne Hutchinson was an American visionary, pioneer, and explorer who epitomized the religious freedom and tolerance that are essential to the nation's character' (*American Jezebel: The Uncommon Life of Anne Hutchinson, the Woman who Defied the Puritans* (San Francisco: Harper Collins, 2004), p. xvi).
19. The last line of the English novel often bewilders commentators and critics: 'although Tamara's final remark is hard to understand and leaves lots of room for different interpretations, in many ways it puts the entire novel in perspective. [...] Even after his disappearance and in the hypothetical world of imagination, Herman is not free from Tamara's tenacious grip' (Kyeong Hwangbo, 'Trauma, Narrative, and the Marginal Self in Selected Contemporary American Novels' (unpublished doctoral dissertation, University of Florida, 2004)).
20. Isaac Bashevis Singer, *Enemies: A Love Story*, trans. by Aliza Shevrin and Elizabeth Shrub (New York: Farrar, Straus & Giroux, 1972).
21. Isaac Bashevis Singer, *Enemies: Une histoire d'amour*, trans. by Gilles Chahine and Marie-Pierre Bay (Paris: Stock, 1975).
22. Sarah Blacher Cohen, 'From Hens to Roosters: Isaac Bashevis Singer's Female Species', in *Recovering the Canon: Essays on Isaac Bashevis Singer*, ed. by David Neal Miller (Leiden: Brill, 1986), pp. 76–86 (p. 81).

23. Isaac Bashevis Singer, *Shosha*, trans. by Joseph Singer and Isaac Bashevis Singer (New York: Farrar, Straus, Giroux, 1978).
24. Valerij A. Dymshits. 'Satana v detalyakh', *Narod knigi v mire knig*, 81 (2009), 9–14 (p. 11).
25. Fishl Shneerson, *Der veg tsum mentsh: Di yesoydes fun mentsh-visnshaft un di lere fun nervezishkayt* (Vilno: Vilner farlag fun B. Kletskin, 1927). For more details about the book see Michail Krutikov, 'Nachwort', in Fischl Schneersohn, *Grenadierstraße*, trans. by Alina Bothe (Göttingen: Wallstein, 2012), pp. 248–68.
26. Florence Noiville, *Isaac B. Singer: A Life* (Evanston: Northwestern University Press, 2006), p. 56.
27. Iris Parush, *Reading Jewish Women: Marginality and Modernization in Nineteenth-Century Eastern European Jewish Society* (Waltham: Brandeis University Press, 2004), pp. 40–41.
28. A term from Jewish rabbinic literature that refers to a person of an unknown sex.
29. Itskhok Bashevis, 'Neshome-ekspeditsyes', *Forverts*, 14 November 1974, p. 3 (my translation).
30. Itskhok Bashevis, 'Neshome-ekspeditsyes', *Forverts*, 3 October 1974, p. 3 (my translation).
31. Itskhok Bashevis, 'Neshome-ekspeditsyes', *Forverts*, 12 September 1974, p. 3 (my translation).
32. Itskhok Bashevis, 'Neshome-ekspeditsyes', *Forverts*, 4 May 1974, p. 3 (my translation).
33. Itskhok Bashevis, 'Neshome-ekspeditsyes', *Forverts*, 17 May 1974, p. 3 (my translation).
34. Goran Lester, *The Bright Streets of Surfside: The Memoir of a Friendship with Isaac Bashevis Singer* (Kent, Ohio, and London: Kent State University Press, 1994).
35. Ofer Dynes, ' "Der toyt fun Oto Veyninger: filosofisher shund-roman" — a fargesn bashutfesdik verk fun Arn Tseytlin un Yitskhok Bashevis-Zinger', *Yerusholayimer almanakh*, 29 (2012), 393–402.
36. Itskhok Bashevis, 'Neshome-ekspeditsyes', *Forverts*, 2 July 1974, p. 3 (my translation).
37. Itskhok Bashevis, 'Sonim: Geshikhte fun a libe', *Forverts*, 16 July 1966, p. 3 (my translation).
38. Zainab Bahrani, *Women of Babylon: Gender and Representation in Mesopotamia* (New York: Routledge, 2001).
39. Janet Howe Gaines, *Music in the Old Bones: Jezebel through the Ages* (Carbondale: Southern Illinois University Press, 1999), p. 27.
40. In 1984, commenting on Barbara Streisand's film *Yentl*, Bashevis ironizes its happy ending and Yentl's departure to America. He reconstructs her possible American future: she will work twelve hours in a sweatshop with no time for learning, marry a salesman, and rent 'an apartment with an ice box and a dumbwaiter' (Isaac Bashevis Singer, 'I. B. Singer Talks to I. B. Singer about the Movie *Yentl*', *The New York Times*, 29 January 1984, p. 2A). A counter-argument is advanced by Steven Sater, who says that Yentl will 'be able to study Talmud as a woman' in America (Steven Sater, 'Debating I. B. Singer's View of *Yentl*', *The New York Times*, 12 February 1984, p. 34).
41. J. David Hoeveler Jr, *The Postmodernist Turn: American Thought and Culture in the 1970s* (New York: Twayne, 1996), pp. xiii–xiv.

CHAPTER 8

The Forbidden Fruit: Gender and Desire in David Hofstein's Early Poetry*

Sabine Koller

Gelibte!
Di velt hot itst in undz fargesn
Vi frier mir in ir ... (David Hofstein)

[Beloved!
The world has now forgotten us
Just as we had forgotten about it before ...][1]

David Hofstein, born in 1889 in Korostyshev, near Kiev, was a leading member of the Kiev Kultur-lige ((Yiddish) Culture League). Along with his literary peers, most notably Peretz Markish, Leib Kvitko, Der Nister, and David Bergelson, he significantly contributed to the Jewish cultural revival movement during the burgeoning years of the 1910s and 1920s. His poems in the anthologies *Eygns* [One's Own] or *Baginen* [Dawn], and his cycle *Bay vegn* [At the Roads] (1919), were powerful manifestations of his sober and modest poetic style. Hofstein, together with Markish, Kvitko, Bergelson, Itsik Fefer, and other prominent Soviet Jews, was shot on 12 August 1952, following the secret trial of the leading figures in the Jewish Anti-Fascist Committee. It was only years later that his second wife, Feige, learned how and when the life of her husband came to this brutal end.[2] In her memoirs, *Mit libe un veytik* [With Love and Grief], written in Kiev and Tel Aviv, Feige recalls Hofstein's gentle character, his confidence and helpfulness, his affection for children and books, and his forgetfulness — once, he even left the one wedding ring he and his wife had in a friend's house.[3] She first got to know him through his poetry, which she read with friends during the Polish occupation of Kremenets in 1919. His famous poem 'In vinter farnakhtn' [In Winter's Dusk] (1912) made a deep impression on her.[4] During the last years of Stalin's rule, when it was forbidden to pronounce Hofstein's name in public, that poem became a kind of shibboleth, a secret code for the lovers of Yiddish literature.[5]

---

* I would like to thank Lauren Ganz and Holger Nath for their help in translating this paper into English.

Hofstein's poetry was received with great enthusiasm by Yiddish readers and critics, not only in the Soviet Union. The American poet Yankev Glatshteyn crowned Hofstein as the 'father of the modern Yiddish word'.[6] In Hofstein's refined schemes of versification and elaborate use of poetic devices, literary critics recognized the influence of Alexander Pushkin, and they considered him the most classical among Yiddish modernist poets.[7] Drawing his inspiration from Yiddish, Russian, Ukrainian, Hebrew, and European poetic traditions, Hofstein made full use of the classical tradition *and* of the innovative modernist potential in his verse.[8] Using the key image of the *navenad*, a wanderer figure, Hofstein created a highly philosophical landscape poetry, as indicated by the emblematic title *At the Roads* of his first collection (published in 1919). His sensitivity to the radical historical and cultural changes which were in store for the Jews, and to the multilayered poetic language of modernism, gave the imagery of pilgrimage a new quality in his poetry. The image of the wanderer who used to travel across the fields and forests now reappears as a *flâneur* in an urban setting, for example in the 1919 poem 'Shtot' [City]. Here, Hofstein translates the exciting and at times painful experience of the big city into a vibrant and expressive Futurist rhythm. According to the Soviet critic Hersh Remenik, this was a new feature in the young Soviet Yiddish poetry of that time.[9]

In addition to his landscape and urban poetry, Hofstein's praise of femininity in the poetry of his early years is a remarkable innovation for Yiddish poetry and language.[10] His bright and laudatory love poems offer a whole range of innovative and exciting representations of gender.[11] They form part of a larger and compelling trend in Jewish art and literature: the discovery of the female and (female) corporality.

Context: Femininity, Nudity, and Eroticism in Jewish Art and Literature

Up until the nineteenth century, a Jewish woman was not allowed to show any part of her body in public; her voice was not allowed to be heard. Women's presence was mostly restricted to the private sphere of the family and home, but some of them were active in business or were running shops.[12] With the modern Jewish renaissance in Eastern Europe, women began to appear on the artistic and literary scene. In her series of poems *Froyen lider* [Women's Songs] (1924), Kadia Molodowsky 'examined the modern legacy of the Biblical Matriarchs'.[13] The artist Sore Shor contributed powerful cubist paintings and illustrations to the Kiev-based Jewish avant-garde.[14] She was close to Hofstein and made an excellent portrait of him for a collection of poetry published in 1923.[15] Corporality and the female body became an important topic for Jewish artists and sculptors. While experimenting with cubism, expressionism, or constructivism in the visual arts, these artists created a highly aesthetic modern (Jewish) identity as well. A lascivious naked woman appeared on Max Weber's cover for David Ignatoff's novella *Fibi* (1918) in the US.[16] In 1920, the Polish Jewish artist Henrik Berlewi presented a Secession-inspired nude on his cover for Shmuel-Yakir Londinski's *Flamen* [Flames] (1920). In

1923, he designed an abstract, geometric cubist nude for *Albatros*, the mouthpiece of the Warsaw Khalyastre (Gang) literary group. Marek Szwarc, another Polish Jewish illustrator of the journal, created a gloomy expressionist portrait of three women.[17] Mark Epstein, who, like Hofstein, is closely associated with the Kulturlige in Kiev, created sculptures of bulky nudes and elegant cubist drawings of slim female water-carriers. Issachar Ber Ryback, who witnessed a pogrom in his birthplace, Elizavetgrad in the Ukraine, presented terribly distorted, grotesque, blood-smeared female nudes in a series of nine drawings in mixed technique (1918–20). (In one of them, a pregnant woman with a cut-off breast reveals the terrible violence perpetrated against women and mothers.) In sharp contrast to these painful reactions to anti-Semitic violence, Joseph Chaikov illustrated Peretz Markish's collection of poetry, *Shveln* [Thresholds] (1919), with a whole series of naked, muscular men and women. These figures in elegant, dance-like positions are among the most powerful and confident contributions to avant-garde images of the new (Jewish) man, the new *adam kadmon*, at a time when two revolutions were underway, a socialist and a Jewish one.[18]

In prose, with his unhappy Mirl Hurvits in *Nokh alemen* (1913; translated as *The End of Everything*), David Bergelson created a Jewish counterpart to Emma Bovary and Anna Karenina. Joseph Opatoshu caused a sensation with his audacious depictions of seductive women involved in orgies in the Hasidic milieu of Kotsk in his *In poylishe velder* [In Polish Woods] (1921). In the first part of his novel trilogy *Farn mabl* [Before the Flood] (1929–31; translated into English as *Three Cities*), *Petersburg* (1929), Sholem Asch revealed the seductive femininity of a mother and a daughter and their sexual rivalry.

In poetry, Kvitko vaguely alludes to the beginning of a love affair and the lyric subject's yearning for a woman in his first collection, *Trit* [Footsteps] (1919). The critic Shmuel Niger describes him as a 'poet of the night' exploring the realm of the uncanny where Lilith appears.[19] In Markish's *Di kupe* [The Heap] (1921–22), women appear as victims in brutal episodes of violence and death. His main concern is history, though, not gender. Unlike Kvitko's unsettling 'poetry of black and white' (Dobrushin), and unlike Markish's impetuous expressionism, Hofstein is a 'poet of light'.[20] The critic Bal-Makhshoves contrasts Kvitko's fascination with darkness with Hofstein's optimism.[21] The latter's serenity, his orientation towards the hymnic as opposed to the tragic or melancholic, determines his representation of the other sex (with one striking exception; see below). Hofstein opts for positive gender roles. He never reduces women to mere objects of (poetic) satisfaction, but shows them as attractive *agents* of gender roles, for example as free women or mothers. They do not need to be legitimized through religion. Hofstein models the female as the incarnation of beauty, as the muse, as the beloved, or as the mother, not as the femme fatale. He investigates representations of women which include nudity without being voyeuristic, and eroticism without being pornographic. His gender poetry is a poetry of the sublime. In elaborate poetic and phonetic harmony, he represents women by explicit depiction or by subtle insinuation. The poetic perfection in rhyme, verse, and rhetorical tropes that the author is aspiring to —

Dobrushin has high regard for Hofstein's 'modest, [...] truly Yiddish versification' — is the framework for his respectful and dignified conception of women.[22]

Hofstein's Poetry and Femininity: A Classification

The cycle of poems *Bay vegn* (1919), *Royte blitn* [Red Offshoots] (1920), *Zunen-shleyfn* [Sunbeams] (1921), *Oyf likhtike ruinen* [On Bright Ruins] (1927), and, to a lesser extent, *Fun ale mayne veltn* [From All of my Worlds] (1929) contain a significant number of gender-relevant poems with various kinds of imagined femininity.[23] It is striking to see how, within Hofstein's minimalist and balanced system, desire and poetic devices, sense and semantics, are interconnected.[24]

In one of Hofstein's early poems, 'In Armenye' [In Armenia] (1912), published in 1919 in *Bay vegn*, the lyric subject is attracted by 'eylbert-oygn' [olive eyes].[25] Women's eyes make his heart sing 'mit heyser freyd' [with ardent joy].[26] A decade later, his 1929 collection *Fun ale mayne veltn* carried the poem 'A shorfer shotn oyf der vant' [A Distinct Shadow on the Wall], dedicated to Feige, who at that time lived in Palestine. A shadow on the wall reminds the lyric I of the woman he loves. His desire for her makes him drunk like 'heyser vayn' [hot wine].[27] This time, the lyric I cannot look into the woman's eyes. She is far away from him. The lyric I's perception shifts from a close reading of an anonymous woman to the dark imagination of his love in order to bridge a huge geographical distance.

Hofstein's earlier poem, 'In Armenye', is a cautious approach to the other sex. It combines femininity and landscape with discrete eroticism accentuating the magic of dark eyes. The later piece, 'A sharfer shotn oyf der vant', is an outburst of sexual desire within his own, the lyric I's body, an almost physiological study of passion while remembering the woman, his beloved. It speaks of glands and a limb. These two poems, which are representative of Hofstein's early poetry and function as cornerstones of this paper, introduce the reader to a wide range of images of femininity. Intimate gender images clearly outweigh official socialist cliché poems about women fighting for equality.[28] His images of women extend from female archetypes (Eve) and allegories (the Muse) to concrete personae: poems are dedicated to his mother, to his sister, Shifre Kholodenko, herself a poet, and — above all — to his wives, Hinde and Feige. In some of them, eroticism and motherhood are combined. The topic of motherhood includes poems about his wives.[29] It also covers poems about Hofstein's own mother, whom he lost, along with other relatives, in the massacres at Babi Yar.[30] In 'Fun Moskve der hoyptshtot' [From Moscow the Capital] and in 'Mame' [Mother], the lyric I, despite the distance between rural space and city, tradition and modernity, elaborates intimately on the mother giving birth to a son who is born to be a Yiddish poet.[31]

Women and the Poetic Wor(l)d

In his portrait of Markish, Kvitko, and Hofstein, 'Dray dikhter' [Three Poets], Dobrushin points to Hofstein's striking sensibility for sensual impressions, to his *khush hashmie*, his sense of hearing, and his *khush harie*, his sense of sight.[32] The result is a rich synaesthetic poetry. 'Kh'hob derzen zi baym taykh' [I Saw Her at the River] is a key text in this respect. It elaborates on the topos of love at first sight. It is part of series of poems in *Bay vegn* about the lyric I's most intimate experience of falling in love with a woman, of making love, of becoming a father. It might have autobiographical roots and be a tribute to his first wife, Hinde:

> Kh'hob derzen zi baym taykh
> Unter tsvaygn,
> Unter grinem, mit himl farlatetn dakh.
> In a por tsendling trit,
> Oyf dem erdishn shvaygn
> Hot geshtumt dort a shteyn,
> A farakshenter glid
> Fun mayn urlands tsezeytn, tseshtoybtn gebeyn ...
>
> Kh'hob derzen zi in naketer freyd fun ir layb,
> In tseflosener kroyn fun di duftike hor,
> Kh'hob derhert fun di tifn fun uryunge yor:
>   — Ot o-di ruft men vayb!
>
> [I saw her at the river
> Under branches,
> Under the green, sky-patched roof.
> Several dozen steps away,
> Upon the earthly silence
> There a stone was mute
> A stubborn limb
> From my old country's bones, scattered and turned to dust ...
>
> I saw her in the naked joy of her flesh,
> In the disheveled crown of her fragrant hair,
> I heard from the depths of age-young years:
> This is what one calls a wife!][33]

The poem is a hymn to naked female beauty in a natural setting.[34] At the same time, it is an impressive manifestation of world and word culture. The text is saturated with rich associations with how bathing women are represented in art and literature. Manifold representations come to mind, be it Botticelli's Aphrodite rising from the sea; Picasso's *Young Ladies of Avignon* (1907); *The Water Sprite's Farewell to Carevna Volkhova* (1899) by the Russian symbolist painter Mikhail Vrubel; or, first and foremost, Rembrandt's *A Woman Bathing in a Stream* (1654).[35]

The image covers centuries of how bathing women were imagined, be it Shoshana in the apocryphal Daniel 13 or Bathsheba at her bath (II Samuel 11); be it the water nymphs of Slavic folklore, the Russian rusalka or her Ukrainian counterpart, the long-haired mavka; be it modern Ukrainian or Russian literature.[36] Russian poetry had a major impact on Hofstein, who was much more orientated towards high

Russian culture and literature than, for instance, the rather folkloristic Kvitko. Hofstein, celebrating the beauty of the water maiden (Hinde?), might have been acquainted with Nikolai Gumil'ev's love poetry, in which Gumil'ev's wife, the famous poet Anna Akhmatova, appears as a kind of Eve, or as a mermaid.[37] In fact, since the preceding poem 'An epl' [An Apple] establishes an overt connection between fruit and desire ('A bis — farfaln ...' [One bite — and doomed ...]), powerful associations with Khave are apparent in Hofstein's poem as well.[38]

'Kh'hob derzen zi baym taykh' is Hofstein's act of creation, his *breyshes* regarding his praise of the female. It is not a creation *ex nihilo*. The landscape poetry preceding the poem already contains all the lyrical, metaphorical, and euphonic features characteristic of Hofstein's classical verse. Yet his explorations of the female body in a poetic realm reveal a specific Yiddish relation between language and love, between female physicality and phonetics. Yiddish has the advantage that *vayb*, 'woman', and *layb*, 'body', rhyme.[39] Beyond ontology and semantics, femininity and corporality are bound together by their sound qualities.

For Hofstein, the poetical shaping of women-related themes is, primarily, a matter of euphony, rhythm, and rhyme. In the second strophe of the poem, this is demonstrated by repetition, anaphor ('Kh'hob derzen' / 'Kh'hob derhert'), embracing masculine rhyme, and the rhythmic prosody of the four-footed anapaest. The last line is an exception. Here, the verse system is cut short in the middle. This organic break in the verse system accentuates the emotional and semantic peak of the whole poem, a euphoric exclamation: 'Ot o-di ruft men vayb!'.

Within a highly saturated acoustic structure, Hofstein establishes a powerful visuality in the poem. It is twofold and highly effective: A concrete image — the naked woman — is combined with astonishing metaphors. The naked beauty is standing under a roof which is not made of slats, but of the green colour of twigs and the blue sky. With the synaesthetic metaphor 'In tseflosener kroyn fun di duftike hor', which combines the senses of sight and smell, the speaker alludes to the metaphorical representation of women as the crown of creation and points to the woman's flowing hair no longer tamed by a bun (due to religious observance, one might add). The divinization of a completely secular and erotic image is all the more evident in the associations of a crown with the *keter Tora*, the crown on the Holy Scrolls.

Hofstein's Imagination of Gender between Europeanness and Jewishness

Dobrushin realized that Hofstein had made a quantum leap forward for Yiddish poetry: the poet's perception of world and women emerges from a general cultural history, an 'unprecedented "Europeanness" born of education in the deepest sense'.[40] The portrayal of naked women makes Hofstein, in Dobrushin's words, the first 'non-national poet': 'No woman, unclothed from national-subjective elements, was treated like this by us artistically. Moreover, we were still unable to poetically comprehend people or objects, whether it be in a secular [*veltlikh*] or global [*veltish*] way.'[41]

Hofstein's poetic imagery of women is set in a secular context, in natural settings, or in the private home. Women and nature form a unity through metaphors. Femininity is shown in all its vitality, including sexuality, pregnancy, maternity, and breastfeeding. For example, in 'Vi troyerik-zis iz mentsh tsu zayn' [How Bitterly Sweet It Is to Be a Human Being], the lyric I is fascinated by the fact that the baby's nose is sinking into his mother's breast while he is drinking: 'Itst moyl un brust shoyn darfn zayn inaynem' [Now, mouth and breast already have to form one whole].[42] Hofstein stresses naturalness, simplicity, and secularity (*veltlekhkayt*). The woman is part of a rural or an urban space, but not of a shtetl. We almost never read of synagogues or rituals linking the gender topic of the poem to the Jewish religion.[43] Gender representation is transferred into a universal, dejudaized context. This erasure of an overt connectedness to Jewish tradition explains Dobrushin's enthusiasm about Hofstein's poetry. It 'transcended any parochial national frame and participated in something more "general" and "European" — yet it was precisely from this fact that it derived its decisive national significance'.[44]

Hofstein, the Yiddish modernist, clearly strives towards universalism (*veltishkayt*) and European high culture. Yet we have to consider the other side of the coin, Hofstein's *yidishkayt*, his rootedness in Jewish religious texts and culture. 'Kh'hob derzen zi baym taykh' and 'An epl' contain subtle allusions to the Jewish tradition disguised in metaphors and a modern textual structure. Taking into account the hymnic tone of his poems about women and the general affinity of his poetry with prayers, we discover how David, the poet of the modern Jewish renaissance in Eastern Europe, continues the tradition of his (symbolic) forefather and namesake, the King David of the Tanakh.[45] In a secular context, Hofstein enacts at least two of David's roles in modern times, as David the singer and David the seduced man (and perhaps also, facing the Nazi menace, David the warrior). These enactments shape his poetry about women.

In the poem 'Fun fenster kegniber' [From a Window on the Opposite Side], the lyric I stages a situation that is well known from II Samuel 11. As David fell in love with Bathsheba, Uriah's wife, so too the lyric I is dazzled by the breathtaking beauty of his neighbour's wife. In the Bible, the story ends with Uriah's death and David's appropriation of Bathsheba. In the poem, we have a balanced presentation of male desire (the lyric subject's penetrating glance at the woman) and elevated femininity.[46] His goal is not physical appropriation, but the emotional pleasure of perceiving pure beauty: 'Nu klayb, mayn harts, un klayb, | Di likht fun layb!' [Gather, my heart, please gather | The light of her body!].[47] Again, the aesthetic transformation of feminine appeal is central: thanks to the alliteration, 'likht' [light] and 'layb' [body], the two leitmotifs of the poem, merge into a single entity.

A close reading of several of Hofstein's intimate poems about women, including 'Fun fenster kegniber', unveils hidden layers in the text revealing ultimately the 'urtext' of love poetry, the *Shir ha-shirim* [Song of Songs].[48] It is an integral part of Hofstein's sophisticated dialogue between European and Jewish poetry. His poetic praising of eyes, of hair, of arms has famous counterparts in the Song of Songs. Yet it dispenses with the traditional religious symbol system of God and his bride,

Israel. In 'A remez oyf ir' [An Allusion to Her], a poem dedicated to Feige, the lyric I compares her beauty mark to 'a simen fun troyb oyf a kindersher brust' [a grape-shaped mark on a child's breast].[49] This is reminiscent of 'thy breasts' being similar to 'clusters of grapes' ('ke-eshkelot ha-gefen'; *Shir ha-shirim*, 7. 7). In 'Du bist fun di, vos' [You Come from Those Who], the line 'Du bist fun di, vos darf mit zilber-shtik nit klingen' [You come from those who should not jingle with silver coins] is reminiscent of Solomon's vineyard, for the protection of which every man had to bring a thousand pieces of silver (*Shir ha-shirim*, 8. 11–12).[50] In the poem 'Nu, zog mir nor, mayn fraynd' [Ey, Just Tell Me, my Friend], the lyric I introduces the beautiful metaphor of 'heldzer-shvanen' [long-necked swans].[51] It recalls hymnic depictions of the woman's neck in the Song of Songs (1. 10, 4. 4), in which the neck is compared to David's tower. The swans' necks are the place where the poet's grief finds its home (here, the metaphor becomes concrete). It combines the feminine body with the blue sky where the beautiful swans' necks are reminiscent of the beloved and of the poetic word. The yearning for the beautiful woman is projected into the sky and into poetry. 'Nu, zog mir nor, mayn fraynd' is generally based on several Yiddish reprises of the formula 'ha-yafa banashim' [thou fairest among women] (*Shir ha-shirim*, 1. 8): 'Di sheyne tsvishn froyen'. 'Di sheyne tsvishn froyen' appears at the beginning of every stanza of the poem. With this formula, Hofstein rhythmizes his eulogy and, as in the Song of Songs, combines the quality of beauty with the treasure of true friendship. The poem ends surprisingly: the article 'di' is changed into the pronoun 'du'. The change of a vowel turns the lyric I's description of the woman's beauty into an intimate declaration of love.

With this rich repertoire of love topoi and gender-relevant poetic images, Hofstein inscribes his universal, secular hymn of the female into the sacred Jewish tradition. Apart from the modernity of his language and versification, his poetics has an almost sacred quality and consists of 'profoundly pious lines'.[52] Hofstein's poetry is erotic and spiritual. It is both universal and Jewish. The origin and the poetic result of this jubilant experimentation is femininity.

The Female Body between Metaphor and Mimesis

The oscillation between a mimetic and a metaphorical use of language in Hofstein's poetry opens up fascinating spaces where the text hides more than it says. It is this tension between what is said and what remains unsaid that evokes female corporality. In the poem 'In engn tsimer' [In the Cramped Room] of the cycle *Bay vegn*, abandoned clothes (the said) point to the intimacy of the lovers' naked bodies (the unsaid). Clothes cast off turn into silent witnesses of a man, the lyric I, and a woman making love:

> In engn tsimer
> Oyf shvartse shtrenge benklekh tsvey
> In onmakht lign undzere tsekneytshte kleyder ...
>
> [In the cramped room
> On two austere black benches
> Our creased clothes lie unconsciously ...][53]

The impression of intimacy and passion is all the more evident as the poet elaborates on appealing images of seductive femininity which he introduced in the preceding two poems. In 'An epl', Hofstein refers to the powerful image of the 'forbidden fruit' offered by the first woman of all women. Indeed, in 'Kh'hob derzen zi baym taykh', the bathing woman appears naked like Eve. In 'In engn tsimer', the concrete semantics of the bathing woman and water of 'Kh'hob derzen zi baym taykh' turn into metaphors of love. The clothes of the two lovers are waiting 'Vi oyf a breg | Oyf zamd' [Like on a riverbank | On sand].[54] The lyric I, engulfed by waves (of love) — 'Un khvalyes yogn zikh un otemen mit shoym' [And waves chase each other and breathe foam] — swam away from every earthly limitation, be it the walls of a house, be it towns, into a cosmic space.[55] Hofstein transforms strong sexual feelings into a chain of metaphors; as Shmuel Niger writes, 'the cooler the thread of his creation, the more one feels the heat of the molten cloth'.[56]

Usually, the point of departure for Hofstein's eroticism is the (female) body. The author describes a woman's face, her eyes and lips, her smile, hair, fingers, and arms. Most of the time, the male counterpart of this anatomy of love is the lyric I's heart. In 'Git dayn blik a vildn blank ' [Your Glance is Casting a Wild Sparkle], a poem included in the cycle *Zunen-shleyfn*, this physical dialogue of the male and female body results in a fusion of the interior and exterior world, of corporal movement and emotion.[57] Again, Hofstein's spiritualization of the physical turns the poems into erotic prayers. The lyric subject's heart is ready to follow every movement of his beloved, leaving its original place behind. The heart of the speaker begins its own journey. The topography of these wanderings is fixed by a double metaphor linking nature with the female body and male feelings:

> Greyt durkh vald fun dayn hor
> Zikh tsu raysn tsu dayn oyer,
> Dort, vu s'shimert reyn un klor
> Tsarter shoym fun mayn fartroyen.
>
> [Ready, through the forest of your hair
> To rip through to your ear,
> There, where it glimmers pure and clear
> The tender and foamy crest of my trust.][58]

The first metaphor ('vald fun dayn hor') in this last stanza of the poem associates femininity with forest. This rather uncommon image in love poetry is part of a whole series of metaphors which appear in other poems.[59] The second metaphor in the closing line of the poem ('Tsarter shoym fun mayn fartroyen') combines water (the foaming crest) and strong emotions (confidence). The two audacious metaphors are bound together by rhythm and rhyme. At the end of his journey across the female body, the lyric I discovers his own inner state of mind. All that he has whispered to her and for her (his anxieties as well as his confessions of love) has been preserved in her ears, the visible and tangible archives of his invisible words.

'Git dayn blik a vildn blank' is one of the most harmonious of all the gender-related poems written by Hofstein examined here. This harmony is accomplished by a regular alternation of masculine and feminine rhymes, by a regular four-footed trochaic metre, and by the regular use of crossing rhymes. Its euphonic structure ('blik' — 'blank', 'vild' — 'vald', and the repetition of 'sh' in 'shlaykht' — 'shmeykhl' — 'shlank' — 'shrayen' — 'shimern' — 'shoym') evokes whispering (in Yiddish: *shushken zikh, shepshtshen*) and stresses the intimacy of the lovers' low-voiced dialogue. The pronouns 'mayn' [mine] and 'dayn' [yours] shift places in such a way that they seem to dance through the stanzas. One cannot help thinking of Nikolai Gumil'ev's poetic confession in his poem 'Sunlips': 'I speak and think in rhymes | While I am dreaming of you.'[60]

David Hofstein's Poetry between Two Women

In the collection *Oyf likhtike ruinen*, we find a poem dedicated to Hinde and a poem dedicated to Feige side-by-side.[61] It is a unique instance in Yiddish literature (and maybe not only there) of a poet juxtaposing two poems for his wives.

Hofstein married Hinde-Gitl Khayit in 1914. Shammai, their first son, was born in February 1915, Hillel in November 1916. The poem 'Nemen' [Names] is a famous homage to them. In 1920, Hinde died. Hofstein moved from Kiev to Moscow at the end of that year. He met Feige Biberman, his second wife, during the Civil War in the town of Khimki, near Moscow, where his two sons went to a sanatorium in the summer of 1921. In the spring of 1925, Feige and David travelled to Palestine, where they married. In February 1926, their daughter Levia was born. In March 1926, Hofstein returned to the Soviet Union. Feige and their little daughter were unable to join him until 1929.[62]

'Nekht' [Nights], dedicated to Hinde, is a two-part poem of melancholy and grief.[63] It does not fit into the established scheme of Hofstein's poetry about women. It is elegiac, not hymnal. The prevailing conjunction of eroticism, the female body, and joy is replaced by the strange vision of a sad woman who is physically untouchable (the speaker's bodily presence in the poem is all the more obvious). Like bright stars shining from above, the woman's tears fall upon the quiet shadows of the lyric I's sadness ('Di shtile shotns | Fun mayn niderik gemit'). Playing with the polyvalence of *shtern*, in the second stanza the lyric I caresses the forehead of the woman's teary face. Eventually, the vision of her face dissolves in his desire within a cosmic context ('unter zun un shtern' [under the sun and under the stars]).[64]

The poem is an unsettling conjunction of his passion and her pain. It is full of ambivalence: the speaker's fever connotes real illness and desire. His caresses evoke intimacy but are restricted to her face. The salt of her tears is sweet ('di zise zalts'), his heart beats in two chests ('harts in mayne bayde brustn'). Is the imagined woman real or an illusion? She is concretized by self-referential intertexts linking 'Nekht' to the central poem 'Kh'hob derzen zi baym taykh'. Yet the lyric I abstains from sexuality and has a tendency towards spiritualization.[65] The key word is 'otem' [breath]. The representation of the female in 'Nekht' is rooted in the sphere of *rukhnies* (spirituality), not in *gashmies* (corporality). In sharp contrast to the author's former exuberant expressions of maternity, this poem ends with a complex and ambivalent image of pregnancy:

> Az alts fun otem daynem
> In trogn iz fargangen,
> Fun otem daynem
> Iz geboyrn ...
>
> [That everything of your breath
> Vanished during pregnancy,
> Of your breath
> Was born ...][66]

Hofstein's poetic minimalism shifts towards existential philosophy. Death and birth form a circle. One can only speculate about this conjunction, but one reason might be Hinde's early death, maybe during a third pregnancy. Yet by ending the poem with the word 'geboyrn' [born] — which is also the title of a joyful poem about the birth of both men and words — the female as guarantor for the continuation of life prevails.[67]

The poem written for Feige is entitled 'A remez oyf ir'.[68] Once again, symmetrical and harmonious structures correspond with the beautiful object of reference, the beloved woman ('mayn libe'). The poem is composed in regular amphibrachs in which every second and fourth line rhyme and feminine and masculine closing rhymes alternate. Similarly to the first poem (for Hinde), this poem focuses upon a woman's (Feige's) face. It refers to lashes, lips, and a beauty mark. Unlike in 'Nekht', the gender markers are neither tears nor death, but a 'pintl' [beauty mark] and 'kheyn' [charm].[69] 'A remez oyf ir' is a poem of revelation: the previously hidden is uncovered by the 'pintl' which turns into the sign and symbol for the joy of the flesh. Affection and desire are expressed by a chain of asyndeta. The restless passion of the lyric subject settles in a single place on the woman's body:

> Un mayn zukhn, mayn garn, mayn libe,
> Mayn umru, mayn benken, mayn dorsht —
> Oyf pintl fun kheyn iber lipn
> Zikh ale gefinen an ort.
>
> [And my search, my yearning, my love,
> My restlessness, my desire, my thirst —
> All this finds its place
> In the beauty mark over her lips.][70]

The love poetics of homecoming is framed by a play with words. Because of the similarity in sound, 'pintl' and 'lipn' are intertwined. The — attractive — noun between these two words is 'kheyn'. It moves from one word to the other: 'Iber lipn fun kheyn host a pintl' [Above lips of charm you have a beauty mark] in the first strophe is changed into 'Oyf pintl fun kheyn iber lipn' [In the beauty mark over her lips].[71] As a result, the woman's body and erotic pleasure are bound together.

Conclusion: (Un)Gendering Language for a Modern Yiddish Poetry

The traditional gendering of Jewish languages describes Yiddish as a language for women (and uneducated men) and Hebrew as a language for educated men.[72] Thanks to authors like Sholem Yankev Abramovitsh (Mendele Moykher-Sforim) who turned to Yiddish as a viable literary language, the whole literary polysystem and Hebrew–Yiddish diglossia were reorganized.[73] This process reflects

> a much larger upheaval of traditional Jewish practices and social norms. In a society in which gender relations were regulated by Jewish textual practices, the new orientation of Jewish literary culture addressed and reflected new relationships to gender. Jewish writers took up the mantle of both languages with the hopes of addressing newly sex-integrated communities of readers.[74]

As a part of the gender-related restructuring of literature and culture, Hofstein's poetry breaks up the traditional conjunctions of language and gender. His vehicle is a modern Yiddish poetic tongue which goes beyond stereotyped Jewish gender attributions. It is addressed to a modern and secular Jewish reader and includes both sexes.

Hofstein's poetic devices are the product of desire and the result of a beautifully arranged interplay of female *and* male categories of language and versification: of melody and rhythm, of feminine and masculine nouns and end rhymes, of embracing and pair rhymes. Sound and body, *klang un kerper*, sense and sensuality are closely intertwined.[75] Being aware of its double existence as something physical and metaphysical at the same time, Hofstein conveys to the reader a corporal and almost erotic feeling for language where, as George Steiner puts it, 'language and eros mesh at every point'.[76] The Yiddish language in this double existence, freed from former gender-related pejorative associations, becomes the vessel for Hofstein's double experience of love and femininity as something physical and spiritual.

Following a long period in which Yiddish love poetry was rather mystical or decadent (as inspired by Heinrich Heine, Peretz, and the Bible), Hofstein models the new literary topic of eroticism in poetry *and* the appropriate linguistic devices. According to Dobrushin, the poet overcomes the influence of the elevated Hebrew *melitsa* style, Bialik's poetics, and David Einhorn's sentimental neo-Romanticism.[77] Hofstein opts for clarity, concreteness, and solemnity. His poetic programme is reminiscent of Acmeism.[78] In their content and their harmonious, neoclassicist aesthetic form, Hofstein's early poems about love and women were an important contribution to a full-fledged modern Yiddish poetry. It was only a few years later that the prudish Soviet (literary) system began to vigorously oppress the playful union of language, eros, and femininity which Hofstein used so convincingly.

Notes to Chapter 8

1. David Hofstein, *Bay vegn* (Kiev: Kiever farlag, 1919), p. 58. Translations in this article are my own unless otherwise indicated.
2. Feige Hofstein (Feyge Hofshteyn), *Mit libe un veytik: Vegn Dovid Hofstein* (Tel Aviv: Reshafim, 1985), pp. 52–58.
3. F. Hofstein, pp. 14, 20, 62.

4. F. Hofstein, p. 8.
5. Hersh Remenik, *Shtaplen: Portretn fun yidishe shrayber* (Moscow: Sovetski pisatel, 1982), p. 25; Chaim Beider, 'In vinter farnakhtn ...', *Forverts*, 18 June 1999, p. 14.
6. Jacob Glatstein, *In tokh genumen* (New York: Matones, 1947), p. 42.
7. See Elizer Podryatshik, *In profil fun tsaytn* (Tel Aviv: Perets, 1978), p. 35; Remenik, p. 25.
8. See Remenik, p. 28.
9. Ibid.
10. Hofstein's contemporary and friend, the literary critic Yekhezkel Dobrushin, perspicuously analysed his poetry in 'Dray dikhter', *Oyfgang*, 1 (1919), pp. 71–97. Remenik, p. 35, discusses Hofstein's innovative love poetry as well.
11. Methodologically, this paper is based on Sabine Bovenschen's gender study, *Die imaginierte Weiblichkeit: Exemplarische Untersuchungen zu kulturgeschichtlichen und literarischen Präsentationsformen des Weiblichen* (Frankfurt a.M.: Suhrkamp, 1979). It considers and analyses representations and images of women by male authors.
12. For further discussions of women in Jewish society, see *Life Is with People: The Culture of the Shtetl*, ed. by Mark Zborowski and Elizabeth Herzog, 5th edn (New York: Schocken, 1967), esp. pp. 71–188, 269–405; Monica Rüthers, 'Frauenleben verändern sich', in *Luftmenschen und rebellische Töchter: Zum Wandel ostjüdischer Lebenswelten im 19. Jahrhundert*, ed. by Heiko Haumann (Cologne, Weimar, and Vienna: Böhlau, 2003), pp. 223–307; Luise Hirsch, *Vom Schtetl in den Hörsaal: Jüdische Frauen und Kulturtransfer* (Berlin: Metropol-Verlag, 2010).
13. David Roskies, 'Modern Jewish Literature', in *From Mesopotamia to Modernity: Ten Introductions to Jewish History and Literature*, ed. by Burton Visozky and David Fishman (Boulder: Westview Press, 1999), pp. 233–59 (p. 249). Molodowsky's *Froyen lider* are included in her first book, *Khezhvndike nekht* [Nights of Heshvan] (1927). For a survey of women's poetry in Yiddish, see Avraham Novershtern, 'Yiddish: Women's Poetry', in *Jewish Women's Archive* <https://jwa.org/encyclopedia/article/yiddish-womens-poetry> [accessed 26 January 2017].
14. Cf. reproductions in Hillel Kazovsky, *The Artists of the Kultur-lige/Khudozhniki Kul'tur-Ligi* (Moscow and Jerusalem: Mosty kul'tury/Gesharim, 2003), pp. 254–73; *Futur antérieur: L'Avant-garde et le livre Yiddish (1914–1939)*, ed. by Nathalie Hazan-Brunet (Paris: Skira Flammarion, 2009), pp. 156–61.
15. See Hofstein, *Gezamlte verk: Ershter band: Lirik* (Kiev: Kultur-lige, 1923), p. 3.
16. Max Weber, born in Białystock in 1881, moved to America in 1891. For a discussion of *Fibi*, published in New York, see Eitan Kensky's paper in this volume.
17. Cf. *Futur antérieur*, ed. by Hazan-Brunet, pp. 198–99, 201.
18. Cf. *Futur antérieur*, ed. by Hazan-Brunet, p. 165.
19. Cf. the poem 'Far sheydim' [For Demons], in Leib Kvitko, *Trit* (Berlin: Yidisher literarisher farlag, 1923), pp. 135–40. Mikhail Krutikov reads Kvitko's dark poetry as an eclectic assembly of voices of chaos and as emanations of the unconscious. See Mikhail Krutikov, '1919 god — revoliucija v evrejikoj poėzii', in *Mirovoi krizis 1914–1920 godov i sud'ba vostochnoevropeiskogo evreistva*, ed. by Oleg Budnickii and others (Moscow: ROSSPEN, 2005), pp. 318–41 (pp. 327–33); Mikhail Krutikov, *From Cabbalah to Class Struggle: Expressionism. Marxism, and Yiddish Literature in the Life and Work of Meir Wiener* (Stanford: Stanford University Press, 2011), pp. 111–12.
20. Dobrushin, pp. 84, 96.
21. Bal-Makhshoves, 'Dray lirishe poetn', in Bal-Makhsoves, *Geklibene verk* (New York: Cyco, 1953), pp. 302–06.
22. Dobrushin, p. 91.
23. I refer to the following editions: David Hofstein, *Bay vegn* (Kiev: Kiever farlag, 1919); David Hostein, *Royte blitn* (Kiev: Kiever farlag, 1920); David Hofstein, *Oyf likhtike ruinen* (Moscow: Shul un bukh, 1927); and David Hofstein, *Lider un poemes*, 2 vols (Tel Aviv: Yisroel-Bukh, 1977), I, which includes important portions of *Fun ale mayne veltn*.
24. This article is part of a larger research project on Hofstein. It seeks to explore his literary evolution, his poetic devices and principles as a poet and translator, and his place in Yiddish (Soviet) culture.
25. D. Hofstein, *Bay vegn*, p. 41. The poem is part of a series of poems written during Hofstein's military service in the Caucasus; see Krutikov, *From Cabbalah to Class Struggle*, p. 111.

26. Krutikov, *From Cabbalah to Class Struggle*, p. 111.
27. D. Hofstein, *Lider un poemes*, II, 62–63.
28. One rare example of a socialist conception is 'O, froy!' [Oh, Woman!], in D. Hofstein, *Royte blitn*, p. 13.
29. Cf., for example, 'Vi troyerik-zis iz mentsh tsu zayn' [How Bitterly Sweet It Is to Be a Human Being], in D. Hofstein, *Bay vegn*, pp. 60–61; 'Der mames — shvartse' [The Mother's Eyes Are Black] in D. Hofstein, *Oyf likhtike ruinen*, p. 94.
30. F. Hofstein, pp. 32–33. Cf. also 'S'hot mayn mame' [My Mother Has], in D. Hofstein, *Bay vegn*, p. 51; 'Mayn muter' [My Mother], in Hofstein's last cycle, *Ikh gleyb* (Moscow: Melukhe farlag 'Der emes', 1944), pp. 15–16.
31. F. Hofstein, pp. 32–33. The starting point of this 'second birth' takes place in the poem 'In vinter farnakhtn'. In 'Mame', Hofstein even mentions *Bay vegn*. The intention and style of the poem is reminiscent of Sergei Esenin's 'Pis'mo materi' [Letter to my Mother] (1924). Esenin was an important author for the Yiddish modernist poets.
32. Dobrushin, p. 90. One might add the tactile sense, the *khush hamoyshekh*; cf. the poem 'A remez oyf ir' [An Allusion to Her], discussed below.
33. D. Hofstein, *Bay vegn*, p. 55. Trans. by Chana Kronfeld in her *On the Margins of Modernism: Decentering Literary Dynamics* (Berkeley, Los Angeles, and London: University of California Press, 1996), p. 214.
34. For a discussion of the poem, see Kenneth Moss, *Jewish Renaissance in the Russian Revolution* (Cambridge and London: Harvard University Press, 2009), pp. 101–06; Kronfeld, pp. 213–18.
35. Rembrandt's model was probably Hendrickje Stoffels (c. 1625/26–1663), who became his wife and bore him a child; see Christoph Driessen, *Rembrandt und die Frauen* (Regensburg: Pustet, 2011).
36. Cf. Pushkin's little tragedy *Rusalka* [The Water Nymph] (1830) or Lesya Ukrainka's *Lisova pisnia* [The Forest Song] (1912).
37. See Amanda Haight, *Anna Akhmatova: A Poetic Pilgrimage* (New York and London: Oxford University Press, 1976), p. 8.
38. D. Hofstein, *Bay vegn*, p. 54. In 'Nekht' [Nights], a later poem dedicated to his first wife, Hinde, the lyric I uses 'shvartsaplen' (pupils) for his own eyes; cf. D. Hofstein, *Oyf likhtike ruinen*, pp. 87–88. Khave reappears as the prototype of all women in the poem 'O, froy!', in D. Hofstein, *Royte blitn*, p. 13.
39. D. Hofstein, *Bay vegn*, p. 55. It would be intriguing to write a gender-based history of love literature whose points of departure are words rhyming with 'woman'.
40. Dobrushin, p. 94; Moss, p. 105.
41. Dobrushin, p. 95.
42. D. Hofstein, *Bay vegn*, pp. 60–61. In the poem 'Un vos bin ikh shuldik' [And What Am I Guilty Of], which is part of the 1927 cycle *Oyf likhtike ruinen*, the act of breastfeeding becomes part of an erotic image (p. 91). Izi Kharik, in his poem 'Kh'hob plutslung haynt dem toyt derfilt' [Today, I Suddenly Felt Death] (1926), compares death (by hanging) with a baby taking the breast; cf. *A shpigl oyf a shteyn*, ed. by Chone Shmeruk, 2nd edn (Jerusalem: Magnes, 1987), pp. 653–54.
43. One of the rare exceptions is the motif of *shabes* (Sabbath) in 'In vinter farnakhtn'.
44. Moss, p. 105.
45. See Dobrushin, p. 93, and Podryatshik, pp. 35–52, who discusses the biblical subtext of Hofstein's poetry. Marc Chagall, who illustrated Hofstein's pogrom cycle *Troyer* [Grief] (1922), repeatedly identified with King David in his paintings.
46. D. Hofstein, *Oyf likhtike ruinen*, p. 96.
47. Ibid.
48. In the *Shir ha-shirim*, the beloved 'mashgiakh min-hakhalonot' [looketh forth at the windows] (2. 9). Translations here are given from the King James Bible.
49. D. Hofstein, *Oyf likhtike ruinen*, p. 89.
50. Ibid., p. 111.
51. D. Hofstein, *Lider un poemes*, I, 218–19. This version contains one more stanza than D. Hofstein, *Oyf likhtike ruinen*, p. 93.

52. Dobrushin, p. 96.
53. D. Hofstein, *Bay vegn*, p. 54.
54. Ibid., p. 56.
55. Ibid.
56. Shmuel Niger, 'Dovid Hofshteyn', in Shmuel Niger, *Yidishe shrayber in sovet-rusland* (New York: S. Niger Book Committee of the Congress of Jewish Culture, 1958), pp. 49–55 (p. 51).
57. D. Hofstein, *Oyf likhtike ruinen*, p. 112.
58. Ibid.
59. Other examples of the metaphorical relation between the forest and creation (of words) are the poems 'Du host mir dertseylt' [You Told Me], 'Fun ale velder, vos ikh hob gezen' [From All the Forests That I Saw], 'Redstu, klingstu brustik shverlekh' [When You Speak, the Sounds Come Heavily from your Chest], and 'Do arum — alts shtile flakhn' [Around Here — the Plains Are All Quiet] from the series *Zunen-shleyfn* (D. Hofstein, *Oyf likhtike ruinen*, pp. 103, 105, 107, 113).
60. Nikolai Gumil'ev, *Polnoe sobranie sochinenii v odnom tome* (Moscow: Terra-Alpha, 2011), pp. 268–69.
61. Another poem dedicated to Feige is entitled 'Fun shoys fun daynem gibn mir a grus' [From That Womb of Yours, Send Me a Greeting] (D. Hofstein, *Oyf likhtike ruinen*, p. 92).
62. The biographical data are taken from Joseph Sherman, 'David Hofstein', in *Dictionary of Literary Biography* (Detroit: Gale, 1982–), cccxxxiii: Writers in Yiddish, ed. by Joseph Sherman (2007), pp. 98–107; Khaim Beyder, *Leksikon fun yidishe shrayber in ratn-farband* (New York: Alveltlekher kultur-kongres, 2011), p. 114; and particularly from F. Hofstein, pp. 8–16.
63. D. Hofstein, *Oyf likhtike ruinen*, pp. 87–88.
64. Ibid., p. 88.
65. Cf. Dobrushin, pp. 92–93, on Hofstein's transformation of strong emotions into a sober, spiritualized poetic expression.
66. D. Hofstein, *Oyf likhtike ruinen*, p. 88.
67. Ibid., pp. 97–98.
68. Ibid., p. 89.
69. Other meanings of kheyn are 'grace' or 'appeal'.
70. D. Hofstein, *Oyf likhtike ruinen*, p. 89.
71. Ibid.
72. See, in particular, Naomi Seidman, *A Marriage Made in Heaven: The Sexual Politics of Hebrew and Yiddish* (Berkeley: University of California Press, 1997), pp. 11–39.
73. Itamar Even-Zohar, 'Polysystem Studies (Revised)', in Itamar Even-Zohar, *Papers in Culture Research* (Tel Aviv: Unit of Culture Research, 2010), pp. 41–50.
74. Allison Schachter, *Diasporic Modernisms: Hebrew and Yiddish Literature in the Twentieth Century* (New York: Oxford University Press, 2012), pp. 8–9.
75. On Hofstein as a poet of great musicality, see Niger, pp. 52–53.
76. George Steiner, *After Babel: Aspects of Language and Translation* (London: Oxford University Press, 1975), p. 38. Hofstein's conceptualization of language and the female body comes close to Octavio Paz's perception of poetry as verbal eroticism; cf. Octavio Paz, *The Double Flame: Love and Eroticism*, trans. by Helen Lane (New York, San Diego, and London: Harcourt Brace, 1995), p. 2.
77. Dobrushin, pp. 94–95. Bialik's and Hofstein's poetry about women provides interesting material for a comparison of style (Romanticism and decadent symbolism vs neoclassicism), motifs (e.g. eyes), and images of the female (e.g. Eve). For an analysis of Bialik's eroticism in poetry, see Khamutal' Bar-Iosef, *Khaim Nakhman Bialik: Evropeiskii dekadens i russkii simvolizm v tvorchestve evreiskogo poeta* (Moscow and Jerusalem: Mosty kul'tury/Gesharim, 2013), pp. 234–75.
78. In March 1912, the Tsekh poetov (Guild of Poets) was founded with Nikolai Gumil'ev at its head and Sergey Gorodecky, Mikhail Kuzmin, Anna Akhmatova, and Osip Mandelstam as the most prominent members. Their focus on concreteness and the anchoring of the poetic world in reality are a more important frame of reference for Hofstein's poetics than Aleksandr Blok and his symbolist yearning for the Eternal Feminine, his mystic conceptions of a feminized wisdom (derived from the Greek word *sofiia*), or his ecstatic visions of the Unknown Beauty

(Neznakomka). Akhmatova's poetry had a tremendous effect at the beginning of the twentieth century. In his poem 'Katerinke' [Barrel Organ], Izi Kharik quotes her famous lines from her poem 'Pesnia poslednei vstrechi' [Song of the Final Meeting] (1911): 'The glove that belonged to my left hand | I unconsciously put on my right' (trans. by Andrey Kneller, in *A shpigl oyf a shteyn*, ed. by Shmeruk, p. 650).

CHAPTER 9

'Ikh hob lib shlangen':
Virility and Di Yunge

Eitan Kensky

Mani Leib was dead. Mani Leib (1883–1953), perhaps the most lyrical of all the poets associated with Di Yunge, had been dead for weeks, but his passing was withheld from Reuven Ayzland, his literary partner, close friend, and confidante: 'mit klugshaft un getrayshaft bahaltn' [hidden wisely and hidden out of loyalty].[1] But during that period, the period when Mani Leib was dead but before Ayzland knew, Ayzland routinely saw Mani Leib in his dreams. Above all, Ayzland thought constantly about the last time that the two of them were together.

The last time: all their friends had left the room, and the two were alone. Mani Leib was in bed, presumably his deathbed, although whether it was then understood as such is key to understanding what happens next. In that final moment, the two of them joined:

> Ikh oyfn rand fun bet un du lebn mir. Un undzere hent tsunoyfgeflokhtn un undzere blikn magnetish bahoftn.
> Un plutsem hob ikh zikh ongeboygn un dir heys a kush geton in a hant un du host zikh a vorf geton un a geshrey geton.
>
> [I [was at] the edge of the bed and you were next to me. And our hands joined, and our eyes magnetically united. And suddenly I bent over and, heatedly, gave you a kiss on the hand, and you jolted and gave a shout.]

There are five distinct acts — hands coming together, bending, kissing, jolting, shouting — but the action all transpires in a single sentence, as if to mark one seamless movement. The two join and come apart. They intertwine and separate. All the actions are impulsive. Hands and eyes move as if of their own accord, as if compelled by other forces. The last joining is the most explicit, described with the verb *baheftn* instead of *baheftn zikh*, uniting instead of copulating, though the later meaning is clearly present and intended. How else to explain the attempt at romance that follows? How else can we interpret the awkwardness of the phrasing 'dir heys a kush geton in a hant'? The final 'in a hant' reads almost as an explanation, an internal attempt to be precise about exactly where the kiss was — as if a kiss on the hand were entirely innocent — a physical relocation that serves as a clarification of meaning. Not passion, but friendship. Comprehension then becomes the explicit subject of the next part of the prose poem. 'Du vunderlekher farshteyer, host nit farshtanen, vos der kush hot batayt' [You, wonderful comprehender, you didn't understand what the kiss signified], Ayzland continues. 'Mit gvaldikn tsar hob ikh derfilt, az mir zaynen tsuzamen tsum letstn mol, az mer veln mir zikh nit zen' [With forceful sorrow, I sensed that we were together for the last time, that we would not see each other again]. But then Ayzland adds as a postscript, 'nor hob ikh es den azoy gemeynt?' [but is that what I meant at that moment?].[2] The prose poem becomes an exercise in — and a meditation on — intention: how we read a scene, the tools and concepts that we bring to bear on the object of study, how we interpret actions and the lack of action.

There are, of course, two ways of comprehending the poem's last line — and Ayzland presumably intends us to understand both readings and to reflect on their critical difference. Reading 1: Ayzland was in denial that Mani Leib was on the verge of death. He earnestly believed that he would see Mani Leib again. Reading two: Ayzland is in denial of his passion for Mani Leib. He wonders if, at that moment, he really intended his kiss as the long goodbye, or if, secretly, he actually understood its hidden meaning and what it expressed: not magnetism but animal magnetism, a repressed love awakening. And it is also worth considering the interplay of these two forces, love and death, which figure so prominently in the American novel, and the specific role that Mani Leib's death plays in the prose poem's narrative. In 'The Storyteller', Walter Benjamin names death as the validating force of story. 'Death is the sanction of everything that the storyteller can tell. He has borrowed his authority from death. In other words, it is natural history to which his stories refer back.'[3] Death certainly plays a critical role in the presentation of this moment. The prose poem appears as an epilogue to a larger chapter about Mani Leib. It is typeset in a different font and style, and identified as a poem in honour of Mani Leib's *shloshem* — the end of the thirty-day period following the death of a loved one. The poem is in all ways — artistically, thematically, and formally — tied to Mani Leib's death. Yet only a shading of Benjamin's dictate applies. The overall sanction for storytelling is not death, but fame. Mani Leib's celebrity validates all telling of his natural life, validates the entire chapter on Mani Leib. Death sanctions/justifies/excuses only the final revelation: a passion that must otherwise go unspoken, actions that must otherwise go uninterpreted.

The subject of this paper is virility and Di Yunge. As a concept, virility's meaning is unfixed. It refers to perceptions of action and character and implied ideals of masculine strength rather than action, character, and strength themselves.[4] The modernist era was a time when Jewish male sexuality was debated and thematized by Jewish authors and non-Jewish authors. Indeed, the post-Otto Weininger feminine conception of Jewish maleness and the Zionist attempt to build a new Jewish body have both been extensively documented by scholars.[5]

Critically, however, the meaning of 'virility' shifts extensively with time *and* space. Like their counterparts in Israel and Warsaw, Jewish immigrants to the US sought answers to the questions 'what is Jewish masculinity?' and 'what is Jewish virility?'. Yet the members of the New York Yiddish modernist group Di Yunge did so under the looming presence of America and American notions of masculinity and virility.⁶ Explaining the allure of Ernest Hemingway to the American man, Mike Gold, the author of *Jews without Money* (1929), wrote,

> The young American 'liberal' writes advertising copy meekly all day, then at night dreams of Hemingway's irresponsible Europe, where everyone talks literature, drinks fine liqueurs, swaggers with a cane, sleeps with beautiful and witty British aristocrats, is well informed in the mysteries of bullfighting, and has a mysterious income from home.⁷

Gold's article is clearly intended as a critique of the class that reads Hemingway ('a whole group of tired, sad, impotent, young Americans, most of whom work in offices every day') and their values — but the language of the class critique is unavoidably gendered, contrasting the 'meek' and 'impotent' office drones of America with the 'swagger' of Hemingway's characters, versed in the sacred performance of bullfighting.⁸ As Sarah Imhoff has argued, 'Jewish manhood was not identical with normative American manhood, but neither was it wholly a denigrated deviation'.⁹ If we hope to understand Di Yunge not only as Yiddish modernism on American soil but as a branch of a multilingual American literature,¹⁰ then we also have to consider how American literature and American art, and the themes and preoccupations of American writing, touched Di Yunge and affected its members as writers — and how they varied. When American literature went west, for example, did Di Yunge seek out other frontiers?

In Di Yunge, as in American fiction of the 1920s, we sometimes find a flamboyant, performative virility (think Hemingway). A telling example comes from Moishe Nadir's newspaper column, 'Fun mentsh tsu mentsh' [From Person to Person]. Here Nadir, renowned for how he dressed, describes the power and significance of one of his signature accessories, an item explicitly mentioned by Gold in his review of Hemingway, his cane or 'staff'.

> Zenen di lezer bakant mit mayn shtekn?
> A shod!
> Zey voltn im badarft kenen!
> [...]
> Nobeler shetekn!
> Er dikhtet nisht, redt nisht keyn loshn hore, trinkt nisht keyn bilikn vayn un iz zeyer solid.
> Men kon im nisht farlirn azoy laykht, vi a gelibte oder a shtele in a redaktsye.
> [...]
> Ikh rot ale lezer, zey zoln perzenlekh bakenen zikh mir mayn shtekn, velkher iz a teyl fun mayn talent.

> [Are readers familiar with my staff?
> A shame!
> They ought to get to know it!
> [...]
> Noble staff!
> It doesn't write poetry, it doesn't gossip, it doesn't drink cheap wine and it is very solid.
> It isn't easy to lose, unlike a lover or an editorial job.

> [...]
> I advise all readers to personally become acquainted with my staff, which is a part of my talent.]¹¹

The sexual overtones are unavoidable, and clearly intentional. Moishe Nadir's self-presentation as the one true aesthete in Yiddish literature relied on a gendered shorthand.¹² In a review of Ibsen's *Hedda Gabbler*, for example, we find him challenging his rival critics to draw their swords: 'Horkht, ir brider fun der kritik! Nemt arunter di shverdn fun ayere lendn un lomir geyn af a dul derfar vos ikh derveg mikh tsu zogn az ayer gelibte mume ibsen iz shreklekh langvaylik' [Listen, ye brothers in criticism! Draw the swords at your belts and let's embark on a duel. For I dare say that your lover Aunt Ibsen is horrendously boring].¹³ Nadir gives the audience reading the review what he claims they missed at the theatre: action, spectacle, even naughtiness. I have translated the Yiddish 'nemt arunter di shverdn fun ayere lendn' as 'draw the swords at your belts' in order to fit the overall language of a duel. But 'lendn' are more accurately 'loins'. Nadir, here, is reversing and subverting the biblical command to 'gird up your loins'.¹⁴ Nadir demands his rivals take out and show him their manhood.

What interests us here, however, is not the explicit display of virility, but rather virility with a question mark over it — and the concomitant identification of masculinity and certainty. Ayzland says of the poetry of Mani Leib's second period that he was 'menlekh-zikher in zayn klorkayt',¹⁵ thereby equating masculinity, certainty/assuredness, and the aesthetic quality of clarity. Critically, we find this dynamic throughout the writing of Di Yunge. Lamed Shapiro's 'Nyuyorkish' (1931) proves a telling example. The story has attracted significant critical attention for its portrayal of an urban sexual exchange, the politics of language, and the politics of race. Noting the presence of racialized imagery within the story, Hana Wirth-Nesher interprets the strained dalliance between the Yiddish-speaking immigrant Manny and the Hispanic Jenny (renamed Dolores by the Jewish man) as a commentary on the uncertainty of racial borders in the supposedly open America where the Jew is both perceived as white and denied whiteness.¹⁶ 'In Shapiro's story, the encounter with English constitutes an encounter with America's racial binary and the ambiguous location of the Jew on its racial map', she writes.¹⁷

Yet there are important sexual and gender elements at play in the story that deserve more thorough study, and which collectively underscore the role and themes of indecisiveness and interpretation. Shapiro's narrative features two critical scenes that call on the male protagonist to interpret the meaning of his relationship with Jenny/Dolores. In the first, Dolores outs herself as a part-time prostitute. She solicits him:

> He was upset, and paced impatiently around her.
> 'What kind of a man ...' she wondered.
> 'What kind of man? A man like other men. Not a lot worse than other men ...'
> Suddenly he had an idea.
> 'Listen', he said, 'I understand ...' He put his hand into a pocket ... He understood, and stood still, discouraged.¹⁸

Though Shapiro uses the Yiddish *mentsh*, 'person', and not *man* 'man', Larry Rosenwald rightly translates the dialogue in a way that highlights the questioning of Manny's masculinity: is he man enough to carry their date to its conclusion?[19] Shapiro twice uses the verb for 'understand' and a phrase that refers to comprehension ('im iz plutsem epes ayngefaln'),[20] as if calling on the reader to give full interpretative weight to this moment — to understand the nature of the exchange that Manny is being asked to interpret — and to the broader thematic resonances. There is an added clue in the original Yiddish. The word Rosenwald virtuously translates as 'discouraged', *ophentik*, can also be used to mean 'impotent',[21] and it also carries the literal meaning/sense of being un-handed: 'Vos iz azoy vi mit aropgelozte hent, vi on hent' [With hands dropped down, as if without hands].[22] Manny is forced to decide what kind of man he is, and, in deciding to pursue Jenny/Dolores, he takes agency and is no longer *ophentik*: 'In automobil hot er zikh arumgenumen mit ayn *hant*, zi hot zikh tsugetulyet tsun im' [He embraced her with one *hand*, she snuggled up to him].[23] He regains his hands. His mental clarity provides him with masculine virility.

Yet the scene's ambiguity dangles until we reach the climax. A new interpretative rift forms in their relationship. A financial transaction seems to have transformed into a genuine moment of romance and intimacy. Manny attempts to pay her, only for Dolores to attempt refusal. She expresses a kind of genuine affection for Manny: 'I ... this time I went — for myself'.[24] But the protagonist insists on paying, adopting a mock courtly affect: 'He took her hand, and brushed her fingers with his lips. His manner was both playful and ceremonious, the proud knight, it seemed, in his dressing gown, a shiny bald spot on top of his head [...].'[25] As Wirth-Nesher so aptly describes, their entire relationship was a kind of ethnic role play — of whiteness and of darkness[26] — and was doomed to failure from the outset. The encounter was by its very nature nocturnal and bound to fade in natural light. Yet Shapiro has chosen to depict their parting with intense layers of irony. He juxtaposes sexual confidence (taking her hand, performed chivalry) and domestic comedy (the dressing gown and the bald spot)[27] in order to set up the story's final joke: Manny does not seem to comprehend that Dolores could have found him desirable. The story closes: 'My God! What's all this? What was all this?'.[28]

What is the source of the confusion? Is it their ethnicity: the idea of a Hispanic woman being attracted to a Jewish man? Is it his body? Clearly, Shapiro's allusion to Manny's bald spot is meant to signal Manny's own physical insecurities, and echo earlier dialogue about a character she found pathetic. Could she have ever really found this body appealing?, he might be asking. Regardless, the most significant element is the act of questioning. Whatever certainty and clarity of action the protagonist possessed evaporates. Instead, he moves back to a position of indecisiveness and aesthetic indeterminacy, and the reader is left to sift through the various contradictory meanings.

Ambiguity defines Dovid Ignatov's 'Fibi'. First published in *Shriftn* in 1914, 'Fibi' [Phoebe] marks the symbolic beginning of Di Yunge, and one of its first serious, sustained prose engagements with the American landscape. 'Fibi' is a love story of sorts, the story of a doomed romance in New York City and northern New England. As Phoebe is half-Jewish, half-Christian, critics, following Noyekh Shteynbarg, have understood the work's central 'romance' as a symbolic treatment of Jewish–Christian relations in America. 'Es ken nokh zayn an ander oystaytsh far vos di ersteylung hoybt zikh on mit: "ikh hob lib shlangen". Dos kon onnemen vern als a simbol tsu erklern dem helds batsiung tsu kristentum' [There may be another explanation as to why the story begins with 'I love snakes'. This can be understood as a symbol to explain the protagonist's attraction to Christianity], Shteynbarg writes.[29] This thematic approach to their relationship has since been taken by Ruth Wisse and Jessica Kirzane.[30]

Yet the focus on the inter-religious aspect of the two characters' relationship obscures other aspects of the novella, namely the intensity of its American thematics and the surreal gender dynamics and sexual politics that dominate their relationship. Phoebe the character is supposed to 'make a man', out of the nameless protagonist,[31] and the two engage in an extended, frequently one-sided flirtation in which Phoebe contrives scenarios for the protagonist to be her physical rescuer. She, in other words, provides him ample opportunity to be strong and masculine. But instead of exciting him, these solicitations only set off his nerves and anxiety. The two can only begin to come together physically when their romance leaves the American setting and enters the symbolic plane of Jewish myth. This realization of virility, however, only leads to its own unwinding.

For the nameless protagonist of 'Fibi', the initial question is whether he has any sexual desire whatsoever. When the narrative begins, his sole interest is riding his bicycle and his only desires are for *breytkeyt, vaytkayt,* and *roym* — width, distance, and space. 'Ikh vil az der veg far mir zol af shtendik blaybn reyn un breyt un vayt' [I want the path before me to always remain pure and wide, and vast], he says.[32] Instead, an ironic *shiddukh* (match) with Phoebe is suggested. Indeed, the promise that she will 'make a man out of him', was preceded by the claim that his desire for width, distance, and space was immature. 'Ot vi groys ir zent, zent ir nokh fort a kind' [You may be big, but you are definitely still a child].[33] Phoebe will force him to mature emotionally and, presumably, sexually. The novella's plot then centres on his relationship with Phoebe, and his own attempt to escape and find boundless space. He flees New York for a farm in Vermont, only to realize that regimented farm life in Vermont is the furthest thing from his desires. And, because of the machinations of a friend, he ends up at a farm belonging to Phoebe's parents: an intermarriage of a Jewish woman and an evil, Irish farmer who mistreats his workers. Phoebe herself later comes to the farm. At the opening of the novella, we read 'ikh hob lib shlangen' [I love serpents], and the (never subtle) connection between serpents, Christianity, and Phoebe is made explicit over the course of the novella.

Although I have already described a rich American setting, it is important, however, that we understand the intense Americanness of the novella. The early pages engage in what Borekh Rivkin referred to as territorializing America for Yiddish. The narrator describes the Grand Concourse, a beautiful monument with elegant figures,[34] and there is an extensive, luxurious description of tennis in the park. But these pages also create a distinctly American protagonist. The desire for space, width, and vastness is the longing for the frontier that runs through much of classic American literature.[35] Indeed, what is striking about this novella is how closely portions map onto Leslie Fiedler's classic, if slightly-out-of-fashion paradigm of American literature developed at length in his *Love and Death in the American Novel* — and how portions schematically depart from Fiedler's analytic story. In Fiedler's paradigm, a white male flees civilization, often embodied by the figure of a woman, and heads to the frontier. There he establishes a deep relationship with a male, racial other.[36] Fiedler even highlighted the imagination of childhood and adolescence in these stories: 'the mythic America is boyhood', he writes.[37] Although there are critical divergences, the protagonist of 'Fibi' embarks on this journey.[38] He escapes the city and leaves for the country, but he flees in the wrong direction: north instead of west. His landscape is not the frontier but already conquered space. The protagonist encounters a number of possible Christian others to befriend, but they are all avatars of brutality and petty thievery. To further confound things, the woman he is attempting to flee, Phoebe, appears at the farm.

As previously noted, Phoebe's attempt to 'make a man' out of the protagonist is not emotional or spiritual, but physical. Three times she attempts to provide him with the opportunity to be her rescuer. The first is when he saves her from a car; the second is when she pretends not to know how to ride a bicycle. Her final attempt at seduction continues Ignatov's devolution of technology: she asks our hero to help her mount her horse. Symbolically, she provides him with the chance to be her courtly, chivalrous hero. Instead the scene plays out as tragicomedy. He takes her by the hand and helps her mount her horse ... only for her to fall into his arms. She laughs. It happens again a second time, and Phoebe, smiling, bursts into an even more beautiful sounding laughter ('un fibi hot zikh nokh klingender un shener tselakht').[39] Finally, it happens a third time, and he remembers the other times he has been forced to come to her rescue. 'Ikh hob zikh dermont on dem velosiped un der kar vos hot zikh a yog geton af ir. Ikh hob zikh dershrokn un bin in kas gevorn un gezogt — vos iz der mer mit aykh, mis o'nelson! Ir kent nit forn, to vos zhe hot ir geheysn zotln?' [I remembered the bicycle, and the care which chased after her. I grew frightened and angry and — What is it with you, Miss O'Nelson! If you can't ride, why did you order me to saddle the horse?].[40] Phoebe has tried to cast him as her hero — only he cannot quite understand the full meaning of her actions. He is not mature enough, not enough of a man, to recognize and interpret her game of attraction.

Their 'romance' would likely have ended at this indeterminate point if the text's space did not suddenly swerve. Ignatov stops describing an actual American landscape, one rich with the thematic resonances of American literature, and begins to transform Vermont into mythic Jewish space. Suddenly, the protagonist has a new role on the farm, one borrowed from biblical heroes: that of shepherd. Suddenly, he tends a flock in a pasture high in the mountains, in an open garden at the edge of the forest. Phoebe and the narrator are both astounded by the beauty of the forest's deer, a romantic symbol lifted directly from medieval Hebrew love poetry.[41] And then, after he has helped heal a cow with a wounded udder, and mended the fence that wounded her, and after Phoebe asks if he has come to hunt deer, he lowers the axe from his shoulder and they sit together on a stone and begin their half-consummated love affair.[42]

Although the novel set out to explore America, there is nothing American about their joining. America does not sanction their relationship; if anything, the protagonist rejects the possibility of the interfaith relationship afforded him, to whatever extent, by America. The relationship begins in earnest only when he accepts the fundamental transgression, when he sees Phoebe as a *shlang*, as a serpent, as Eve in the Garden. The novella does not model a new kind of interfaith romance; rather, the novel reinscribes a Jewish fear of the Christian women and her ability to prey on him. Yet the scene of the two characters joining also marks a striking display of decisiveness and certainty for this otherwise indecisive character: having cast himself as David, he embraces his passions. Within the novella's terms, he foregoes Jewish restraint and adopts Christian wildness. Or, perhaps, the Christian layer is superfluous. He ceases to be a child, embraces the role of man, and comes together with Phoebe. And by being with her physically, he starts to heal certain psychological wounds, certain sexual traumas that he has long felt. The novella, however, refuses to sustain this decisiveness and clarity. Ignatov thrusts us back into ambiguity: after a short love affair, Phoebe may or may not commit suicide. At the end of the story, we cannot clearly state whether or not Phoebe is alive. In fact, her suicide is a hyper-realization of the protagonist's inability to make meaningful, long-term decisions. To some degree, however, the novella was always destined to end in ambiguity. The narrator cannot be with Phoebe and return to the actual American landscape. Their coupling is predicated on the creation of an imaginary space, one where he can uncover a lost, more Jewish masculinity. Implicitly, Ignatov appears to define virility as decisiveness — but there is no real, early twentieth-century space for the narrator to be decisive and for the pair to be together.

Ayzland's narrative of Mani Leib gives us the clearest answer to the question, what is virility for the American Jew? In Ayzland's narrative, virility is not the ability to father children. Indeed, the ability to father children is the imagined opposite of virility. When Mani Leib first considers leaving his wife, the two have four children together. Later, a fifth child is born. But she has long since ceased to attract him, nor does anyone else find her attractive. Mani Leib had met his wife in Europe and brought her to America. Their romance crossed geographical borders. In the Eastern European context, the mark of virility might have been the quantity of children produced. His four or five children would have made him a man. Now, however, the test of Mani Leib's virility is whether or not he can embrace the relative sexual freedom afforded him by America, whether he can leave his wife, who he has began to see as little more than a womb and who he compares to an animal.[43] The question is, can he begin new, *licit* love affairs? Can he bring his actions into alignment with his temperament and internal feelings?

Mani Leib's flirtations with other women reached a nadir during a period when

Mani Leib hosted Ayzland at his apartment. At that time, Mani Leib would stay out late into the night with women and he would sneak into the house in the early morning. At first he sneaks into his son's bed, but it is too small, and he sneaks into Ayzland's bed instead.[44] Mani Leib's wife tolerates this, but she eventually confronts him one morning. He jumps out of bed; she blocks the door to Ayzland's room, preventing him from escape, and berates him. 'Ober do dos kleyne, shtendike shtume vaybele plutsem bakumen loshn un tselozt zikh hoykh afn kol' [But here, that small, always silent wifey suddenly received language and she let him have it loudly].[45] Words had been his power. But at this moment, when he is cowering in Ayzland's room, she gains a voice. She retakes the voice of moral authority, and gains the power of action. Mani Leib is cowed.

Ayzland's narrative of Mani Leib's relationship with his wife neatly parallels Ayzland's interpretive framework for Mani Leib's poetics. In the first periods of his time in America and his writing, Leib suffers from a surfeit of passion for women, falling in love repeatedly. As a result, Mani Leib advances the aesthetic argument that the true poet is emotional, in a constant state of unrest, and in a constant state of desire.[46] His poetry is not, in other words, marked by surety, but by confusion and intellectual agony. Ayzland tells us that Kolye Teper later criticized Mani Leib's poetry as too feminine. Mani Leib responded with a stuttering 'yo', which characterized his state of near-agreement with the speaker.[47] But suddenly he turned on Tepper. 'Un bald deroyf hot er take kolyen sharf an entfer geton, az nor tsekrokhene, nishtike mener shrekn zikh aroystsuvayzn veykhkayt un tsartlekhkayt, men zol zey nit halt far vayblekh' [And quickly he actually answered Kolye sharply, that only weak, insignificant men are afraid to display softness and tenderness, lest people consider them too feminine].[48] Although there is unquestionably truth to Mani Leib's response, Ayzland-the-storyteller refuses to allow Mani Leib the last word. Ayzland surprises us by agreeing with Kolye Tepper. 'Mani Leyb iz in zayn ershtn period gants oft geven tsu vayblekh' [In his first period, Mani Leib was frequently too feminine].[49] Ayzland then returns to an argument he made earlier: that Mani Leib's first period was characterized by *nepl*, 'fog', whereas his new, second period embraced a clarity of action. Now, however, Ayzland genders these poetic characteristics: 'Fun itst on iz er zunik un klor in kemat alts vos er shraybt, un menlekh zikher in zayn klorkayt' [From then on he was sunny and clear in almost everything that he wrote, and masculinely assured in his clarity]. As evidence of his new clarity, Ayzland offers a decisively masculine poem that Mani Leib wrote in quasi-revenge on his first wife.

> Ikh hob lib di meuberese vayber
> mit di beykher farshpitst un geshvoln,
> ven zey shlepn di toplte layber
> vi di ki oyf di grozike toln.
>
> [I love pregnant women
> With bellies pointed and swollen
> When they shlep their doubled bodies
> Like cows over grassy valleys.][50]

Once again his wife has lost her womanhood, her personhood, and been transformed into something more bestial. She is no longer the mother of his children but a sexual fetish.

Rather than defining virility as a set of actions, Ayzland defines virility as clarity in aesthetic and mental states. At the moment when he is confronted by Kolye Tepper, Mani Leib has already left his wife. But he lacks the strength and internal clarity to be completely true to his rejoinder and to truly embrace the idea of softness as an aesthetic virtue, as evinced by his stuttering 'yo'. Within the narrative, having taken action, having displayed masculine clarity, does not transform Mani Leib into Mr Virility. Rather, it underscores the common perception of him as *eydl*. We opened this paper with his sudden rejection of Ayzland's kiss. Would Mani Leib have responded to Reuven Ayzland in quite the same way if he had not constantly been forced to prove his masculinity, if he had not constantly been forced to defend his gentleness, his softness, his tenderness, his *eydlkayt*, his delicateness?[51]

While the specific language linking masculinity, certitude, and clarity was borrowed from Reuven Ayzland, the dynamic and fraught link between all three elements is at play in the writing of all four members of Di Yunge studied in this paper. In Moishe Nadir, we see the uncritical adoption of this notion, not as a problematized virility but as the acceptance of its logical premise. Shapiro highlights the role that interpretation plays in making sense of interpersonal dynamics and in navigating the city as a male Jewish immigrant. Ignatov, writing at the beginning of Di Yunge, at the outset of Di Yunge's discovery of America, uses scenes of sexual power and a near-impossible relationship to delve into the psyche of the American Jewish man, one not yet ready to make decisions and to comprehend the meanings of actions, and to discover what it might mean to be all those things jointly and separately: 'American', 'Jewish', and 'Man'. While there is the danger of reading Ignatov prescriptively, we can nonetheless read him as arguing for the discovery of an internal, Jewish definition of virility. Perhaps he argues that we can reach within, carve a Jewish space, and embrace certain classical motifs of Jewish masculinity. A shepherd who tends to his flock, not only a warrior. The frontier was open. By contrast, Ayzland wrote the encomium for Di Yunge. He is left to sort out the contradictions and make sense of them: restrained passion; strength in weakness. He is left to parse emotional uncertainty and fog as an aesthetic aim. Ayzland is left with ambiguities that are still ambiguities. He advances the premise that masculinity, certitude, and clarity are all linked, even as he acknowledges another, potentially forceful declaration of masculine poetics: one that embraces *veykhkayt un tsartlekhkayt*, softness and tenderness. It is worth pondering, however momentarily, why Ayzland insists on rejecting Mani Leib's argument to Kolye Tepper. It is possible that Ayzland simply believes in the inherent manliness of aesthetic certitude. But it is also possible that Ayzland denies Mani Leib's proposition because of the nature of his narrative. Ayzland's telling relies on a neat parallel between actions and personal story and aesthetics. To change one of them, and to accept alternative values for one of them, would require rebalancing and altering the other. Indeed, the ultimate aesthetic success of his treatment of Mani

Leib is its narrative dislocation of the question mark: it is the teller of the tale who may finally reveal his passion for another man — but we largely do not consider the teller. It is the teller of the tale who seems to be internally riven by debates about the nature of maleness. Instead, we ponder the other man's masculinity.

Notes to Chapter 9

1. Reuben Eisland, 'Mani Leyb, Mani Leyb! Tsu zayne shloshem', in Reuben Eisland, *Fun undzer friling: Literarishe zikhroynes un portretn* (New York: Inzel, 1954), pp. 65–108 (p. 107). Unless otherwise indicated, all translations from Yiddish are my own. Further, a note on names: I am choosing to use Library of Congress authority names for bibliographic purposes. I will, however, refer to authors within the text using YIVO transliterations, so 'Ayzland' instead of 'Eisland' and 'Ignatov' instead of 'Ignatoff'.
2. In *From our Springtime*'s larger Mani Leib narrative, Ayzland describes one of the quintessential acts of their friendship: late night meals at a deli or dairy restaurants followed by endless walks through the streets of New York. Given the focus on intention, is it wrong to hear the Prufrockian echo? 'Of restless nights in one-night cheap hotels | And sawdust restaurants with oyster-shells | Streets that follow like a tedious argument | Of insidious intent | To lead you to an overwhelming question | Oh, do not ask, "What is it?"'
3. Walter Benjamin, 'The Storyteller', in Walter Benjamin, *Illuminations*, ed. by Hannah Arendt, trans. by Harry Zohn (New York: Shocken, 1968), pp. 83–109 (p. 94).
4. My use of the term is borrowed from Cynthia Ozick. In her 1971 short story 'Virility', virility is closely linked to literary talent and success (Cynthia Ozick, *The Pagan Rabbi and Other Stories* (New York: Knopf, 1971), pp. 219–70). The poet Edmund Gate sleeps with women, fathers children, and brings poems into the world. Each of his collections of poems bears the title *Virility*. The emotional tenor of his poems is praised as masculine until it is revealed that they were actually composed by a woman. At that point, the final volume of Gate's poetry is considered mere women's writing.
5. See, for example, Daniel Boyarin, *Unheroic Conduct: The Rise of Heterosexuality and the Invention of the Jewish Man* (Berkeley: University of California Press, 1997); Sander Gilman, *The Jew's Body* (New York: Routledge, 1991). There have also been some attempts by scholars to understand the authorial play with sexual themes and the image of the Jewish male as sexual icon; see, for example, Jonathan Friedman, *Klezmer America: Jewishness, Ethnicity, Modernity* (New York: Columbia Univeristy Press, 2008).
6. If defined only by official publications, Di Yunge lasted from 1907 until the mid- to late-1920s. This paper, however, follows the approach to dating taken by Ruth Wisse in her history of Di Yunge, and uses the term to refer more generally to the members of the group and their collective works ('This book covers a period of approximately fifty eventful years'; Ruth Wisse, *A Little Love in Big Manhattan* (Cambridge: Harvard University Press, 1988), p. x).
7. Michael Gold, 'Hemingway — White Collar Poet', in *Mike Gold: A Literary Anthology*, ed. by Michael Folsom (New York: International Publishers, 1972), pp. 157–61 (p. 159).
8. See the discussion of 'macho criticism' in James Penner, *Pinks, Pansies, and Punks: The Rhetoric of Masculinity in American Literary Culture* (Bloomington: Indiana University Press, 2011).
9. Sarah Imhoff, *Masculinity and the Making of American Judaism* (Bloomington: Indiana University Press, 2017), p. 19.
10. As implied by the work of Werner Sollors. Of especial relevance are *Multilingual America: Transnationalism, Ethnicity, and the Languages of American Literature*, ed. by Werner Sollors (New York: NYU Press, 1998); Werner Sollors, *Ethnic Modernism* (Cambridge: Harvard University Press, 2008).
11. Moishe Nadir, 'Bikher, meydlekh, un nokh epes', in Moishe Nadir, *Geklibene verk*, 5 vols (Vilna: Kletskin, 1927–28), I (1928): *Fun mentsh tsu mentsh*, pp. 118–24 (pp. 123–24).
12. For more on Nadir's aestheticism, see Eitan Kensky, 'Facing the Limits of Fiction' (unpublished doctoral dissertation, Harvard University, 2013), ch. 2.

13. Moishe Nadir, 'Heda Gabler', in Moishe Nadir, *Zeks bikher*, 2 vols (New York: Mayzl, 1928), II: *Mayne hent hobn fargosn dos dozike blut*, pp. 110–16 (pp. 110–11).
14. See, for example, Yehoash's translation of 1 Kings 18. 46, 'un er hot ongegurt zayne lendn'. Available online via Haifa University's *World of Yiddish* website, <http://yiddish.haifa.ac.il/texts/yehoyesh/tanList.htm> [accessed 27 June 2019]. Yehoash's translation was first published in two volumes in 1937–38.
15. Eisland, p. 101.
16. In this way, the story is thematically similar to John Fante's *Ask the Dust* (1939), which imagines an interethnic romance between a Mexican woman and an Italian American.
17. Hana Wirth-Nesher, 'Encountering English', in *The Cambridge History of Jewish American Literature*, ed. by Hana Wirth-Nesher (Cambridge: Cambridge University Press, 2015), pp. 41–61 (p. 49).
18. Lamed Shapiro, 'New Yorkish', trans. by Larry Rosenwald, in *The Cross and Other Jewish Stories*, ed. by Leah Garrett (New Haven: Yale University Press, 2007), pp. 198–212 (pp. 206–07).
19. 'Should I, after tea and cakes and ices | Have the strength to force the moment to its crisis?'
20. Lamed Shaprio, *Nuyorkish un andere zakhen* (New York: Aleyn, 1931), p. 25.
21. *Comprehensive Yiddish–English Dictionary*, ed. by Solon Beinfeld and Harry Bochner (Bloomington: Indiana University Press, 2013), p. 110.
22. *Groyser verterbukh fun der yidisher shprakh*, ed. by Yudl Mark, 4 vols (New York: Komitet farn groyser verterbukh fun der yidisher shprakh, 1961), IV, 1770.
23. Shapiro, p. 27; Shapiro, trans. by Rosenwald, p. 207 (my emphasis).
24. Shapiro, trans. by Rosenwald, p. 211.
25. Ibid., p. 212.
26. 'For Lamed [...] the charged word that remains untranslated is "darky"' (Wirth-Nesher, p. 48).
27. This latter element foreshadows the volume's closing story, 'Dak', about a parvenu Jewish, immigrant doctor with few real morals: 'Beni milgroym hot ongehoybn kultivirn a plikh nokh in di studentishe yorn' (Shapiro, p. 127).
28. Shapiro, trans. by Rosenwald, p. 212.
29. Noyekh Shteynbarg, *Yung Amerike* (New York: Lebn, 1917), p. 26. I have standardized the spellings to confirm with YIVO transliteration, but have preserved Shteynbarg's lexical forms, i.e. here 'ertseylung' instead of 'dertseylung' or 'ertsehlung'.
30. Ruth Wisse, '*Di Yunge* and the Problem of Jewish Aestheticism', *Jewish Social Studies*, 38.3/4 (1976), 265–76; Jessica Kirzane, 'Intermarriage and the Uncanny in the Literary Imagination of *Di Yunge*', American Academy of Religion Annual Meeting, Atlanta, 21–24 November 2015. My sincere thanks to Jessica Kirzane for sharing her conference paper with me.
31. ' — gerekht, tokhter! Me darf im take zen bakenen mit fibi'n. Yo, zi vet shoyn fun im makhn a mentsh!' [— that's right, daughter! He ought to be introduced to Phoebe! Yes, she will make a man out of him!] (David Ignatoff, 'Fibis roman', in David Ignatoff, *Romanen, dertseylungen, legenden, un vunder mayses*, 3 vols (New York: Farlag Amerike, [n.d.]), III: *Tsvishn tsvey zunen: A bukh in fir teyln*, pp. 3–78 (p. 9)).
32. Ignatoff, p. 9.
33. Ibid.
34. As Mikhail Krutikov notes, this monument is itself a symbolic presence and a clue to Ignatov's inspirations. Ignatov describes a real statue, built in honour of Heinrich Heine, and it features a large impression of 'Lorelai'. See Mikhail Krutikov, 'Lorelay in di bronks', *Forverts*, 11 October 2013 <http://yiddish.forward.com/articles/172955/lorelei-in-the-bronx/> [accessed 28 June 2019].
35. For his part, Shteynbarg, p. 11, takes this aspect of the novel seriously. His chapter on Ignatov includes a fantastic description of travelling to the (then) outer neighbourhoods of Brooklyn to visit Ignatov, which he connects to Ignatov's language of 'roym un vaytkayt'.
36. 'Yet there is a relationship which symbolically joins the white man to nature and his own unconscious, without a sacrifice of his "gifts"; and binds him in life-long loyalty to a help-meet, without the sacrifice of his freedom. This is the pure marriage of males — sexless and holy, a kind of counter-matrimony, in which the white refugee from society and the dark-skinned

primitive are jointed till death do them part' (Leslie A Fiedler, *Love and Death in the American Novel* (New York: Delta, 1966), p. 211).
37. Leslie A. Fiedler, 'Come Back to the Raft Ag'in, Huck Honey!', *Partisan Review*, June 1948, pp. 664–71 (p. 666).
38. Given Ignatov's later translations of Native American chants for *Shriftn*, it is worth speculating as to whether Ignatov could have read *The Last of the Mohicans*. Fenimore Cooper's novel was translated into Russian in 1833. (A Yiddish translation was published in Warsaw in 1921.). On Ignatov's translation of Native American chants, see Rachel Rubinstein, *Members of the Tribe: Native America in the Jewish Imagination* (Detroit: Wayne State University Press, 2010), ch. 2.
39. Ignatoff, p. 49.
40. Ibid.
41. See Raymond Scheindlin, *The Gazelle: Medieval Hebrew Poems on God, Israel, and the Soul* (Oxford: Oxford University Press, 1999).
42. Ignatoff, p. 60.
43. 'Far zey iz genug ven zey hobn farn oyskumenish far di kinder un konen zey balekn vi ki, vos balekn zeyere kinder' [For them it's enough to sustain the children, and to be able to lick them like cows who lick their children] (Eisland, p. 77).
44. The reader's interpretation of this scene takes on new shades after the final prose poem.
45. Eisland, p. 95.
46. 'Dermit hot er gemeynt tsu zogn ershtns, az an emeser poet iz nor der, vos iz shtendik emotsyonel un in shtendikn umru un in shtendikn epes veln' [With that he intended to say, first, that a true poet is he who is always emotional and in constant unrest and in a constant state of desire] (ibid., p. 74).
47. Ibid., p. 101.
48. Ibid.
49. Ibid.
50. Ibid.
51. Consider the sexualized language used even in the criticism of Leib and Di Yunge: 'the *Yunge* made a virtue — some said, a fetish — of stillness, softness, silence, and this poem [Leib's 'Shtiler, shtiler'] assumed the importance of a manifesto' (Wisse, '*Di Yunge*', p. 271).

CHAPTER 10

Gendered War in Aharon Reuveni's *Yerusholayim in Shotn fun Shverd*

Yaakov Herskovitz

A Brothel in Shanghai

A short and relatively little-known story by Aharon Reuveni, 'Der libhober' [The Lover] tells of a visit to a brothel in Shanghai by two men.[1] This short story is part of the first period in Reuveni's career, which began when he was living in the United States, writing short Yiddish prose. The story tells of two men in transit, Shloyme Karbel and Fyodor Petrovich Eirling, travelling by sea from Shanghai to Singapore. Eirling, a stout brutish type, is a cook seeking work in Singapore, while Karbel, the narrator, is a smaller Jewish man, contemplative and gentle. The nexus of the story is not the travels but rather the exploits of men in transit; within a frame story of the two sitting on the deck of the ship, the narrator recalls the last night the two spent in Shanghai, namely a visit to a brothel.

The story, told from the view point of the Jewish man, is imbued with sexual dread; the narrator recalls the entry to the brothel and how the pimp displays three prostitutes before the two men, all young women of 'seventeen or eighteen years of age'.[2] The narrator tells how his companion insists, demands, to have sex not with the Chinese prostitute, a child herself, but with her younger sister, a child of ten years or so. The pimp and Eirling get into a heated discussion, which the narrator at first interprets as opposition on the part of the pimp before realizing that the exchange is a negotiation of a steeper price for the younger girl.

From this point on, the story unfolds at a growing pace with ominous dread. The narrator, as appalled as he is, is not deterred so far as to openly oppose his friend, who leads the ten-year-old girl up to a room while the narrator accompanies her sister to another room. The narrator seems to have forgotten what just occurred in the hallway, and so the sexual act and the following conversation proceed uneventfully, while the reader is constantly bothered by events in the adjacent room, which the two seem oblivious to. But this oblivion is short-lived when the two are startled by a blood-chilling scream from the other room and race in to find that

> Eirling was sitting on the edge of a wide bed in a filthy unbuttoned shirt, his hairy feet on the floor. Under his feverishly shaking hands a flimsy sobbing

body was spasming. The eyes of the cook from Riga were dazed and more bulging than usual. Spit was running down from his mouth towards his chin. [...] 'What have you done?' Shloyme was screaming hysterically. [...] he was shocked, the blood rushing to his head, his heart dizzy. He raised his hand, punched Eirling in the forehead and kicked him to the ground.[3]

But this is a belated intervention, and thus very strange: the Jewish traveller was not driven to action by his compatriot's haggling to acquire intercourse with the ten-year-old child. Nor was he deterred or put off from having sex with the sister of the girl being molested in the nearby room. Shloyme is only driven to action once the act, the acts, have been done, and his violence does little more than add pain with seemingly nothing to gain. Not prevention of pain and violence is on his mind, but appearances and appeasing his own conscience. In fact, the recollection of the night in Shanghai ends abruptly, and the story reverts back to the two men on the deck of the ship, Eirling talking on and Shloyme contemplating the strange occurrences of the previous night, not forgiving but not upset, musing on human nature and its quandaries.

This is a good point at which to return to the beginning of the story and to what must now seem an even more peculiar title, 'Der libhober'. It is possible that this is an ironic title, motioning towards the coarseness and sexual violence which are to follow. But it may also be a very real self-perception of the narrator, pegging himself as a lover, one who truly enjoys his night in the brothel, barring the uneasy incident at the end. Without the punch and kick he had to administer, it seems that Shloyme would not have seen any problem in the whole situation, just as he saw no problem in the grown man leading a ten-year-old girl off to a room. The uneasiness, the sense of dread throughout the story, belongs to the readers, and the tame title only exacerbates this dread and the violence to come.

This early story, a story of travel and of sexual violence, shows how, from the earliest stages of his career, Reuveni had a fascination with, and an acute eye for, gender imbalance, male and female tension and contention, and the role a 'good man' can play in situations of peril to women. This comes up in the early story set in Shanghai, but also, more so, in Reuveni's magnum opus, the trilogy *Ad Yerushalayim* (1919–23), which will be the focus of this paper. The gender roles in these three novels were very much presaged in the short story with a male protagonist who is attracted to sexual violence on the one hand and appalled by it on the other. Thus, in the novels, men find use for women insofar as they allow them easier life in the harsh reality of wartime, making empty gestures at equality, always too late, always at the expense of women.

The Life of Reuveni; or, How Shanghai Entered Jewish Literature

The many travels, trials, and tribulations of Aharon Reuveni's life chart out one of change and cultural sensibilities. Born in Poltava, now Ukraine, in 1886, he was reared in the Russian language, learning Yiddish only upon arriving in the United States in 1904. In the year he spent in Chicago, he not only learned the language but mastered it, starting a period in which he wrote over a dozen short stories in

Yiddish which remain a highpoint of his oeuvre. Shortly after returning to Russia hastily following the 1905 Revolution, Reuveni and his father were exiled to Siberia for the illegal possession of arms. If this imprisonment can in any way be seen as fortuitous, that is because it led to an escape through Manchuria and China to Palestine, travels which served as inspiration for stories such as 'Der libhober'. Famously, Reuveni ceased writing Yiddish upon his arrival in Palestine in 1910, and published only in Hebrew. This chapter in Reuveni's career culminated in the trilogy *Ad Yerushalayim*, novels depicting World War I in Palestine.[4]

Between the short story discussed above and the novels to be discussed shortly, Reuveni's writings chart an artistic life marked by displacement and war. The through-line I wish to add to these themes is that of gender. Specifically, I wish to see how the fog of war and displacement allows for women to be marginalized and utilized more than usual, how they become not only foils for the men around them, but literally aids in the survival of men in these times of hardship. Hardship for all, and survival of the fittest — or in this case the men.

Gendered War in Palestine

World War I would turn out to be both the catalyst of Reuveni's artistic pinnacle, and the demise thereof: between the years 1917 and 1923, Reuveni set out to write a tetralogy of life in Palestine during the Great War. But, as Reuveni reflected later in his life, this ambitious feat was cut short due to the depression which seized him in the aftermath of the deadly riots of 1920.[5] At the time, he was writing the third part of what amounted to a trilogy, and he decided to end the undertaking. Thus, the narrative spawned by war was also extinguished in violence, reaching its premature end with the novel which was published in 1924 under the Hebrew title *Shamot* [Devastation]. This novel ends many years' journey of depicting war and violence in the final demise of a protagonist and a narrative.

Before moving on to the narrative itself, I wish to touch on one of the more peculiar aspects of the trilogy: language. Written seven years after his arrival in Palestine, Reuveni composed the trilogy in what was his writing language of the time, Yiddish. Yet it took over four decades for it to be published in that language. Instead, with the help of other writers, help which diminished as the cycle progressed, Reuveni self-translated the novels into Hebrew, publishing them all, and only, in this language. By the time the third novel came round, Reuveni felt confident enough in his Hebrew faculties to translate it himself — to translate, but not to write it in Hebrew, for his artistic sensibilities and prowess were still firmly within his primary writing language, Yiddish. And yet, even though the process was similar, Reuveni's decision to translate the third novel on his own produces a text which has moments, in the Hebrew version, which are more Yiddish than Hebrew, and the Hebrew text of the novel as a whole is markedly different from that of the previous two novels.

This was all a preface for the delayed and belated first publication of the novel in Yiddish some forty years after it was written. In 1963, the New York publisher

Der kval[6] published a novel by Aharon Reuveni, *Yerusholayim in shotn fun shverd* [Jerusalem in the Shadow of the Sword]. In the afterword to the novel, the chief editor of Der kval, Yisroel London, discusses the process of publication; in this short epilogue, 'Etlekhe verter' [Several Words], London announces that it is with the greatest of pleasures that Der kval is publishing the novel, for it will allow the Yiddish reader to be better acquainted with Hebrew literature: 'To enrich Yiddish literature and make whole once again the important saying by Bal-makshoves: one literature — two languages.'[7] Of course, this is a reversal of the very well-known statement by Bal-makshoves, and is no slip of the tongue(s). The world of Jewish literature, in 1963, was in no way one, and the two languages were hardly two participants in a solidified literary system. But London is correct in his unique positioning of Reuveni's novel, even if he fails to fully divulge its unique position, one that involves Hebrew and Yiddish in complex ways.

Following the hyperbolic opening, London goes on to commend Reuveni for his beautiful idiomatic Yiddish, which tells the story in a way readers can relate to.[8] Again, what this statement omits is that the relationship here to the authentic, the idiomatic, the original is not that simple. Aside from the omission of the true nature of the relationship between the language of writing and the language of publication, there is also an omission regarding the decision of what to publish: *Yerusholayim in shoten fun shverd* is the third part of a trilogy, a trilogy published in Hebrew under the title *Ad Yerushalayim* [To Jerusalem]. Yet London treats it in his introduction as a standalone novel, and a Hebrew one to boot. The decision to publish a Yiddish version of the third part, and only the third part, will be an issue I wish to keep in mind throughout the discussion. For now, suffice to note that the last novel of the said trilogy has a sensationalist aspect to it that the other parts of the trilogy did not contain. Moreover, the last novel foregrounds gender roles and their implications in fascinating ways — a bold, but perhaps wise choice in 1963 New York.

Another issue that is crucial to my discussion is that the beautiful idiomatic Yiddish translation by Reuveni, to quote the editor, is not a translation at all. As mentioned above, between 1916 and 1923 Reuveni wrote a trilogy, in Yiddish, about the Great War, World War I, in Palestine. This was translated into, or rewritten in, Hebrew almost simultaneously by Reuveni, with varying help from other writers due to his insufficient and definitely not idiomatic Hebrew.[9] Reuveni was determined to publish the novels in Hebrew, and only then, if ever, in Yiddish. After initially abstaining from Yiddish publication, Reuveni laboured for decades to find a Yiddish publisher for the entire trilogy, until 1963 and Der kval came along. These facts make London's comments on the authenticity and natural feeling of the Yiddish more complex. If it sounds natural in Yiddish, that might be because it was always already Yiddish, and the façade of Hebrew, or more precisely of Hebrew literature for a Yiddish readership, is just that, a façade.

The trilogy as a whole tells the story of three protagonists, all men, in Jerusalem during World War I. Each one of the three in turn deals with the implications of life in Palestine in times of war. *Be-rayshet ha-mevukhah* [When Confusion Began], *Ha-oniyot ha-akhronot* [The Last Ships], and *Shamot* [Devastation], the three novels comprising *Ad Yerushalayim*, are different in form, pace, and protagonists. Yet together, the three comprise a sprawling narrative which aims to portray the complexity of Jewish life in Palestine during World War I, producing an ambitious narrative unlike any written before, or even after, in Hebrew literature.[10] The first novel, *Be-raishit ha-mevukhah*, focuses on the accountant Aharon Zifroviz, who works for a Hebrew newspaper in Jerusalem, and portrays the collapse of his life in Palestine, ending with him leaving the country. In *Ha-oniyot ha-akhronot*, which opens following Zifroviz's departure from Palestine, the trilogy shifts to focus on Gedalyah Berenchuk, a writer at the same newspaper, thus keeping the narrative continuous even though Zifroviz has departed. Berenchuk, like Zifroviz, attempts to leave Palestine, but ultimately fails, and the novel ends with this failed flight. *Shamot*, the final novel in the trilogy and the one which will be discussed below, focuses on yet another protagonist, Meir Funk, a young carpenter who fought locust attacks alongside Berenchuk, once again linking characters while shifting focus. This novel too ends in failure, with Funk committing suicide.

Yerusholayim in shoten fun shverd is a detailed and focused account of the life and death of Meir Funk, a Russian-born carpenter living in Jerusalem. The novel focuses on the trajectory of Funk's demise by attempting to evade the draft and ultimately, failing to do so, committing suicide while stationed in the desert. The story of Meir Funk is intertwined with that of the family he rents a room from, mainly with the three siblings: Esther, whom Funk falls in love with, her sister Chaya, and their brother Leyzer.

In the rare occasions where previous scholarship has paid attention to female protagonists in the trilogy, it has highlighted the fact that this third novel stands out from the rest of the trilogy in that female protagonists are more than just a foil to the men in the centre and are fashioned, in this novel alone, as independent and compelling agents.[11] My reading will re-evaluate such claims in an attempt to see what exactly the realm of women's life is, what the spectrum of action which the novel grants them is. Once again, this is a perspective associated with the fact that *Yerusholayim in shoten fun shverd* is a single novel, isolated from the previous two.

The most crucial driving force in the novel is the war and the issue of the Ottoman draft, which induces many of the conflicts in the narrative; from the onset of the trilogy, the demand on all foreign citizens is to Ottomanize and renounce their previous citizenship. The Ottomanization process is the trajectory of the trilogy as whole. In the first novel, there is an option to be deported voluntarily from Palestine or to Ottomanize, which lays bare a dilemma of Zionist implications: to refuse to Ottomanize means deportation and Zionist failure, but to agree to Ottomanize carries with it serious ramifications, which will become clear shortly. The second novel, *The Last Ships*, charts the moment of the shift, when the ports are shut.

Regardless of the options in the first two novels, the third contains no such possibility of voluntary deportation; the time for that has passed. Therefore, the only option is to Ottomanize, which means quite simply, for men of a certain age, being drafted into the army. This is an unbearable result for Meir Funk, and more so for Esther, who is no longer just the daughter of the landlord but now Funk's wife-to-be. The draft into the Ottoman army is a dangerous prospect for any young man, let alone a Jewish one, as we will later learn through Leyzer, Esther's brother.

With Ottomanization becoming an inevitable reality, a new struggle emerges, the struggle to evade the draft, which quickly becomes a family effort for Esther and her sister Chaya. The draft, which seemingly affects only Funk, produces serious consequences for the sisters by proxy. While Esther works as a seamstress, Chaya does not work at all, yet she has for some time been a key contributor to the household, bringing home meat and white bread, black-market food, for her whole family. The family is obviously, as always, the last to put together the hints and rumblings of the neighbours and acknowledge that this food comes through Chaya's prostitution. Even after the realization, this fact does not deter the family, or Funk, from continuing to enjoy the food. But the profiteering intensifies when the implicit demands become explicit, and the stakes become higher as Funk and Esther turn to Chaya to produce the money that will help Funk evade the draft, or at least delay it. Thus, the whole family, and Funk, effectively pimp Chaya out while positioning themselves above her, as morally better than her. They rely on Chaya to supply the bribe which will allow Funk to evade the draft, but will not even acknowledge the price she pays in order to supply this money.

Funk is not the only one who has draft trouble, and is not the only one evading it at the expense of women: Leyzer, Esther and Chaya's brother, is also on the run from the army; on a short period of leave, he left his base and never returned.[12] Again, similarly to the case with Funk, Leyzer's evasion of the draft has implications not only for him but for a whole ecosystem that supports his decision. The closest thing in the novel to a hedonist, Leyzer was probably not an epitome of work ethic before the war. But now, with the excuse of the danger in going out to work while being on the run from military service, Leyzer stays mostly indoors, at Rosa's, his lover. Rosa chooses to provide for Leyzer and, as does Chaya, his sister, she does so through prostitution. Leyzer lives comfortably in Rosa's home, well fed and safe, while she goes around town to supply these luxuries. Leyzer acts as an in-house pimp, and Rosa uses her body to allow his army-dodging days to continue.

Thus, once again in this novel, though the draft is exclusive to men, it still burdens women in ways that are comparable to, and even exceed, the hardships brought upon men, seeing as both Leyzer and Meir are able to stay out of the army for the time being by the graces of the benefactor women in their lives. Or so matters might have continued if Leyzer had not pushed his luck: while living with Rosa, he starts frequenting the house of another woman, Zlatka, cheating on his sponsor with her. The frequent absences from home spark Rosa's suspicions, until one day she follows Leyzer over to Zlatka's home to catch him red-handed.

What happens next is surprising: instead of taking her anger out on Leyzer, the one who is cheating on her, Rosa attacks Zlatka: '"You think I'm a whore? Me?!" Rosa screamed at Zlatka like an ox being slaughtered, like she heard these words for the first time ever. With a red face she continued: 'And you ... you ... carrion, skeleton, skin and bones — who do you think you are?!'.[13] What starts out as a verbal quarrel escalates quickly into a bloody battle between the two women, during which Leyzer sneaks out and scurries home — to Rosa's home, that is. Before he departs, to add insult to injury, he steals Rosa's gold watch, which flies off her wrist in the altercation.

Before turning to the consequences of this scene, I want to take a moment and point out the breakdown of female solidarity in the face of male infidelity: both women in this scene are prostitutes, both using their body to support this one man, Leyzer the deserter. In the face of his infidelity, they turn not against him but against one another, inflicting once again pain upon the female body, violence which allows Leyzer to flee the scene — under the cover of female suffering, just as he fled the draft.

Yet this escape by Leyzer is not to last long, for once Rosa returns to her apartment and sees Leyzer there, calmly eating lunch, she sends him away. This eviction would have been enough for her, but when she sees that Leyzer left with her gold watch, she runs outside to the police station. The next day, the narrator reports, the thief is arrested and sent back to the army.

Failure is also the end of Funk's draft evasion, but this turns out to be self-inflicted. After attempting to raise money to finally bribe his way out of the draft, Funk gives up and goes willingly. This comes after he has sex with Tzipora, a colleague of Esther, who promises him the money he needs in exchange for sex. He goes through with this, but is so repulsed by what he has done to get this ransom that he immediately gives it away to Chaya to help her escape the city and the trouble she herself is in. The story here reaches what seems to be a rare equilibrium, with Funk and Chaya changing places, both using their bodies to get money. But this equation is eschewed; while Funk used the money Chaya gave him at the outset of the novel, here he refuses to enjoy the fruits of his own prostitution, giving away the money so as not to be reminded of his transgression. Through this, he recognizes his original acceptance of Chaya's money as tainted.

So off to the army Funk goes, overcome with shame for his actions, taking on the mantle of army service as the cross he must bare for his sexual transgressions, for prostituting himself. This self-righteousness, which is not awarded to any women who does the same thing in the novel, places Funk on a self-proclaimed higher moral level. Yet once again, this excessive morality comes at the expense of a woman: his martyrdom reaches its zenith with him committing suicide, and the novel ends with the image of an oblivious Esther, as a character reports in the final lines: 'I saw Esther last night, her and the child, three months old. She knew not of the death, not yet. And the child — so healthy! Same nose, same forehead.'[14] With Chaya on the run, Leyzer in the army, and Funk dead — her whole family gone — Esther is not allotted any escape route that others are afforded. She is left with a child in the image of Funk, with no knowledge of what tomorrow holds.

In *Gender Camouflage*, Laurie Weinstein and Francine D'Amico argue that wars occur because power hierarchies grounded in constructions of not only gender but also ethnicity, nationality, and sexuality require them. War sustains gender hierarchy, oligarchy, and heterosexism because difference is deployed to justify domination.[15] In fact, more often than not, wars not only occur to sustain power hierarchies; they have the result of masking who the victims are. Not only those who lose their lives are victims, though they are the most obvious ones. With Esther left alone to care for a baby at the end of the novel, with her family crumbled around her, it seems that the war has succeeded in victimizing her: all that has occurred has pinned Esther down, neatly fastened under dominant hierarchies. That this destruction was wrought by war is self-evident. But it was also wrought by the roles and opportunities wartime allowed and allotted to women; they evade a draft which seems unevadable, perhaps at a cost greater than imagined. In this novel, women's activism is restricted to the realm outside of the draft, and yet it is strongly linked and influenced by it.

To come full circle, war and the gender problems it emanates from and reaffirms make this novel an important and understudied text, one which transcends decades and languages. It is an important publication in Hebrew in 1920s Palestine, and an important return to Yiddish in 1963 New York. We may never have a definitive answer as to why this last book of the trilogy was selected as best suited for a Yiddish readership of the early sixties, one of only fourteen books that Der kval published in New York. London chose this novel, and also chose to characterize it as an insight into Hebrew literature, yet it was not a portrayal of Hebrew literature, neither of the time nor of the 1920s. Rather, it was a reclaiming of a Yiddish classic, one which resounds with a long-lasting truth of war and gender domination.

To end the discussion of the novel, let us reflect on literary historiography and field bias: in the scholarly work dealing with the trilogy, all of which, incidentally, deals with the Hebrew version, the issue of gender comes up seldom, albeit in interesting ways when it does. By now it should come as a surprise that Esther, Rosa, Chaya, and Zlatka are barely mentioned, and not discussed at all, in these scholarly works.[16] Four men are at the centre of these studies: Funk, Leyzer, Berenchuk, and Zifroviz. This focus on masculinity raises some warranted questions: what, for example, does the treatment of this novel as a Hebrew novel, and only a Hebrew novel, dictate when reading it in the context of gender? The young male protagonist, be he uprooted or a good Zionist, is the focus of so many studies in the field of Hebrew literature to the point of myopia. In this sense, there are new options, new readings, which arise through reading this novel on its own, in Yiddish, without the overbearing norms of Hebrew literary studies.

This issue also allows a return to the initial question, and a reversal of it: reading this third novel on its own allows for women to appear, magically, as if out of thin air. The one published Yiddish novel reframes the narrative of the trilogy as a whole, focusing on the war as a backdrop not for the story of men, but for the circumstances and culture of domination that allowed the cliché of great men to be established in the first place. Viewed as such, the third novel is not a fraction of a trilogy but a work which puts forward a complex fabric of war, gender, and language.

Conclusion; or, Who Failed Better?

Thinking back to 'Der libhober', we can see the path to Palestine was paved with violence at the expense of women. In this sense, the arrival in the Promised Land was no change: in the Palestine of the novel, men are blazing a path to redemption and it is once again women who pay the price. But unlike in 'Der libhober', here the men fail along with the women, albeit in another fashion altogether. Men are expelled, imprisoned, and dead at the end of this story, rather than escaping violence by ship. In this sense, there might be merit in the claim that women are more wholly represented in *Yerusholayim in shotn fun shverd*: while the first two novels of the trilogy end with flight by men leaving their troubles behind, similarly to the short story set in the Far East, the third novel of the trilogy ends with failure all round. Funk is dead; Esther is alone and with child.

Yet imbalance still remains in the question of who failed more squarely, who failed better? And, as to agency, has the balance really shifted in this last novel, is there a dynamism to Esther that her predecessors lacked? The end of the trilogy would have us believe so, with Funk dead and Esther surviving him. But if we reconsider the repeated flight of men from the plight which befalls women, Funk's death may be seen as a better failure. He has truly escaped the war of his own volition, through suicide, while Esther, for all her efforts, is no better off than she was to begin with, before she met Funk. Failure too is a privilege, awarded to some, not so much to others.

Notes to Chapter 10

1. (The title could also mean 'The Amateur'.) The story, first published in Yiddish in 1914, was later translated by Reuveni himself and republished in Hebrew. Yet, and this is no doubt due to the disturbing subject matter, this story is seldom included in collections of Reuveni's prose. There has been no scholarly work written on this short and intense story, possibly due to the dark subject matter, possibly due to the fact that it appears only in two collections of Reuveni's work, Yiddish and Hebrew respectively: Aharon Reuveni, *Gezamlte dertseylungen* (Jerusalem: Magnes, 1991) and Aharon Reuveni, *Kol hasipurim* (Jerusalem: Reuven Mass, 1967).
2. Aharon Reuveni, 'Der libhober', in Aharon Reuveni, *Gezamlte dertseylungen* (Jerusalem: Magnes, 1991), pp. 87–96 (p. 92). 'Der libhober' could also mean 'The Amateur'.
3. Ibid., pp. 94–95.
4. For a much more extensive account of Reuveni's life, see the monograph by Yigal Schwartz, *Lekhyot kedai lekhyot* (Jerusalem: Magnes, 1993).
5. This is from the acceptance speech for the Bialik prize in 1969, published in *Davar*, 19 December 1969, p. 8.
6. Not to be mistaken with the Viennese publisher by the same name which was active in the years of World War I. Yisroel London, the editor in chief and publisher of the New York publisher, had played an active role in the Viennese publisher before its demise.
7. Yisroel London, 'Etlekhe verter', in Aharon Reuveni, *Yerusholayim in shoten fun shverd* (New York: Der kval, 1963), pp. 221–25 (p. 223).
8. Ibid., p. 225.
9. This is what Rebecca Walkowitz has described as a 'born-translated' novel, where translation is not merely a vehicle of language transfer but an inherent part of the creative process of writing and many times a part of the narrative itself. See Rebecca L. Walkowitz, *Born Translated: The Contemporary Novel in an Age of World Literature* (New York: Columbia University Press, 2015).

10. Here, once again, the complexity of the translingual standing of the trilogy complicates such statements. While Hebrew literature is all but devoid of vast trilogies such as *Ad Yerushalayim*, Yiddish literature is no stranger to such narratives, Asch's *Farn mabl* being a more or less contemporaneous example. However, *Ad Yerushalayim* was never *published* as a trilogy in Yiddish, which makes this statement all the murkier.
11. This claim is most neatly laid out by Ruth Kartun-Blum, 'Ha-kol tzafuy ve-harashut netuna', in *Aharon Reuveni: Mivhar maamre bikoret al yetsirato*, ed. by Yigal Schwartz (Tel Aviv: Hakibbutz Hameuchad, 1992), pp. 207–13.
12. The text hints that this sick leave was granted due to a sexually transmitted disease Leyzer contracted in the army. This is an implicit explanation of the dangers which awaited young Jewish men in the Ottoman army.
13. Reuveni, *Shoten*, p. 157.
14. Ibid., p. 219.
15. Francine D'Amico and Laurie Lee Weinstein, *Gender Camouflage: Women and the U.S. Military* (New York: New York University Press, 1999), pp. 253–62.
16. In this, I am thinking of works which appear in *Aharon Reuveni*, ed. by Schwartz. This collection contains most of the Hebrew scholarship on the trilogy. Another example of a male-centred reading can be found in Philip Hollander, 'Rereading "Decadent" Palestinian Hebrew Literature: The Intersection of Zionism, Masculinity, and Sexuality in Aharon Reuveni's "Ad Yerusholaim"', *AJS Review*, 39.1 (2015), 3–26. The exception to all of these is the aforementioned article by Kartun-Blum.

CHAPTER 11

The *Kmoy*-Conquest of South America: Yankev Botoshansky and the Masculine Imaginary of Yiddish Literature

William Gertz Runyan

Un ven undzere shiflekh zenen tsugekumen tsum fond fun der bukhte Garibaldi un mir hobn gezen di tsvey rizike gletshers, di tsvey groyse berg fun shney, vos zeen oys vi makhnes matseyves, oder gor vi rizike lukhes — glaykh toyznter Moyshes gibn do naye toyznter toyres — hobn mir shoyn gor gefilt, az mir zenen nisht in ayz un shneyland, nor in Fayerland. Alts brent do ...

[And when our boats reached the edge of Garibaldi Fjord and we saw those two immense glaciers, those two great mountains of snow that looked like hosts of tombstones or even immense tablets — just as if thousands of Moseses gave thousands of new Torahs here — we now distinctly felt that we were not in ice-and-snow land, but in Fire Land. Everything burns here ...][1]

This passage to a degree captures the performative sensibility of Yankev Botoshansky's travel narrative entitled 'Fayerland' [Tierra del Fuego], dated February 1933 and published two months later in Warsaw's influential Yiddish weekly *Literarishe bleter* [Literary Pages].[2] Here, the Buenos Aires-based journalist and belletrist momentarily transposes the reality before him into Jewish lore in a manner reminiscent of Abramovich's quixotic hero Binyomin Hashlishi.[3] In this case, however, the mythic template does not serve to orient the traveller in an unknown geography. Rather, as soon as two glaciers have come into view, they give way to intimations of death and a thousandfold revelation that in its absurd excess would shatter the mythic mould, dwarfing the topography and drama of Exodus. The larger narrative contains no further biblical flourishes, but persistently shrouds Tierra del Fuego in a discourse of ineffability. Initially, the traveller locates himself at the edge of two oceans, on a journey amid gulfs, bays, fjords, glaciers, mountains, and waterfalls, and proposes to sketch a single indescribable outing. The narrative of the approach to and arrival at Garibaldi Fjord further dramatizes the terrain — cast as primitive and unforgiving, forged in a struggle between fire and water — until finally an encounter with the sublime occasions a meditation on the limits of representation.

The circumstances of Botoshansky's journey are opaque to the reader of the *Literarishe bleter*, and from the ends of the earth the middle-class tourist casts himself in the role of intrepid explorer to address the journal's well-defined reading public — itself dispersed across some two dozen countries.⁴ The thrill and mortal peril of expeditions to the South Pole, as sensationally reported and chronicled in preceding decades in the international press, resonate in Botoshansky's narrative, and the expeditions of Magellan and Charles Darwin in earlier centuries are not far from his mind.⁵ However, he stops short of adopting the posture of discoverer qua Man of Science, and instead places an educated German in this role in order to pit his own folksy observations and poetic wonderment against naturalist reason. This allows him to construct the modestly grandiose position of discoverer qua Yiddish Man of Letters, tasked with discovering the wonders of Tierra del Fuego in and for Yiddish. During his own experience of sublime nature, Botoshansky recalls the poet David Frishman's appreciation of the Finnish Imatra Rapids, but finds this model lacking:⁶

> Azoy kon men zingen bay der Imatra, in der bukhte Garibaldi darf men Valt Vitmans kol ... un efsher volt dos oykh geven tsu shvakh. Dos shtarkste gezang kon do zayn dos shvaygndike ...
> Shvayg ikh haynt oys dos ershte yidishe gezang tsu Fayerland un tsu der fayerlendisher bukhte Garibaldi ...
>
> [One can sing this way at Imatra — in Garibaldi Fjord one needs Walt Whitman's voice ... and even that might be too weak. Here the most powerful song may be the silent one ...
> Today I mutely voice the first Yiddish song to Tierra del Fuego and to its Garibaldi Fjord ...]⁷

In this way, Botoshansky lays claim to the first Yiddish word commensurate with Tierra del Fuego in a silent appreciation of a landscape so rugged and immense, it would seem, that it cannot be tamed into poetry even by a manly, vitalist Whitmanesque yawp.

This posture represents, in an exaggerated form, a significant tendency in the Yiddish literature and press of the early twentieth century: the description, figuration, and performance of Yiddish literature's transformation from a regional into a worldwide literature as a species of conquest. What may at first appear to be a sporadic rhetorical tendency to appeal to a masculine fantasy of mastery over space amounts to something more than that — a sustained colonial conceit in Yiddish literature and criticism. This is a phenomenon that resists neat circumscription or summation, as it entails a whole repertoire of reading, writing, and editorial practices — part mindset, part representational regime, part market force.

Decades after the publication of 'Fayerland', Botoshansky would reaffirm the pioneering nature of his visit to Tierra del Fuego in a short autotext titled 'Azoy ze ikh zikh aleyn' [This Is How I See Myself] (1955), later revised as 'Vi ikh ze zikh' [How I See Myself] (1962).⁸ In both versions, the writer casts himself as a restless wanderer, half-gypsy in appearance and in spirit by merit of his origins at the southern limit of Bessarabia with Romania.⁹ Apart from the central role he claims in ridding the Argentine Jewish community of its notorious 'pimp infestation', the accomplishments Botoshansky cites are mainly linked to travel.[10] These include his presence at landmark events in Jewish and general history: the ten-year anniversary of the Institute for Jewish Research (YIVO) in Vilna in 1935, the 1939 World's Fair in New York, the establishment of the United Nations in San Francisco in 1945, and the founding of the state of Israel in 1948. Alongside these moments, Botoshansky adds: 'Ikh bin geven der ershter yidisher shrayber in der gantser velt, vos iz geven in Fayerland, dos vunderlekhe indzl, vos hot dem letstn yishev afn veg tsum zid-pol' [I was the first Yiddish writer in the entire world to be in Tierra del Fuego, the wonderful island that holds the last settlement on the path to the South Pole].[11] This retrospective comment once again evokes the figure of the explorer-discoverer — the witness of the very edge of human civilization — only now this role is cast as one of historic proportions.

Grandiloquent as Botoshansky's statement may appear, it reflects what was likely a much broader sensibility about Yiddish literature and print culture, grounded less in daring exploits than in the ceaseless circulation of new publications, correspondence, and manuscripts that defined it. At editorial desks in New York, Warsaw, Buenos Aires, and elsewhere, figures such as Samuel Margoshes, Nakhmen Mayzel, and Botoshansky himself sorted through such materials from around the Yiddish-speaking world to harness an intercontinental cultural sphere and mould it into an encompassing vision for their readers.[12]

As co-editor of the daily *Di prese* [The Press] in Buenos Aires, Botoshansky ensured that readers of this, the more progressive of the city's two rival Yiddish papers, would see the Yiddish literary and cultural developments of New York, Warsaw, and Moscow play out right before their eyes. This perspective was in part the product of Botoshansky's own frequent reviews of new books and coverage of ongoing cultural debates, but was principally achieved by reprinting essayistic, critical, and literary works from major newspapers abroad. Meanwhile, Mayzel periodically featured contributions from Mexico, Cuba, South Africa, Palestine, and Argentina in the *Literarishe bleter*, which otherwise privileged contributions from or about writers in the major centres. The great disparity between these two editorial gazes was that Mayzel looked from centre to periphery and Botoshansky the other way round. Where Botoshansky could offer a bit of prestige, a wider readership, and a meagre honorarium in Argentine pesos to foreign writers printed or reprinted in *Di prese*, editors and critics in Warsaw and especially New York were in a position to act as real brokers of economic and symbolic power for literary writers and journalists across the world — and in particular for those who aspired to be more than merely local writers.

Botoshansky was just this kind of aspirational writer, and early on learned in rejection letters from New York that there was a need not for additional cultural criticism, opinion pieces, or European travelogues, but instead for gripping contributions about South America. When he visited New York for the first time in 1931, full of fresh impressions from extensive travel in Poland and Romania, *Der tog* had little need for such material, as staff writers Shmuel Niger and Joseph Opatoshu had been in Poland at the same time. Instead, *Der tog* published long pieces from Botoshansky about Buenos Aires and Rio de Janeiro, in effect confirming the status of Argentina and all of South America as a repository of exciting and therefore publishable material.[13] In this light, Botoshansky's later 'Fayerland' may be seen as both a symptom of and a conscious attempt to satisfy a metropolitan desire for distant unfamiliar regions. In the medium of print, the Yiddish language and, vicariously, the Yiddish reader are endowed with the agency of exploration and conquest.

Antecedents of such a worldly appetite on the part of a Yiddish readership may include the early nineteenth-century Yiddish adaptations of Joachim Heinrich Campe's *Entdeckung von Amerika*, a late eighteenth-century retelling of the deeds of the Spanish conquistadors for young adults, or Daniel Defoe's *Robinson Crusoe*, or even the many works of Jules Verne adapted from the late nineteenth century up to the early 1930s in both Warsaw and New York. Such adaptations underscore the basic fact that most Yiddish readers and writers had not only come of age in empire — whether Russian or Austro-Hungarian — but lived in an increasingly colonized world often shrouded in the romance of European exploration and conquest. When Jewish mass migration out of Eastern Europe in the late nineteenth and early twentieth centuries occasioned the arrival of Yiddish writers, as migrants or tourists, to destinations throughout the world, it is possible that their experience itself was already underwritten by the imagination of European expansion old and new.

Less speculative are the intimate ties between Yiddish literature and the many shades and textures of Jewish territorialism that had developed by the early twentieth century. The various strands of Zionism that looked to Ottoman and Mandate Palestine are only the most conspicuous examples. Also well documented are the efforts of the Paris-based philanthropic Jewish Colonization Association, which arranged agricultural colonies for Eastern European Jews in Argentina, Brazil, Canada, and Ottoman Anatolia. Similar Jewish agricultural colonies were established in the Kherson Governorate and elsewhere in the Russian Empire, while in the Soviet Union Stalin designated a Jewish autonomous region (Birobidzhan) along the border with China's Amur province. No less significant are the various failed diplomatic projects of establishing a Jewish territory in locations as varied as Madagascar and Suriname.[14]

Every facet of Yiddish print culture was saturated with debate, speculation, and reportage about real and projected territorial projects, which would become increasingly thematized and figured in literary production. By the 1890s, territory and territorialism were already recurring themes in the Yiddish press, and only became more pronounced throughout the interwar period. Somewhere between the fragmentary reality, alluring possibility, and acute lack of Jewish territory, an expansionist imagination emerged in Yiddish literary discourse, echoing the colonial models that informed Jewish territorialism in theory and practice.

The most explicit evidence of this influence is to be found in the critical vocabulary introduced by the critic Borekh Rivkin in his *Grunt-tendentsn fun der yidisher literatur in Amerike* [Basic Tendencies of Yiddish Literature in America].[15] With this work, Rivkin sought to reconcile the seeming abnormality of the Jews as a nation in material terms — lack of a state and national economy — with the existence of an apparently normal and even robust national, Yiddish literature. Blending Herderian and materialist sensibilities, he wondered how, if all other national literatures are based on a territorially grounded economy, could Yiddish literature so closely resemble them? To answer this question, Rivkin devised a theory of Yiddish literature as a technology that, through a material–spiritual dialectic, compensated for the absence of real Jewish national territory with *kmoy-teritorye* (quasi-territory): the same firm ethereal footing that religion had once afforded Jews on real ground. For Rivkin, the postulation of modern Yiddish literature's homologous relation to territory necessarily implied a quasi-colonial tendency toward expansion, an inexhaustible drive to accumulate more territory. His account of the development of Yiddish literature is thus a history of virtual territorial conquest, beginning with Eastern Europe and reaching the US.

Yankev Botoshansky may be seen as carrying this conquest southward to claim new territory for Yiddish literature: not in the sense that Rivkin proposed, as a means of orienting the subjects of the multimillenary *klal-yisroel* (Congregation of Israel) in the world, but instead for sale and ephemeral mass consumption. Thus, with my appropriation of Rivkin's *kmoy*-conquest, I name a fanciful subjugation driven not by the vital national force of Yiddish literature he imagined, but by a literary mass market centred in New York and Warsaw. And it was during Botoshansky's first stay in New York in the summer of 1931 that he conceived of and wrote a novel entitled *Buenos Ayres* for *Der tog*, where it was serialized from October 1931 to January 1932.

In the minds of most Yiddish readers of the time, Buenos Aires was little more than a metonym for the notorious Jewish 'white slave trade', which obtained mythic proportions thanks to the exaggerations of both the international press and European morality crusaders.[16] This sensational journalistic fodder is exactly the stuff of Botoshansky's sensational newspaper novel, which depicts the plight of young Jewish men and women ensnared in a sprawling transnational criminal net that leads them inevitably to the Argentine capital. At the same time, the novel depicts the plight of the Jewish pimps, or *rufianes*, of Buenos Aires as they are pursued by self-styled *erlekhe yidn* (upstanding Jews), as well as by the federal police, until they are finally ousted. With this double movement, *Buenos Ayres* at once allows readers to indulge in a lurid fantasy of the eponymous city and moralistically divides a tainted past from a redeemed present.

In a way, this novel is akin to Botoshansky's 'Fayerland' narrative. Although it does not share the same rhetorical trappings of exploration and discovery, it lays before the reader an eminently consumable version of Argentina. The novel takes great lengths to domesticate for a normative — foreign — Yiddish audience not only the city of Buenos Aires but a wide range of unfamiliar, 'exotic' phenomena. These include the rugged pampas or steppes of Argentina and their customs, the dark skin and ostensible backwardness of indigenous Argentines in the provinces, the particular Spanish and Yiddish spoken in Argentina — and also the very real, protracted conflict between Jewish pimps and moralists that reached its spectacular denouement in a 1930 legal campaign. The necessary conditions for the creation of such a novel, flagrantly distasteful to a local Argentine audience for which any mention of the reviled *tmeim* (tainted ones) was anathema, went far beyond a mere spirit of exploitation on the part of Botoshansky.[17] Necessary too was the colonial exuberance of the popular Yiddish press in the US and Poland, which demanded and rewarded the production, in novel form, of a consumable world extending as far and wide as the aspiring novelist's eye could see.[18]

As evidenced by Yiddish daily papers from New York, Warsaw, and Buenos Aires, Yiddish readers the world over received and fervently consumed a steady diet of other places. This is true not only with respect to the preponderance of news stories or special articles about Jewish life in diverse locations on various continents, or the widely reprinted travel writings of leading literary figures, but also with respect to the serialized novels that appeared in virtually every Yiddish paper.[19] Botoshansky's novel too was part and parcel of the robust literary economy at work in the global Yiddish press, which commoditized places familiar and foreign in narrative form and put them into circulation. Although much of the novel is set in Buenos Aires and to some extent in the Argentine interior, *Buenos Ayres* takes as its setting a much greater swathe of the world as events unfold from the first years of the new century until 1930. Roughly one third of the novel's 110 daily instalments are set outside of Argentina, aboard several ships and in locations as diverse as Rio de Janeiro, Paris, the Romanian town of Piatra Neamţ, Constantinople, and a Romanian Jewish agricultural colony in Anatolia. Botoshansky's variously intimate and more superficial knowledge of these places allows him to sketch a grand panoramic view that invites readers to join in the act of surveying space as the novel's events unfold.

In contrast to this expansive sense of space, the narrative of *Buenos Ayres* itself emphasizes frequent obstacles to mobility — above all for women, whose mobility is almost exclusively determined by men. The greatest degree of mobility goes to the pimps who ferry both willing and unwitting Jewish women from Eastern Europe to Buenos Aires; they have the means to travel, bribe officials, and forge the migration documents without which their Jewish collaborators and victims would be stranded within Russian or Romanian borders. The movements of the novel's anti-hero, the reluctant pimp and seducer Itsik, are wide-ranging but circumscribed by the debt he owes to his bosses. His first victim and love interest, Feygele, is confined shortly after her arrival to Buenos Aires, and is subsequently forced to move from brothel to brothel in small towns throughout the provinces. Back in Constantinople, Itsik's abandoned wife and daughter gain mobility through a new marriage, then wartime deportation and another marriage. The Polish prostitute Janet circulates through the seedy leisure spaces of Buenos Aires only in the company of Itsik, her *khosn* (protector). Such examples of restricted or qualified movement continue to multiply: even in a story within a newspaper within the novel — itself within a real newspaper — we read of a psychically distressed and sexually frustrated Jewish immigrant to Buenos Aires confined to the shop she must tend daily as her husband freely moves about the city.

This profusion of examples reflects a pervasive gendered social hierarchy spanning Jewish Eastern Europe, Ottoman lands, France, and Argentina, a hierarchy of which *Buenos Ayres* offers a limited critique. At an exteriorized extreme, this hierarchy manifests itself in a scene of brutal sexual violence when a defiant Feygele initially refuses to submit to a life of prostitution. Responsibility for this violence is displaced from the Jewish pimps onto their henchman, an indigenous Argentine behemoth whose dehumanization is transparently disclosed in his name: El Tigre (The Tiger). At an interiorized extreme, the immigrant shopkeeper burns with pathological, sinful desire as a result of her socially and economically mandated confinement to the private sphere — a consequence of the confused logic of Argentina's Catholic morality, according to one of Botoshansky's characters. Both ill-conceived morality and 'inhuman' immorality seem to collude, then, in an all-encompassing logic of women's subjugation and confinement.

The status of this logic as a social ill, however, is secondary to its function as a motor of Botoshansky's expansive narrative. Feygele's initial confinement in a pimp's mansion in Buenos Aires is drawn out across several chapters, and the prolonged physical struggle leading to her rape alone spans two chapters. The narrative weaves in and out between scenes of Feygele's confinement and scenes of her family in Romania as they anxiously await her next letter, thus dramatizing the distance between them. This effect is heightened as Feygele attempts to enlist help in sneaking out a letter as her parents across the ocean bicker about the precise number of days it should take the next letter to reach them. Their concern eventually sets off a new epistolary chain, from a rabbi in Romania to a rabbi in Warsaw to a Jewish institution in Buenos Aires and back, prompting Feygele's father to travel to Buenos Aires in an unsuccessful bid to find her, a process that requires him to negotiate the legal implications of his non-citizen status as a Romanian Jew. In this way, Feygele's confinement to a single room mobilizes the dramatic potential of transatlantic distance and sustains a parallel plot predicated on wider Jewish communication networks and the pragmatics of Jewish travel.

In addition to performing a crucial narrative function, Feygele's confinement is unambiguously a lurid spectacle, both in its initial violent form at the pimp's mansion in Buenos Aires and in subsequent passages depicting her life among indigenous prostitutes at a brothel in the Argentine interior. But perhaps the greatest sense of spectacle in *Buenos Ayres* is to be found in another scene of confinement where Botoshansky shows his long-standing penchant for the grotesque. During the height of a legal campaign against the pimps of Buenos Aires, we encounter a historical figure, the police chief Julio Alsogaray, at his precinct.[20] He has rounded up hundreds of Jewish prostitutes, hopeful that they will aid the investigation by denouncing their supposed exploiters, and addresses them in the precinct's courtyard. Their refusal to cooperate, combined with their jeers, enrages Alsogaray, who does not allow the prostitutes to leave. Thus begins a bizarre, almost naturalistic cycle that continues for several days and nights: the prostitutes cry, their make-up runs, they wash with a hose and reapply it, they grow cold at night, hungry, they grow hot in the day, their make-up runs, again to be rinsed away and reapplied. All the while they sing and moan and pray, unnerving Alsogaray with their strange cacophony. He relents and they go free.

This scene, at once carnivalesque and affecting in its depiction of dehumanizing cruelty, serves as little more than a demonstrative embellishment or diversion with regard to the narrative as a whole. In fact, it may be considered a narrative by-product of yet another scene of confinement in that it forms part of an extended journalistic montage that coincides with and mimics Itsik's obsessive reading of the Yiddish newspapers of Buenos Aires during a decade of imprisonment. Together with a Botoshansky-like writer friend and Alsogaray, Itsik had located Feygele in a provincial brothel and returned her to Buenos Aires, in the process being convicted for his initial role in trafficking her. His feverish reading in jail provides the occasion for a whole series of disclosures that summarize and sometimes reproduce the contents of Yiddish newspapers in a timeframe roughly corresponding to the 1920s. Prominently featured here are two historically rooted campaigns against the Jewish pimps of Buenos Aires: first on the part of the broader Jewish community, aimed at expelling pimps from their prominent role as financiers and privileged clients of the Yiddish theatre, and second on the part of the federal police.

This police campaign continues once Itsik is released from prison, living the life of a penitent, newly pious newspaper- and cigarette-vendor. His long time tormentor, the pimp kingpin of Jewish Buenos Aires, Mordkhe Gazlen (a name akin to 'Morty Thug'), is in hiding, unable to leave his diminutive room in a boarding house, or even to move freely, lest the other residents learn of his presence. At a rare opportunity to converse with his collaborator, the landlord, Gazlen reflects on the good old days at the close of the nineteenth century, when he and others of his trade were among the first Jews in an almost provincial Buenos Aires, urban pioneers in a country where most Jewish immigrants were destined for agricultural colonies and shunned the pimps who welcomed them upon arrival. His recollection stretches even further back, to the even broader open space of his childhood, when he accompanied his father, a horse thief, on jobs across the Polish border. Once again, the situation of confinement summons up an inverse sense of expansiveness.

The ways in which male and female characters are subjected to confinement over the course of *Buenos Ayres* are decidedly unequal. Itsik's and Gazlen's loss of agential mobility occurs primarily in relation to a legal framework — in the form of imprisonment or threat of imprisonment. While their confinement is presented in terms of deprivation and personal suffering, each nevertheless adopts an expansive sense of vision through memory and through the window of the newspaper. Feygele, the shopkeeper, and the prostitutes in Alsogaray's custody, in contrast, are defined by the intensity and totality of their confinement, coloured by different shades of indignity. Although each can conceive of escape, and some situations occasion a broadening of the narrative perspective, confinement itself is what fills the scope of the characters' vision and what is on view for the reader.

Despite this disparity, however, each instance of confinement feeds into the novel's broader representational logic by making visible a constitutive openness, mobility, or distance.

The perspectival expansion and contraction on display in the examples discussed above may be considered more broadly as the narrative strategy by which Botoshansky converts Buenos Aires into *Buenos Ayres*, ensnaring the city that in turn ensnares his characters. The symbolic conquest he enacts operates by assimilating both characters and places themselves into an order of novelistic capture. A condensation of Buenos Aires into the city of the Jewish sex trade — and, at its most inclusive, also the city of that trade's opponents — creates the narrative possibility, if not necessity, of reaching beyond those narrow limits across continents and oceans. Paris and Constantinople are similarly subject to a claustrophobic depiction that accentuates a sense of liberating mobility when the narrative eventually delivers the reader from their confines. A certain figure of the author becomes perceptible in the ceaseless interplay between a constricted and expansive sense of space: the savvy international traveller who may mould the spaces he has traversed into a marketworthy product.

Just months after *Buenos Ayres* had finished printing, Botoshansky would compare himself to the single most successful exponent of this kind of popular newspaper novel in a bid to have a second work published in *Der tog*. In a letter to the chief editor, Samuel Margoshes, he presents the following parallelism: 'Sholem Ash [hot]: *Peterbarg, Varshe*, un ikh — *B. Ayres, Rio de Zhaneyro*' [Sholem Asch [has]: *Petersburg, Warsaw*, and I — *B. Aires, Rio de Janeiro*].[21] The reference is to the first two works in what would become the immensely popular urban trilogy of the author Sholem Asch (1880–1957), a sweeping depiction of events leading up to the 1917 revolution. *Rio de Janeiro* was not ultimately accepted by *Der tog*, but the parallel is instructive insofar as it makes explicit that Botoshansky was following a script, even if he fell far short of Asch's stature. This script entailed, first, a recipe for novelistic success: an epic stretch of time and space plus sensational melodrama and morality. Second, it entailed the posture of the worldly author.

Botoshansky's approximations of such an authorial posture in both *Buenos Ayres* and in 'Fayerland' are unmistakably inflected with a fantasy of domination over space, an enactment of *kmoy*-conquest that is underwritten both ideologically and performatively by the model of European colonial masculinity. If there is any doubt that the implicit (*Buenos Ayres*) or explicit ('Fayerland') seeing authorial subject of these texts inhabits such a masculine discourse, one need only refer to the gendered disparity of vision among the confined characters of *Buenos Ayres*. Although the texts examined here are relatively marginal with respect to main currents of modern Yiddish literature, and in their own time would have gained only a fleeting visibility, they are symptomatic of a more pervasive colonial imaginary that accompanied this literature's geographic spread and informed new regimes of writing, criticism, editorial practice, and consumption. More extravagant expressions of this imaginary than Botoshansky's are to be found.[22] However, the fullest significance of this phenomenon will not be understood by assembling a gallery of easily identifiable extremes, but rather by moving toward a more nuanced account of the authorial and editorial logics that accompanied a distinctly global strand in the practice and conception of Yiddish literary culture.

Notes to Chapter 11

1. Yankev Botoshansky, 'Fayerland (rayze ayndrukn)', *Literarishe bleter*, 16 (21 April 1933), 11–12.
2. Botoshansky (1895–1964) resided in Buenos Aires from 1926, where he served as co-editor and eventually chief editor of the progressive Yiddish daily *Di prese* [The Press].
3. Benjamin the Third is the protagonist of a satirical 1878 Yiddish quest narrative in the manner of Cervantes, set in the Jewish Pale of Settlement.
4. The essay printed in *Literarishe bleter* in fact belongs to a larger series of Patagonian travel impressions published in the Buenos Aires Yiddish daily *Di prese*, of which Botoshansky was a co-editor. Following an announcement of Botoshansky's departure from Buenos Aires on 15 February 1933, readers of *Di prese* could vicariously join the journalist on his two-week tour, recounted over the course of at least fifteen instalments. This series as a whole may be productively understood in relation to the history of Patagonian travel writing in English and Spanish. However, the present discussion regards 'Fayerland' as an isolated text, from the vantage point of its second publication in Warsaw.
5. A Yiddish adaptation of a book-length account of one such expedition appeared in *Di prese* of Buenos Aires in the 1920s. Botoshansky explicitly references both Darwin and Magellan in the larger travelogue described in n. 4 above.
6. David Frishman (1855–1922) was a significant writer, poet, and translator in modern Hebrew and Yiddish literature. The Imatra Rapids are located near the Russian border north-west of St Petersburg, and even in Frishman's time had long attracted Russian tourists.
7. Botoshansky, 'Fayerland', p. 12.
8. Yankev Botoshansky, 'Azoy ze ikh zikh aleyn', in *Yankev Botoshansky: Tsu zayne zekhtsik yor*, ed. by Yitskhok Yanusovitsh and Shloyme Suskovitsh (Buenos Aires: Oysgegebn durkh a grupe khaveyrim, 1955), pp. 7–14; Yankev Botoshansky, 'Vi ikh ze zikh', in Yankev Botoshansky, *Di kenigin fun Dorem Amerike* (Buenos Aires: Comite pro homenaje de J. Botosansky, 1962), pp. 75–83.
9. The idea of a physical and temperamental affinity between Romani people and the Bessarabian and Romanian Jews who often lived in close contact with them was a commonplace among the Jews of Eastern Europe. Like the poet Itsik Manger and other writers, Botoshansky embraced this predominantly negative ethnic stereotype by identifying with the romanticized figure of 'the gypsy' prevalent in Yiddish and other literatures. His birthplace, Chilia (now Kiliya, Ukraine) is located on the northern bank of a branch of the Danube that once formed a border between Romania and the Russian Empire. The town has at various moments been subject to Moldavian, Ottoman, Russian, Romanian, and Ukrainian rule.
10. In 1926, Botoshansky used his position at *Di prese* as a pulpit to denounce and decry the influence Jewish pimps exerted over the Yiddish theatre in Buenos Aires as its benefactors and favoured clientele, and simultaneously to promote a campaign for a 'pure' popular theatre. Several years later, when an Argentine federal judge initiated an expansive legal campaign against members of a mutual aid association for Jewish pimps, Botoshansky and *Di prese* were once again vocal participants in a project of 'purification'.
11. Botoshansky, 'Azoy ze ikh zikh aleyn', p. 12.
12. Samual Margoshes (1887–1968) served from 1926 to 1942 as chief editor of *Der tog* [The Day], a New York Yiddish daily modelled after the *New York Times*. Nakhmen Mayzel (1887–1966) played several significant editorial roles in the Yiddish literary circles of Warsaw, and was the sole editor of the *Literarishe bleter* from 1925 to 1939, all but the first year of its publication.
13. The single exception was a piece Botoshansky had written about the Polish town of Chelm, famed in Yiddish lore and literature as a town of fools.
14. These and other bids for a Jewish territory are examined in Adam Rovner, *In the Shadow of Zion: Promised Lands Before Israel* (New York and London: New York University Press, 2014).

15. Rivkin (1883–1945) became an influential critic, principally based in New York after arriving in the US via London in 1911. This major study was first printed in two parts in 1937 and 1938 in the literary anthology *Zamlbikher*, edited by H. Leivick and Joseph Opatoshu, and appeared posthumously in book form: Borekh Rivkin, *Grunt-tendentsn fund der yidisher literatur in Amerike* (New York: IKUF, 1948).
16. On this phenomenon in general, see Paul Knepper, 'International Criminals: The League of Nations, the Traffic in Women and the Press', *Media History*, 20.4 (2014), 400–15. On the case of the Polish Yiddish press, see Mariusz Kalczewiak, 'Buenos Aires Seen from Warsaw: Poland's Yiddish Press Reporting on Jewish Life in Argentina', *Studia Judaica*, 17 (2014), 85–107.
17. One disgruntled commentator in Buenos Aires went so far as to denounce the novel on the basis largely of its title and the fact of its foreign publication. A Buenos Aires novel directed at foreign readers, reasoned Y. L. Gruzman, editor of the weekly *Der shpigl* [The Mirror], could only be scandalous ('Vi azoy un ver se informirt vegn argentiner yidishn kultur-lebn', *Der shpigl*, 155 (1932), 12).
18. The role of the Polish mass market for Yiddish literature is significant in that the novel was pirated from *Der tog* by provincial Yiddish dailies in Grodno and Białystok.
19. An assessment of the importance of the daily press for Yiddish literature is offered in Nathan Cohen, 'The Yiddish Press and Yiddish Literature: A Fertile But Complex Relationship', *Modern Judaism*, 28.2 (2009), 149–72.
20. Alsogaray did in fact play a substantial role in this legal campaign, and wrote a book about it.
21. Letter from Yankev Botoshansky to Dr S. Margoshes, 2 July 1932. New York, Institute for Jewish Research (YIVO), archive of *Der tog — Morgn-zhurnal*, box 30, folder 273.
22. A near-caricature of European colonial masculinity can be found in another migrant to Argentina: the hard-bodied, gun-toting Poalei Zionist adventurer Marcus Paryszewski, whose barely plausible travel accounts of Andean and Central America in the 1920s were authenticated, for Botoshansky, by his powerful handshake.

CHAPTER 12

❖

The 'Bathroom Crisis' in the Shtetl: Transgender Identity and Homoerotic Anxiety in Isaac Bashevis Singer

Alexandra Tali Herzog

It is impossible, as I write this in 2017, to watch the news without hearing about the 'bathroom crisis', which is shaking the US perception of gender binaries and the rights of minority groups. In this new controversy, the prospect of transgender women using women's restrooms is threatening the whole gender system, creating a forceful debate in the media. State legislatures are being flooded with proposed measures to deny transgender people access to restrooms and facilities that accord with what they consider their authentic gender identity, and to compel them instead to use the restrooms matching the sex assigned to them at birth — a gender they consider inaccurate. These bills screaming 'no men in women's restrooms' deny transgender people their identity, open up a debate about what femininity and masculinity entail, and create anxiety about sexual orientation, threatening heterosexuality and heteronormativity at once. By claiming that transgender women are essentially men, the supporters of these bills imply that they will lust over women's bodies and prey on young girls. The blurring of lines evinced by this line of argument is the primary reason we currently have a 'bathroom crisis' in the first place.

This crisis is certainly not new, and the enclosed space of the bathroom suddenly symbolizes the microcosmic representation of the entire structure of our society. It becomes a prime space where gender is being performed. In Jewish culture, the existence of transgender individuals was never repudiated or even hidden. As the literature of the Yiddish writer and Nobel Prize winner Isaac Bashevis Singer (1904–91) reveals, the existence of trans people was not an abnormality but rather a reality of life.

My argument is that Isaac Bashevis Singer writes with an exceptional and startling openness that stems from his deep engagement with Talmudic thought, which recognizes seven genders, suggesting an acceptance of gender fluidity. However, his use of gender and sexuality is complex and fraught with moments of resistance regarding same-sex relations. Through the analysis of three short stories ('Two',[1] 'Androgynous',[2] and 'Yentl the Yeshiva Boy'[3]), I investigate Bashevis's treatment of cross-dressing and transgender characters and his queer representation of gender performance and sexual identity. In ways that anticipate the 'bathroom crisis', Bashevis recognizes the existence of cross-dressing and transgender individuals as long as they do not threaten the heterosexual structure of society by drawing attention to homoeroticism and homosexual relationships. This paper demonstrates that Bashevis's short stories blur the sexual orientation of the characters along with their gender identity, which comprises the biological, social, sexual, and intellectual aspects of gender. While Bashevis is at ease writing about transgender identity, androgyny, and cross-dressing, anchoring his thoughts in a Talmudic tradition that permitted them, he expresses real anxiety when it comes to same-sex relationships.

One of the short stories ('Two') analysed in this paper focuses on the act of cross-dressing, which licenses the characters to engage in their homosexual relationship more easily. In this narrative, the main characters are not necessarily androgynous or transgender, but they rather cross-dress in order to live with their same-sex partner more freely. In contrast, the other two stories ('Androgynous' and 'Yentl the Yeshiva Boy') really investigate the deeper internal phenomenon happening to characters whose soul does not match their body, illustrating the difficult conflict of a preferred gender that does not match the gender at birth. In the case of Yentl, this true androgyny provokes some complications in the plot in terms of sexual preference and homoeroticism. Bashevis leaves the story with an open-ended conclusion in which Yentl leaves the town where she resides and most likely starts her new life as the male scholar she has always wanted to be. The story is not necessarily liberating, as Yentl disappears from the narrative altogether. Like Yentl, Shevach, the main character of 'Androgyny', also possesses hermaphroditic physical features. However, unlike any of the other short stories discussed in this paper, this does not end in death or misery. Interestingly, it is also the only story that does not portray homoeroticism or homosexuality. Even though Shevach is clearly androgynous, she does not express any sexual preferences and remains asexual throughout the story. It is thus not coincidental that Bashevis allows her to live freely in the narrative: she does not represent a threat to the heteronormative system of society.

The Talmud and Its Seven Genders

To see what Bashevis is building upon, it is necessary to turn back to traditional Yiddish literature and to Talmudic thought. Rabbi Alana Suskin contends that the Talmudic rabbis may have recognized seven genders: male, female, *androgynos* (a hermaphrodite[4] or someone with both male and female genitalia),[5] *tumtum* (someone whose gender cannot be determined),[6] *aylonit* ('a female who fails to produce signs of female maturity by the age of twenty'), *saris khama* (a eunuch sterile from birth), and *saris adam* (a castrated eunuch).[7] These classifications are taken directly from the Talmud and shake the sex/gender system as a whole, expressing subtleties that do not exist, even linguistically, in English. The two most prominent concepts in Bashevis's writing are the *tumtum* and the *androgynos*, and one should note that many of his characters would be called 'transgender' in contemporary terms because their gender identity does not match their assigned sex. What we would now consider 'transgender' is described by Bashevis as 'androgynous'. His characters that meet this description do not fit into clear gender categories; they exist freely and are not threatening.

In the original Yiddish of the short story 'Andruginus' [Androgynous] (1975), for example, Bashevis writes that the main character, Shevach, is 'a tumtum oder an andruginus' [a *tumtum* or an androgyne].[8] Sherman's translation describes him simply as a eunuch, blurring the depth of the gender confusion that Bashevis indicates in the Yiddish. It is important to note that the rabbinic scholars dealing with these Talmudic categories were not shocked by these classifications, but that they were instead concerned about the practicality of categorizing them. In Jewish faith, only men are required to observe the commandments of putting on a prayer shawl or wearing phylacteries. It was therefore critical for the rabbis to categorize these individuals as either male or female in order to determine whether they had to follow the commandments prescribed for men.

Additionally, the concept of androgyny and having both male and female features are essential components of Jewish mystical literature. In his introduction to *The Holy Letter: A Study in Jewish Sexual Morality*, for example, Seymour Cohen explains that the contemporary Rabbi Adin Steinsaltz 'speaks about Eve [as] the missing half. The Talmud and the Kabbalah literature are filled with references that Adam and Eve were originally one person with two sides, one male and the other female.'[9] For Steinsaltz, Adam and Eve thus 'try to restore the status of old' where

> male and female are essentially part of a single whole. And though two bodies were separated, the two half-bodies are in constant search for each other. There will never be complete fulfilment until the male and the female are re-joined in a new unity.[10]

Moreover, as Seymour Cohen mentions, the two aspects of the body in the Kabbalistic work *Shiur Qomah* are composed of both male and female (*Shiur* is male and *Qomah* is female): 'The two half-bodies (*du-parzufim*) were also known as androgynes.'[11] Even though Bashevis does not write about the biological aspect of gender, he plays with gender performance. In that respect, it is not so much that his characters have the genitalia of the two genders that matters, but rather that for him this supposed confusion leads to queer relationships.

Defining 'Queer' Identity

This paper refers to many of Bashevis's short stories as well as characters as queer. My use of 'queer theory' or 'queer' in general aligns itself with that of Daniel Boyarin. I do not use 'queer' simply to refer to a gay or homosexual practice, but rather to signify any sexual practice that 'puts into question any praxis, theoretical or political, of the "natural" in sexuality'.[12] What I am interested in are the deviations from the conjugal heterosexual act. Bashevis uses the Talmudic definitions of gender categories and does not consider same-sex attraction unusual.

For him, the world of the Yeshiva scholars is a homoerotic space; however, while he does not condemn gender fluidity, he does not encourage gay sex and punishes his gay characters by killing them at the end of his short stories. Michael Satlow argues that same-sex attraction was not unusual: 'The rabbis [of the Talmudic period] considered male sexual attraction to other males to be unexceptional.'[13] Moreover, according to Satlow, 'no evidence suggests that the rabbis defined people by the gender of the object of their sexual desire'.[14] My use of the gender/sex system also stems from Judith Butler's theories of performance and gender roles. For Butler, gender does not exist objectively: 'Gender reality is performative which means, quite simply, that it is real only to the extent that it is performed.'[15] Butler argues that gender is socially constructed and subject to change: the body becomes its gender only 'through a series of acts which are renewed, revised, and consolidated through time'.[16]

'Two': Cross-Dressing and Homosexuality

'Two' tells the story of an effeminate man called Zissel who falls in love with his study partner, Ezriel. Both men, who are married to women, obtain divorces, and they run off together. In their new town, Zissel dresses as a woman and pretends to be Ezriel's wife. Zissa, as she is now called, is offered a job as an attendant in the bathhouse. Their lives mimic those of a heterosexual couple until Zissa inexplicably feels attracted to a young maiden called Reizl. Following this moment of lust, Zissa tries to seduce Reizl, and both women fall into the waters and drown. Realizing that Zissa is not biologically a woman, the townspeople are enraged and kill Ezriel in retaliation. Both Ezriel and Zissel are then buried in an anonymous grave outside the town. It is evident that sexual orientation plays a decisive role in the ending of this story, which reveals a certain level of anxiety on Bashevis's part.

From the beginning of the story, Bashevis plays with queer identity by explaining that Zissel's father, Yomtov, was effeminate and was 'drawn more to the matriarchs than to the patriarchs'.[17] As it is written, he enjoyed women's texts like the *Ze'enah u-Re'enah* rather than men's literature such as the commentaries, and he 'wore silk dressing gowns and slippers with pom-poms'.[18] The narrator goes a step further by pointing out that Yomtov's feminine side was noticed by everyone in the town: 'You're a soft, Yomtov! Worse than a woman.'[19] And with irony, the text points out that Yomtov wanted a baby girl, but got a boy, even though the midwife had announced the wrong gender at birth:

> The midwife made a mistake and announced to the mother that the baby was a girl, but she soon acknowledged her mistake. Menuha grew terribly upset that between a yes and a no a daughter had turned into a son. Yomtov couldn't bring himself to believe it and demanded to be shown. [...] Since his gowns, jackets, and bonnets had already been prepared, the infant was dressed in them, and when the mother carried Zissel in the street, strangers assumed he was a girl.[20]

In this comedic scene, Bashevis plays with the gender identity of his main character, Zissel, by pointing to not only a kind of biological transmission of gender behaviour through an effeminate father, but also a social reinforcement of gender through feminine clothing and naming. Bashevis does not here describe a biological androgyny, but rather a confusion of genders passed from one generation to the other, as if gender preferences could somehow be transmitted through genes. Not only does the midwife make a mistake by calling Zissel a girl, but his very name is also androgynous. Indeed, Zissel (which is a name 'for both a man and a woman')[21] is named after his great-aunt. Bashevis clearly implies in the story that gender is a social construct as well. The narration explains that Zissel 'spent most of his time with girls and enjoyed their ways and their games', asking his mother: 'Why can't I be a girl?'.[22] He follows in his father's footsteps and becomes a 'girlish boy' who, when no one is looking, puts on 'his mother's dress, her high-heeled shoes, camisole, and bonnet'.[23] Other schoolboys mock him, calling him a 'girl' and trying 'to lift the skirts of his gabardine as if he were really female'.[24] Between the other boys' attitude and his own gender predicament, Zissel becomes 'convinced that to be a male was unworthy and that the signs of manhood were a disgrace'.[25] He stares at women in envy and even tries to pierce his earlobe with a needle, 'dab[bing] his eyes with the edge of a kerchief, as women do'.[26] The comparison to women, once again, illustrates his highly feminine personality and his mimicking of women's gestures.

At the age of fifteen, Zissel marries a beautiful girl from another village, but 'he could not do what he knew he was supposed to', and when women in the morning came to inspect the sheets, 'they did not find what they were looking for'.[27] Similarly to Zissel, Ezriel also marries a woman and has an unsuccessful marriage. Writing to Zissel about it, he calls Zissel 'my beloved and the desire of my soul'[28] and declares his love for him. It is at this point that Zissel decides to run off with Ezriel, changes his name to Zissa, dresses as a woman, and passes as Ezriel's wife, becoming a virtuous and pious woman. When Zissa takes a job as a *mikveh* attendant, Ezriel suddenly begins to argue with him, implying that Zissel has 'accepted his masculinity'[29] by spending all this time with naked women in the bathhouse. In fact, Zissa experiences desire for a woman for the first time in his life as he attends to the beautiful virginal bride Reizl. His desire quickly turns into passion.[30] The most interesting aspect of this tale is that Bashevis plays with gender, using androgynous terms to describe his characters and arguing that their souls are of a different gender than their bodies.[31] Zissel dresses as a woman in order to love Ezriel more freely and because his gender has always been more feminine than masculine. However, the ending of the story, in which Zissel acts on his unexpected desire for a woman and thereby provokes the downfall of three characters, is confusing in this respect. The tale's ending refers to a board with an inscription from Samuel: 'Lovely and pleasant in their lives and in their deaths they were not divided.'[32] If for Bashevis gender identity is fluid, so too is sexuality, because Zissel is attracted to both men and women.[33] Zissel fits the rabbinic interpretation of 'androgynous' because his identity is 'confused' (to cite the actual Talmudic terms), even though he does not have both male and female genitalia. Because his parents have treated him as a female from birth, his biological gender is different from his socially constructed gender.

'Androgynous': 'The body is nothing more than a garment'

'Androgynous' (1975) tells the tale of Reb Mottele, who decides to marry an androgyne named Shevach who was rejected by her first husband, the scholar Leybele, when he found out she was not a woman at birth. The news of their wedding surprises the whole town. However, Shevach quickly becomes a rebbetzin, a rabbi's wife, and the keeper of Jewish commandments, playing with the fluid lines of gender categories. In her androgyny, Shevach straddles both female and male roles. The people of the town come to accept her, and after her husband's death, she carries on writing biblical analysis while living permanently as a man.

'Androgynous' is about men or women who have androgynous souls and do not fit into any gender category. The story treats androgyny as a complicated matter. In contrast to his approach in the other queer stories, Bashevis does not condemn Shevach's lifestyle because he finds justification for her actions in Talmudic precepts and because she remains within the realm of heteronormativity. On his wedding night, Leybele screams that his bride 'is not a woman!'.[34] The text explains that Shevach's body is then examined, and the conclusion reads as follows: 'This Shevach was an androgyne, half man, half woman, neither one thing nor the other.'[35] The narrator adds that 'only now did everyone remember that she had a masculine voice'.[36] Throughout the story, Bashevis explains and dissects the rules behind androgyny in the Talmud. The narrator inquires: 'In what way is an androgyne more a woman than a man? In the same way as the body possesses both genders, so does the soul. There are such things as twin souls.'[37] And in fact, as the narrator explains,

> it would seem that an androgyne can choose for himself what he wants to be, male or female. If he wants to be female, then he is relieved of performing the daily ritual duties demanded of men. If he takes manhood upon himself, then he takes on the obligation of fulfilling all six hundred and thirteen commandments. [...] It appears that not every androgyne is the same. In some, the male qualities are dominant; in others, the female. The kabbalah makes it clear that both male and female attributes are present in every human being.[38]

Again, this passage puts the onus on the rabbis to define whether the androgyne is male or female because of the religious commandments directed at men. It also illustrates that the Talmud in general does not treat this issue as unusual, assuming instead that every human being has attributes of both genders. Note that the Yiddish specifically uses the words 'an androginos ken aleyn oysklaybn vos er vil zayn, a zokher oder a nekeyve' [an androgyne alone can select what he wants to be, a male or a female].[39] The use of 'zokher' and 'nekeyve' refers to male and female genders and not simply to the binary of 'man' and 'woman'; in other words, the phrasing implies a physical choice and not simply a socially constructed role. Bashevis does not imply that androgynes should not have a place in this world. As long as they do not engage in homosexuality, Bashevis accepts their social existence. Shevach is the only queer character who does not die at the end of the story. Part of the reason may be that only her gender identity is unclear, not her sexual orientation.

When her first husband discovers her identity and inquires how she could trick him like that, she answers: 'I don't want to be a woman. I'm a man. [...] I've fooled only myself. I imagined [...] that perhaps if I married, it would help, but I see now that I'm lost.'[40] Towards the end of the story, Shevach begins to behave like a man and puts 'on ritual fringes. It was said that she secretly also put on phylacteries.'[41] At this point, she takes over the beadle's duties after he dies, but she also prepares stews and puddings. However, Bashevis complicates the story by having Shevach alternate between dressing up like a man and like a woman. Moreover, Reb Mottele, who has been a widower for years, unexpectedly declares that he wants to marry Shevach. The narrator explains that rumours promptly spring up in the town and people take sides right away. Some argue that 'Reb Mottele had simply surrendered himself to lust', while some others recognize that 'the whole core of that union was spirit, not flesh. The body is nothing more than a garment.'[42] In this passage, Bashevis privileges the soul over the body, arguing that the body is nothing more than a piece of clothing:

> When they are naming souls in the upper world and they call out 'so-and-so, the daughter of such and such', no body yet exists, not even in the womb. Not only that — what about the couplings in heaven? The books of the kabbalah are full of couplings — face-to-face, back-to-back — all of them mysteries of mysteries, secrets of secrets.[43]

Shevach becomes a celebrity in the community and has both the synagogue and the ritual bath rebuilt. Her role as the rabbi's wife extends to helping him transcribe and publish his words. She becomes a great scholar, and after his death she goes to Warsaw to have his books printed. To communicate with the Hasidic leaders, she dresses as a man. The narration adds that 'the prohibition against cross-dressing does not apply to an androgyne'.[44]

'Androgynous' explicitly uncovers Bashevis's interest in the question of gender performance and the way the Talmud treats sexuality and gender categories. The story is told from the perspective of a person who was young at the time of the events. It ends with the following remarks: 'there are certain lights that must remain hidden' and 'there are certain unions that have no need ever to couple. [...] The real truth is: The whole world is joy. In heaven, the whole year is one long festival.'[45] Bashevis points out the troubles of being an androgyne, but in saying that everything in the world to come is 'one long festival',[46] he refers to a certain confusion of boundaries or a reversal of norms. Here, he may be arguing in favour of the acceptance of difference. His story emphasizes that Shevach leads a holy life, or at least that in heaven the logistical problems she encounters on earth will not exist.

'Yentl the Yeshiva Boy'; or, Learning How to Share Bathrooms

Finally, 'Yentl the Yeshiva Boy' (1963), which is one of Bashevis's best-known short stories, complicates the entire gender/sex system. It tells the story of a young woman named Yentl who decides to dress as a man in order to study in a yeshiva in Eastern Europe. Calling herself Anshel, Yentl falls for her study partner, Avigdor, who is himself in love with the beautiful Hadass. Through complicated plot twists, Anshel is forced to marry Hadass before abandoning her to marry Avigdor. This story is particularly complex because Bashevis is ambiguous about Yentl/Anshel's sexual preferences. Indeed, she is attracted to both Avigdor and Hadass while crossdressing as a man.

As in 'Androgynous', Bashevis emphasizes the soul over the body, showing that physically Yentl does not look like a woman and does not fit into socially constructed gender categories. From the very beginning of the story, Yentl is said to be 'unlike any of the girls in Yanev — tall, thin, bony, with small breasts and narrow hips',[47] and she feels she has the 'soul of a man and the body of a woman'.[48] Yentl's physical appearance is even described as mannish: 'She looked like a dark, handsome young man.'[49] She does not follow the social conventions of her gender either. She does not want to get married, and worse, she dislikes women's tasks:

> But Yentl didn't want to get married. [...] Yentl knew she wasn't cut out for a woman's life. She couldn't sew, she couldn't knit. She let the food burn and the milk boil over; her Sabbath pudding never turned out right, and her challah dough didn't rise. Yentl much preferred men's activities to women's.[50]

For Yentl, a woman's life is mere drudgery, and marriage represents a frightening entrapment that places a woman without education in a miserable condition if the marriage ends. Besides, Yentl does not possess all the skills that are usually required from a girl of her milieu: she does not know how to sew or knit, let alone cook. Miriam Heman Maltz argues that 'the very title, "Yentl the Yeshiva Boy", is an oxymoron, with its opposing feminine–masculine referents yoked together in a conjunction of apparent contradictions'.[51] And indeed, throughout the short story, Bashevis plays with pronouns and confuses Yentl's gender identity. 'Yentl' is the feminine name given to the main character; however, she is defined as 'the Yeshiva Boy', which is clearly masculine. Even though she does not possess the biological features of both sexes, she is hard to categorize and hence fits into the category of the androgyne as defined by the Talmud. When her father tells her she has the soul of a man, she wonders why it is trapped in a woman's body. Surprisingly, Lillian Schanfield argues against the idea that the story talks about androgyny because 'the union of Yentl and Anshel produces a state of unresolvable disharmony, not androgynous harmony'.[52] Although it is unclear what 'androgynous harmony' means, it seems clear that the representation of Yentl in the story does, in fact, fit the Talmudic explanation of androgyny. Bashevis uses the same words to describe Yentl/Anshel in 'Yentl' and Shevach in 'Androgynous': Yentl/Anshel tells Avigdor that 'kh'bin shoyn nish-ahin un nish-aher' [I'm neither one nor the other],[53] and in 'Androgynous' Shevach is said to be 'nisht ahin, nisht aher' [neither one nor the other].[54] This position, according to which Yentl is an androgyne or a character who does not fit into her given biological category, has become more widely accepted in recent years.[55]

The other explanation for Yentl's non-normative gender identity is certainly the education she receives from her father, which sets her apart from other girls. Indeed, the only goal Yentl really cares about is becoming erudite because of all the stories about the men of letters she has heard from her father:

> No, she had not been created for the noodle board and the pudding dish, for chattering with silly women and pushing for a place at the butcher's block. Her father had told her so many tales of Yeshivas, rabbis, men of letters! Her head was full of Talmudic disputations, questions and answers, learned phrases.[56]

This passage expresses the excitement with which Yentl imagines the life of a student. She sees a real separation between women's and men's worlds: women cook, take care of the household, and do 'silly' things, in contrast to men, who dwell in the highest intellectual sphere.

Bashevis often equates the acquisition of knowledge with masculinity and emphasizes that, behind mannish women, there are often men who pass on their masculine knowledge. In a discussion of educated girls in *Isaac Bashevis Singer and the Eternal Past*, Irving Buchen argues that 'all these young girls have scholarly or rabbinical fathers who do not just pass on their knowledge but like dybbuks appear to deposit their natures in the souls of their daughters'.[57] Here, Buchen suggests that a woman with access to knowledge necessarily strives to become what she is not supposed to be according to Orthodox laws. Yet, paradoxically, a setting in which education is highly valued gives a woman many chances to be tempted to pursue knowledge. Indeed, if all the men of a household study to become wise and learned, why would the women not want to follow their path? Many of Bashevis's stories point out this paradox, but they also illustrate the pain inflicted by this lifestyle. There is an interesting parallel between mothers who dress their sons as girls and fathers who teach their daughters Talmud: the parents in both cases defy conventional norms.

In his interview with his biographer Paul Kresh, Bashevis claimed that he left the story of Yentl ambiguous and did not want to deal with Yentl's sexual orientation. However, the Yiddish text presents Hadass and Anshel's wedding night with relative clarity: 'Anshl hot gehat gefunen a fortl vi azoy ibertsuraysn bay Hodesn di psulim. In ir gantskeyt hot Hodes nisht gevust az epes iz do nisht vi es badarf tsu zany' [Anshel had found a trick for cutting in two her virginity. In her wholeness, Hadass did not know that this was not as it was supposed to be].[58] The published English translation of this passage reads: 'Anshel had found a way [a trick] to deflower the bride. Hadass in her innocence was unaware that things weren't quite as they should have been.'[59] Both in Yiddish and in English, a sexual act between the two protagonists unequivocally occurs. Even though Hadass, because of her 'innocence' — or, in Yiddish, her 'gantskeyt' (which literally means 'wholeness' but refers to her virginal state, purity, and ignorance of sexuality) — is not aware of the mechanisms of the heterosexual act, one has to deduce from the idea of deflowering or tearing in two her virginity that something has occurred that at least resembles the sexual act. In fact, Bashevis's portrayal of Hadass is a somewhat exaggerated caricature of women's naivety. Indeed, women talked together about such issues. Moreover, in an Orthodox milieu, it was traditional for the bride to be taught by another woman about the laws of marriage, family purity, and *nidah*.[60] It is unlikely that a woman would have had no knowledge at all about sexuality. Bashevis's argument that he left the homosexual act ambiguous can only find its justification in the word *fortl*, 'trick', which he did not explain.

Throughout the Yiddish short story, Yentl's relation to Hadass remains very ambiguous and potentially sexual. Even though Yentl admits her love for Avigdor, she marries Hadass. Without a doubt, Yentl/Anshel feels confused with her sexual identity:

> Anshel looked at her [Hadass] as she stood there — tall, blond, with a long neck, hollow cheeks, and blue eyes, wearing a cotton dress and a calico apron. Her hair, fixed in two braids, was flung back over her shoulders. A pity I'm not a man, Anshel thought.[61]

Yentl/Anshel scrutinizes Hadass's face, moving her eyes up and down along her body, from the silhouette (Hadass is 'tall'), to the face (her 'long neck', 'hollow cheeks', and 'blue eyes'), to her hair and clothing. Yentl/Anshel's gaze is sharp. She also tells Hadass at various times that she is beautiful and that she wants her: 'I, too, want you.'[62] After this comment, the narrator states that Anshel is surprised by her own words: 'Anshel was astonished at what she had said. [...] She knew very well she was getting entangled in evil. [...] Some force kept urging her on.'[63] Note the specific use of 'Anshel' in the following sentence: 'A pity I'm not a man, Anshel thought.' This casts Anshel/Yentl as the subject of the male gaze, which typically privileges the perspective of a male viewer and relegates women to the status of objects.[64] By using the name 'Anshel' rather than 'Yentl', Bashevis here makes Hadass the object of Anshel's male gaze. In short, despite Bashevis's attempt to claim ambiguity, Yentl's attraction to Hadass is implied throughout the short story.

At the beginning of 'Yentl', Bashevis points out that Yentl is non-normative as a woman. After putting on her father's clothes, Yentl studies her reflection in the mirror:

> On Sabbath afternoons, when her father slept, she would dress up in his trousers, his fringed garment, his silk coat, his skullcap, his velvet hat, and study her reflection in the mirror. [...] She looked like a dark, handsome young man. There was even a slight down on her upper lip. Only her thick braids showed her womanhood — and if it came to that, hair could always be shorn.[65]

The statement that 'she looked like a [...] man' implies that cross-dressing does not simply involve wearing the clothes of another gender but is also reinforced by biological features. Yentl is described as a mannish woman who is 'unlike any of the girls in Yanev' and who has 'a slight down on her upper lip'. Moreover, her androgyny is physically inscribed because the only sign of her 'womanhood', her braids, could be easily cut off.

Although she acts like a man, Yentl feels uneasy when she stops at an inn crowded with young men on her way to the yeshiva. She suddenly feels deprived of her ability to speak:

> An argument was in progress over the merits of various yeshivas, some praising those of Lithuania, others claiming that study was more intensive in Poland and the board better. It was the first time Yentl had ever found herself alone in the company of young men. How different their talk was from the jabbering of

women, she thought, but she was too shy to join in. One young man discussed a prospective match, [...] while another, parodying the manner of a Purim rabbi, declaimed a passage from the Torah.[66]

In this environment, Yentl feels estranged because it is the first time she has 'ever found herself alone in the company of young men'. The only expression of her opinion is that the talk of those students is nothing like the 'jabbering of women'. In this animated universe where others argue, praise, talk, discuss, parody, and declaim, Yentl stays mute. She is only driven out of her silence by a student who, poking her shoulder, asks: 'Why so quiet? Don't you have a tongue?'.[67] Yentl is not only shy but is also among male students for the first time when dressed as a man. In Michelle Cliff's words, 'passing demands quiet. And from that quiet — silence.'[68] The students sense Yentl's uneasiness and mock her for it.

Throughout the story, readers are reminded of the gender roles that dictate that a woman should marry by a certain age and that a man should act like a man. For example, after she realizes that she is in love with Avigdor, who is already engaged to another woman (Hadass), Yentl says that she is 'a girl of marriageable age, in love with a young man who was betrothed to another'.[69] Conscious of the expectation that a girl like her will get married, Yentl is torn between the desire to act like a girl and her thirst for education. Yet, pondering whether to confess her feelings to Avigdor or keep them secret, Yentl finds she cannot give up the freedom she has obtained through cross-dressing: 'Anshel could not go back to being a girl, could never again do without books and a study house.'[70] Similarly, the character of Avigdor also reinforces gender norms: when Anshel chokes after a sip of brandy, Avigdor tells her that she is not 'much of a man'.[71]

Later in the story, Yentl even dreams and is brought by her thoughts 'close to madness':

> In her dreams she had been at the same time a man and a woman, wearing both a woman's bodice and a man's fringed garment. [...] Only now did Yentl grasp the meaning of the Torah's prohibition against wearing the clothes of the other sex. By doing so one deceived not only others but also oneself. Even the soul was perplexed, finding itself incarnate in a strange body.[72]

In this scene, the narrator implies that cross-dressing is unnatural and that Yentl will harm herself and the people around her. Furthermore, androgyny is clearly mentioned at the end of this passage in the original Yiddish:

> Er iz eyngeshlofn, zikh ibergevekt mit a tsepl, in kholem iz er geven say a mansbil say a nekeyve. [...] Nisht bloyz nart men dermit yenem, nor oykh zikh aleyn, a shteyger vi di neshome volt zikh ongekleydet in a fremdn kerper. M'vert vi a tumtum oder an androginos.

> [He fell asleep, then awoke with a start. In the dream, he had been at the same time a man and a woman [...] By acting this way, one deceives not only everyone else, but also oneself, cloaking one's soul in a foreign body. And one becomes a *tumtum* or an androgyne].[73]

The verb 'ongekleydet', which literally means 'to wear' or 'to put on', implies the dressing-up of the soul and the cross-dressing of the individual, not only physically but also mentally. The soul is clothed in a foreign body ('ongekleydet in a fremdn kerper').

The published English translation, though accurate, states only that the body is 'strange', not 'foreign' ('fremdn'), which somewhat diminishes the strength of Bashevis's idea. Yentl's body is not merely strange — she does not recognize her own body, which is foreign to her and which does not represent her inner self. To be foreign to oneself is painful and demonstrates Yentl's uneasiness with her body. We must also note that the Yiddish refers to Yentl as 'er' [he] and not as 'she', as in the published English translation. By using the masculine pronoun, Bashevis portrays Yentl as an androgyne, as someone who is both male and female. By using the feminine pronoun, the translation implies that Yentl remains a woman throughout the story.

'Yentl' blurs the construction of gender based on biological features by asserting that Yentl has the 'soul of a man and the body of a woman'. Bashevis uses the Talmudic notion of androgyny to frame Yentl's case. Although his conception of the genders is based on a binary construction, he plays with the instability of this system and the possible deviations from it, defining gender and sexual categories in a nuanced way. He once said he 'wrote the story to show that behind all the strict behavior, behind the long skirts and the rules and regulations, human nature was still there'.[74] He wants Yentl to reject a life in captivity, to accept her difference and live for herself.

At the end of the story, Yentl disappears, leaving Hadass with Avigdor, who names his son Anshel. Marjorie Gerber argues that

> the infant Anshel is a changeling in that he is substituted for [and named after] a figure who herself/himself incarnated change, and was himself/herself exchanged. Yentl becomes 'Anshel' who becomes — in some quite complicated way — Anshel. A memory, a promise, a replacement, and a substitution.[75]

Yentl/Anshel becomes a scholar, while Hadass — now educated — expects to have a more equal relationship with Avigdor. Their child represents the promise of better relations between the sexes. It is the female Yentl, though, who disappears completely from the narrative, leaving the male Anshel on that bright horizon.

While Bashevis chooses to leave Yentl's gender identity uncertain, he also maintains fluidity in the characters' sexual orientation. Hoffman argues that 'in [Bashevis's] universe, unclear gender is almost always a marker of homosexuality'.[76] The Yiddish version of 'Yentl' appears more ambiguous than does the published English translation, blurring the lines of every character's sexuality. Yentl is attracted to both Avigdor and Hadass, whom she eventually even marries. In an interview, Bashevis once declared that the characters of 'Yentl' were 'homosexual persons',[77] but he never defined what he meant. The play with the pronouns and the constant shifting between Anshel and Yentl blur gender and sexual boundaries. One could argue that Anshel and Avigdor share a close bond in the homoerotic space of the yeshiva. For example, when Yentl and Avigdor meet to talk after Yentl has declared her real gender to Avigdor, the Yiddish text reads: 'Er vet oysgeyn fun benkshaft nokh Ansheln (oder Yentlen), ober er hot zikh shoyn nisht dervegt dos tsu zogn' [He [Avigdor] would long for Anshel (or Yentl), but he had not been able to bring himself to say this].[78] However, the published English translation omits the ambiguity by stating that Avigdor would miss Yentl (the female) and not Anshel (the male): '[Avigdor] knew he would long for Yentl, but he dared not say so'.[79] Here, the translator chose to use 'Yentl' rather than 'Anshel', and thus removed the complication of this dual identity. The English version is not completely logical, because it also says that 'a great love of Anshel took hold of Avigdor, mixed with shame, remorse, anxiety'.[80] Note that this time the translation mentions Anshel rather than Yentl, which reinforces or confirms the homoerotic relationship between the two men. In fact, this entire passage goes back and forth between Yentl and Anshel, emphasizing the dual identity and the attraction Avigdor feels for him/her:

> His desire for Hadass was gone now, and he knew he would long for Yentl, but he dared not say so. He felt hot and knew that his face was burning. He could not longer meet Anshel's eyes. He began to enumerate Anshel's sins and saw that he too was implicated, for he had sat next to Yentl and had touched her during her unclean days.[81]

While imagining what his life would be with a woman like Yentl, Avigdor is still sitting next to Anshel, whose eyes he cannot meet any more. The attraction that he experiences is both for Anshel and for Yentl, and, while the Yiddish clearly demonstrates this, the published English version does so only by choosing wrongly one name rather than another.

Even though Bashevis writes about androgyny and transgender identity, his perspective is not necessarily one that defends homosexuality, since all the characters that have gay sex die at the end of the stories. The critic Edward Alexander asserts that, in 'Yentl', Bashevis 'never allows us to forget that whatever else may be said for homosexual relationships, they do not do much for the propagation of the race and perpetuation of the Jewish people'.[82] This brief comment is grounded in the religious idea that the purpose of marriage is to 'be fruitful and multiply',[83] not merely to experience bodily pleasure. Even though Bashevis might have shared this opinion and might not have been a defender of gay rights in the political realm, he nevertheless conceived characters who, with androgynous souls, defy the binary construction of the genders.

In Singer's World, It Is Better to Be 'TQ' Than 'LGB'

While this whole debate about what it means to be a man and what it implies to be a woman is taking place in the US right now, transforming the restroom into a contested political space, it seems clear that sexual orientation is more accepted nowadays and that the problems start when talking about gender redefinitions. Strikingly, for Bashevis the opposite is true. He signals anxiety while writing about sexual orientation, but not about gender. This lack of anxiety about gender is, in part, linked to the vocabulary and theories available to him through the Talmud and through Yiddish, which possess words to describe different states of gender fluidity.

For David Biale, Bashevis's work 'may have appealed to a traditional audience, but it allowed that audience, particularly if it was female, a fictional reversal of gender relations'[84] because of the stories' traditional religious dimension paired with a more subversive one. Moreover, Bashevis's 'sexual subversions frequently rest on reversals of traditional roles'.[85] Bashevis's queer corpus implies that there can be no happy ending for his marginal characters, who are often discarded from the narrative. While contemporary queer theory and LGBT activism have carved out a place for people who cross-dress and have gay sex, the Talmudic system within which Bashevis works does not have space for the cross-dresser who has gay sex or for gay sex in general. The anxiety regarding sexuality is mirrored and extended, of course, in the bathroom controversy. Although the same anxiety about sex exists in both Bashevis's fiction and the political controversy regarding bathrooms, Bashevis's work illustrates the extent to which the Yiddish language and his own aesthetic world possess far greater flexibility in discussing gender.

Bashevis uses cross-dressing to signify homosexuality, but he also deals very explicitly with the Talmudic definitions of gender categories. None of his characters are easy to classify, and none fit the normative structure of traditional Jewish society. 'Two' tells the story of same-sex male partners who cross-dress in order to live as a heterosexual couple and be accepted. This story does not end well, even though Bashevis does not seem to condemn these characters. 'Androgyny' is perhaps the exception to the misery the others experience, since Shevach is the most strictly androgynous and is accepted within her community — maybe because her biology corresponds with (instead of contradicting) her social behaviour. She proves that her dual gender identity does not impact her role in society and that she can live as both male and female. Finally, 'Yentl the Yeshiva Boy' shows Bashevis writing about a character who is a man trapped in a female body, and he complicates both the gender and sex system by adding sexual attraction between both the male characters and the female ones. Anshel is attracted to Hadass while also being enamoured with Avigdor, who feels attraction for Anshel as well. The pronouns illustrate that Bashevis created a very ambiguous story in terms of gender roles and sexual orientation.

Far from arguing that Yentl is simply cross-dressing, Bashevis writes about the more complex phenomenon of a male soul trapped in a female body, or, in contemporary terms, a transgender character. Irving Buchen argues that Yentl dressing up as a man 'dislocates her sexuality'.[86] I illustrate that most of the short stories that engage with homosexuality do so through androgyny and transvestitism. Through cross-dressing, Bashevis alludes to homosexuality and shows his distrust of same-sex relationships. That is truly the equivalent of his own bathroom crisis.

Bashevis's writing is provocative and self-exploring, filled with sexual imagery, gender reversals, androgyny, supernatural forces, and imps — colourful characters that haunt the pages with an enigmatic presence. Although he uses sexuality to oppose the traditional depiction of Eastern European life as a prudish environment, Bashevis also grounds his ideas in the Talmud. By doing so, he anchors himself in an Eastern European tradition that was far more open to permutations of gender and sexuality than is commonly understood. Moreover, in several interviews, Bashevis explained that he wrote about a character like Yentl because he was interested in exceptionality: 'I am interested always in the exception — you might say, almost in freaks. Because through the exception we can learn more about ourselves, about normal people.'[87] This remark suggests that, even though his tale is modern, it is based on the postulate that analysing what is different ultimately serves to reveal what is 'normal'. Bashevis reinforced norms instead of deconstructing differences, though it is not clear to what extent he was aware of doing so.

While issues involving transgender individuals and non-normative gender identities are fiercely debated today, Bashevis offers a refreshing perspective on gender — one that is based on fluidity and openness. He was, however, unable to accept homosexuality. The resulting ambiguities and tensions in his work make it clear that, in today's world, a consistent and thorough acceptance of queer identities cannot be grounded in the exclusion of homoeroticism or same-sex relationships.

Notes to Chapter 12

1. Isaac Bashevis Singer, 'Tsvey', *Forverts*, 17–18 April 1970, p. 2; 24 April 1970, pp. 2, 5; 25 April 1970, p. 2. Translation: Isaac Bashevis Singer, 'Two', trans. by Isaac Bashevis Singer, in Isaac Bashevis Singer, *Collected Stories: 'One Night in Brazil' to 'The Death of Methuselah'*, ed. by Ilan Stavans (New York: Library of America, 2004), pp. 30–43.
2. Isaac Bashevis Singer, 'Andruginus', in *Der shpigl un andere dertseylungen*, ed. by Chone Shmeruk (Jerusalem: Hebrew University, 1975), pp. 180–93. Translation: Isaac Bashevis Singer, 'Androgynous', trans. by Joseph Sherman, in *Beautiful as the Moon, Radiant as the Stars: Jewish Women in Yiddish Stories*, ed. by Sandra Bark (New York: Warner, 2003), pp. 153–70.
3. Isaac Bashevis Singer, 'Yentl der yeshive bokher', in Isaac Bashevis Singer, *Mayses fun hintern oyvn* (Tel Aviv: Peretz, 1982), pp. 131–64. Translation: Isaac Bashevis Singer, 'Yentl the Yeshiva Boy', trans. by Marion Magid and Elizabeth Pollet, in Isaac Bashevis Singer, *Collected Stories: 'Gimpel the Fool' to 'The Letter Writer'* (New York: Library of America, 2004), pp. 439–63.
4. The English word 'hermaphrodite' derives from the name of Hermaphroditos, the mythical son of the Greek deities Hermes and Aphrodite. The most familiar version of the story of Hermaphroditos is recounted by the Roman poet Ovid (43 BCE–17 CE) in Book IV of the *Metamorphoses*. While the word 'hermaphrodite' has been commonly used for centuries, in the last few decades there has been a sustained effort on the part of many activists, medical practitioners, and scholars to replace it with the term 'intersex'. The Intersex Society of North America (ISNA), a leading US-based activist organization that seeks to promote a better understanding of intersex conditions and advocates a patient-centred medical approach, argues for a more clinically based terminology: 'The word "hermaphrodite" is a stigmatizing and misleading word. There is growing momentum to eliminate the word "hermaphrodite" from medical literature and to use the word "intersex" in its place' (<http://www.isna.org/drupal/node/view/16> [accessed 9 January 2017]). For contemporary debates on intersexuality, see Anne Fausto-Sterling, *Sexing the Body: Gender Politics and the Construction of Human Sexuality* (New York: Basic Books, 2000); Judith Butler, *Gender Trouble: Feminism and the Subversion of Identity* (New York and London: Routledge, 1990).
5. Moses Gaster, 'Androgynos (Hermaphrodite)', in *The Jewish Encyclopedia 1901–1906* <http://www.jewishencyclopedia.com/articles/1508-androgynos-hermaphrodite> [accessed 23 July 2018].
6. Alfred Cohen, '*Tumtum* and Androgynous', *Journal of Halacha and Contemporary Religion*, 38 (1999), 62–85.
7. Alana Suskin, 'Bet You Didn't Know ... What the Talmud Says about Gender Ambiguity', *Lilith* (spring 2002), 25.

8. Singer, 'Andruginus', p. 187 (my translation).
9. Seymour Cohen, 'Introduction', in *The Holy Letter: A Study in Medieval Jewish Sexual Morality, Ascribed to Nahmanides*, ed. and trans. by Seymour Cohen (New York: Ktav, 1976), pp. 9–59 (p. 27).
10. Ibid., p. 28.
11. Ibid., p. 29.
12. Daniel Boyarin, *Unheroic Conduct: The Rise of Heterosexuality and the Invention of the Jewish Man* (Berkeley: University of California Press, 1997), p. 14.
13. Michael L. Satlow, ' "They Abused Him Like a Woman": Homoeroticism, Gender Blurring, and the Rabbis in Late Antiquity', *Journal of the History of Sexuality*, 5.1 (1994), 1–25 (p. 18).
14. Ibid.
15. Butler, p. 278.
16. Ibid., p. 274.
17. Singer, 'Two', p. 30.
18. Ibid.
19. Ibid., p. 31.
20. Ibid.
21. Ibid.
22. Ibid.
23. Ibid., p. 32.
24. Ibid.
25. Ibid.
26. Ibid.
27. Ibid., p. 35.
28. Ibid.
29. Ibid., p. 39.
30. Ibid., p. 40.
31. In contemporary terms, we would classify these characters as transgender.
32. Ibid., pp. 42–43.
33. Again, Zissel would be seen as a transgender bisexual.
34. Singer, 'Androgynous', p. 154.
35. Ibid. The Yiddish states: 'Di Shevach iz an androginos, halb mantsbil, halb nekeyve, nisht ahin, nisht aher' [That Shevach is androgynous, half male, half female, neither here, nor there] (Singer, 'Andruginus', p. 187; my translation). In contemporary terms, we would call Shevach an intersex person, but the text categorizes this as one way of being androgynous. An intersex person is not identifiable within the male/female sex binary and may have genital ambiguity. The historian Alice Dreger explains that intersexed individuals 'are born with an anatomical conformation different from "standard" male or female bodies, in that they feature both male and female genital tissue. Their unusual anatomies can result in confusion and disagreement about whether they should be designated female, male, or something else' (Alice Domurat Dreger, *Hermaphrodites and the Medical Invention of Sex* (Cambridge: Harvard University Press, 1998), pp. 3–4).
36. Singer, 'Androgynous', p. 154.
37. Ibid., pp. 156–57.
38. Ibid., p. 157. The Yiddish original of the final sentence reads: 'Es iz do in kabole-sefires az di berina fun zokheres un nekeyves iz do in yedn ben-odem' [It says in the Kabbalah that the qualities of manhood and femalehood are in every human being] (Singer, 'Andruginus', p. 190; my translation).
39. Singer, 'Andruginus', p. 190 (my translation).
40. Singer, 'Androgynous', pp. 162–63.
41. Ibid., p. 157.
42. Ibid., p. 159. Bashevis makes a clear distinction between the soul and the body. In the Yiddish, he writes: 'Der guf iz a guf un di neshome iz a neshome' [The body is a body and the soul is a soul] (Singer, 'Andruginus', p. 188; my translation).

43. Singer, 'Androgynous', p. 159.
44. Ibid., p. 169.
45. Ibid.
46. Mikhail Bakhtin's top–bottom theory of the carnivalesque is useful in understanding Bashevis's self-exploration. Bakhtin introduced the theory of the carnival to describe and interpret a sociocultural mechanism that is subversively disruptive while also regenerative. Through its subversive mechanisms, the carnivalesque serves as a liberating function while it disrupts authority and introduces alternatives. Bashevis's writing, as is seen here, plays with the reversal of normative concepts. He elevates the low in a carnival context and parodies the religious and normative laws of society.
47. Singer, 'Yentl the Yeshiva Boy', p. 439.
48. Ibid.
49. Ibid.
50. Ibid.
51. Miriam Heman Maltz, 'Ambiguity in Isaac Bashevis Singer's *Yentl the Yeshiva Boy*', *Jewish Affairs*, 55.4 (summer 2000), 7–12 (p. 7).
52. Lillian Schanfield, 'Singer's "Yentl": The Fantastic Case of a Perplexed Soul', in *Spectrum of the Fantastic*, ed. by Donald Palumbo (Westport: Greenwood Press, 1988), pp. 185–92 (p. 188).
53. Singer, 'Yentl der yeshive bokher', p. 156 (my translation).
54. Singer, 'Andruginus', p. 186 (my translation).
55. In 2012, for example, the singer-songwriter Jill Sobule made a musical version of 'Yentl' that interprets Yentl as transgender: 'If you read the book, and there was no word for it back then, but I think Yentl was transgender [...]. I mean, it's several times in the book where the father says to her, "You have the soul of a man and the body of a woman"' (quoted in 'New Staging of "Yentl" Tells a Transgender Story', *NPR.org* <http://www.npr.org/2012/02/05/146431727/new-staging-of-yentl-tells-a-transgender-girls-story> [accessed 23 July 2018]).
56. Singer, 'Yentl the Yeshiva Boy', pp. 439–40.
57. Irving Buchen, *Isaac Bashevis Singer and the Eternal Past* (New York: New York University Press, 1968), p. 124. In Jewish mythology, a dybbuk is a malicious spirit or the tortured soul of a dead body that usually enters a person's body and possesses it.
58. Singer, 'Yentl der yeshive bokher', p. 151 (my translation).
59. Singer, 'Yentl the Yeshiva Boy', p. 453.
60. The rules governing menstruation and sexuality.
61. Isaac Bashevis Singer, 'Yentl the Yeshiva Boy', p. 445.
62. Ibid., p. 447.
63. Ibid.
64. Laura Mulvey coined the term 'male gaze' in an 1975 essay in which she argues that, in films, audiences view characters from the perspective of a heterosexual male: 'In a world ordered by sexual imbalance, pleasure in looking has been split between active/male and passive/female' ('Visual Pleasure and Narrative Cinema', in *Film Theory and Criticism: Introductory Readings*, ed. by Marshall Cohe and Leo Braudy (New York: Oxford University Press, 1999), pp. 833–44 (p. 837)).
65. Singer, 'Yentl the Yeshiva Boy', p. 439.
66. Ibid., p. 440.
67. Ibid.
68. Michelle Cliff, *The Land of Look Behind: Prose and Poetry* (Ithaca, NY: Firebrand Books, 1985), p. 22.
69. Singer, 'Yentl the Yeshiva Boy', p. 446.
70. Ibid.
71. Ibid., p. 444.
72. Ibid., p. 446.
73. Singer, 'Yentl der yeshive bokher', p. 141 (my translation).
74. Quoted in Paul Kresh, *Isaac Bashevis Singer, the Magician of West 86th Street: A Biography* (New York: Dial Press, 1979), p. 11.

75. Marjorie B. Garber, *Vested Interest: Cross-Dressing and Cultural Anxiety* (New York: Routledge, 1992), p. 84.
76. Warren Hoffman, *The Passing Game: Queering Jewish American Culture* (Syracuse: Syracuse University Press, 2009), p. 136.
77. Hoffman, p. 176 n. 44, reports this, citing an interview with Cyrena Pondrom.
78. Singer, 'Yentl der yeshive bokher', p. 158 (my translation).
79. Singer, 'Yentl the Yeshiva Boy', p. 458.
80. Ibid.
81. Ibid., pp. 458–59.
82. Edward Alexander, *Isaac Bashevis Singer: A Study of the Short Fiction* (Boston: Twayne, 1990), p. 63.
83. Cf. Genesis 1. 28.
84. David Biale, *Eros and the Jews: From Biblical Israel to Contemporary America* (Berkeley: University of California Press, 1997), p. 166.
85. Ibid., p. 223.
86. Buchen, p. 125.
87. Quoted in Kresh, p. 11.

INDEX

Acmeism 134
Adam and Eve 29, 175
abortion 43–44
Abraham da Sarteano 13
Adler, Eliyana 85
Akhmatova, Anna 128, 136 n. 37, 137 n. 78
Albatros 125
A. Almi (Elias Chaim Sheps) 84, 91 n. 27
Amsterdam 98
Anatolia 165, 167
androgyne 112, 175, 178–80, 183–84, 188 n. 35
Anti-Semitism 37, 75, 94, 118
Argentina 164–68, 172 n. 16, 22
Asch, Sholem 98–99, 106 n. 19 and. 23, 109, 112, 125, 161 n. 10, 170
Ashkenaz 2, 9, 16, 113, 115, 120
Ashkenazi, Shlomo 29, 34 n. 57, 35 n. 58, 59 and 63
Australia 70
Ayzland, Reuven 139–40, 142, 146–49

Babi Yar 126
Bachofen, Jacob 20, 25, 27, 29, 30, 32 n. 6, 34 n. 49
Bal-Makhshoves (Isidor/Israel Elyashev) 125, 135 n. 21
Bebel, August 19– 25, 28–29, 31, 32 n. 3, 33 n. 20, 23 and 24, 35 n. 63
Beckett, Samuel 108
Beecher Stowe, Harriet 61
Berlewi, Henrik 124
Benjamin, Walter 140, 149 n. 3, 103–04, 107 n. 40
Berdichev 82
Berdyaev, Nikolai 85
Bergelson, David 83–84, 123, 125
Bessarabia 84, 163, 171 n. 9
Białystok 28, 172 n. 18
Biale, David 62 n. 2, 186, 190 n. 84
Bible 7, 9, 12, 14, 22, 25, 27–31, 87, 95, 111, 120, 129, 134, 136 n. 48
Birobidzhan 165
blood libel 2, 42, 94
Boccaccio, Giovanni 12
Botoshansky, Yankev (Jacob) 5–6, 117, 162–72
Botticelli 127
Brazil 165, 187 n. 1
Brueghel the Elder 9
Butler, Judith 176, 187 n 4, 188 n. 5
Buenos Aires 117, 162, 164–72

Canada 165
Campe, Joachim Heinrich 165
Casimir the Great 3, 94, 99–102
Chaikov, Joseph 125
Chicago 153
Childbirth 2, 9, 37–39, 43, 56
circumcision 13, 18 n. 29
Cliff, Michelle 67, 183, 189 n. 68
Cohen, Natan 100, 105 n. 3, 172 n. 19
Cohen, Seymour 175, 188 n. 9
Cohen, Tova 86, 92 n. 42, 105 n. 1
Communism 34 n. 46
Constantinople 167, 170
Cook, Blanche 66, 76, 77 n. 7, 79 n. 66
Cunow, Heinrich 20, 22, 29, 32 n. 9

da Genazzano, Elia 13
D'Amico, Francine 158, 161 n. 15
Darwin, Charles 3, 88, 163, 171 n. 5
Der kval 155, 159, 160 n. 7
Der Nister 123
Der tog 164–66, 170, 171 n. 12, 172 n. 18 and 21
Detroit 62 n. 11
Di prese 164, 171
Di Yunge 5, 139–43, 148, 149 n. 6, 150 n. 30, 151 n. 51
Dik, Ayzik Meyer 81
Dobrushin, Yekhezkl 125
Dropkin, Celia 2, 37–39, 55, 62 n. 8 and 9, 64 n. 58
Dubnov, Simon 80, 81, 87, 90 n. 2 and 9, 92 n. 45
Dumas, Alexandre 80
Dykewomon, Elana 72, 78 n. 46
Dynes, Ofer 117, 122 n. 35

Edelman, Marek 75
Einhorn, David 134
Elizavetgrad 125
Engels, Friedrich 19–20, 22–25, 28–35
Epstein, Mark 125
Esther, biblical character 9, 11, 18 n. 29, 93–95, 97, 100

Fain Pratt, Norma 71
Faygenberg, Rokhl 84, 91 n. 26
Feigenbaum, Benjamin 2, 19, 21, 22–25, 30–31, 33
Feminism 3, 37, 44, 47, 53, 62 n 5, 65, 67, 68, 71–72, 76, 77 n. 16 and 20, 78 n. 52, 79 n. 62, 92 n 39 and 44, 108, 110, 112, 118, 119, 121 n. 10 and 11, 187 n. 4

folklore 10, 17 n. 7, 71, 98, 127
Forverts 68, 69, 108, 110, 114, 118
Fox, Harry 8, 16 n. 3, 17
Freeman, Elizabeth 73, 78 n. 53
Frenk, Azriel Natan 84, 91 n. 29
Frenkel, Alexander 120 n. 4
Frieden, Ken 81, 90 n. 8
Frishman, David 163, 171 n. 6

Germany 7, 20, 32 n. 2
Ginsburg, Saul 81
Glatshteyn, Yankev 121 n. 15, 124
Glikl of Hameln 69
Gold, Mike 141, 149 n. 7
Gordin, Abba 2, 19, 24–28, 30–31, 33–35
Gordon, Shmuel-Leib 95, 96, 105 n. 6 and 9
Gordon, Yehuda Leib 98, 106 n. 18
Gorodecky, Sergey 137 n. 78
Gurevich, Grigory 89
Gorin, Borukh 108
Gumil'ev, Nikolai 128, 132, 137 n. 60 and 78

Halakhah 22, 29, 31
Halevi, Judah 86
Hasidism 88, 91 n. 37 114–15, 125, 179
Haskalah, *also* maskil(a) 82, 83, 85, 86, 89, 90 n. 1, 92 n. 41, 95, 98, 99, 105 n. 5
Hebbel, Friedrich 95–97, 105 n. 6
Hebrew 1, 3–5, 7, 13–16, 22, 25–26, 28, 30, 76, 79 n. 62, 80–81, 83, 86–87, 92, 93, 95–100, 104, 105 n. 9, 109, 111, 120 n. 1, 124, 134, 146, 154, 156, 159, 160 n. 1, 161 n. 10 and 16, 171 n. 6
Heine, Heinrich 134, 150 n. 34
Hellerstein, Kathryn 3, 62–64, 67, 70–72, 76–77
Hemingway, Ernest 141, 149 n. 7
hermaphrodite 174, 187 n. 4 and 5, 188 n. 35
Hershfeld, Pessie 2, 38–39, 62 n. 11 and 12
heterosexuality 62 n. 1, 65, 66, 74, 101, 77 n. 9 and 17, 149 n. 5, 159, 173–76, 181, 186, 188 n. 12, 189 n. 64
Hever, Hannan 96, 105 n. 8
Hofstein, David 4, 123–38
Hofstein (Biberman), Feige 126, 130, 132–33, 134 n. 2, 137 n. 61
Hoeveler, David Jr 119, 122 n. 41
Hollander, John 74, 78 n. 54 and 55
Holocaust 103, 113, 118
homosexuality 121 n. 10, 174–76, 178, 182, 184–87

Ignatov, Dovid 5, 143, 145–46, 148, 149 n. 1, 150 n. 34 and 35, 151 n. 38
Irigaray, Luce 47, 63 n. 32
Israel 11, 29, 30, 37, 68, 71, 72, 75, 78 n. 59 and 60, 79 n. 61 and 62, 82, 130, 140, 164, 166
Italy 2, 9, 11–18, 150 n. 16

Jewish Anti-Fascist Committee 123
Jewish Colonization Association 165
Jezebel 108, 111–12, 118, 121 n. 18, 122 n. 39
Judaism 2, 19, 25, 26, 28–29, 36, 52, 79 n. 62, 98, 111, 121 n. 11

Kabbalah 118, 175, 178, 179, 188 n. 38
Kaye/Kantrowitz, Melanie 67
Khalyastre 125
Kharik, Izi 136 n. 42, 138 n. 78
Khayit, Hinde-Gitl 132
Khmelnytsky, Bohdan 114
Kholodenko, Shifre 126
Kiev 82, 123, 124, 125, 132
Klepfisz, Irena 3, 67–70, 72, 73, 75, 76
Klepfisz, Michał 75
Kling, Berta 36, 48, 50
Korman, Ezra 3, 66, 67, 69–71, 77 n. 33
Korn, Rokhl 56, 57, 69
Korostyshev 123
Krantz, Philip 2, 19, 22, 24, 30, 31
Kultur-lige 123, 125
Kuzmin, Mikhail 137 n. 78
Kvitko, Leib 123, 125, 127, 128, 135 n. 19

Laine, Frankie 112
Latvia 84
Le Borg, Reginald 112
Levin, Khana 2, 44, 46, 53, 54, 58, 59, 69
Mani Leib (Brahinsky) 5, 139, 140, 142, 146–48, 149 n. 2
Lerner, Yosef Yehuda 96–98, 106 n. 12
lesbian 3, 4, 65, 66–68, 70, 73–76, 111, 112
Elia Levita (Elye Bokher) 8, 9, 15, 18 n. 25
Lewis, Justin Jaron 8
Literarishe bleter 5, 162–64, 171 n. 4 and n. 12
Litvaks 23, 24, 84, 85
Londinski, Shmuel-Yakir 124
London 98
London, Yisroel 155, 159, 160 n. 6, 172 n. 15
Luria, Esther 69

Magellan, Ferdinand 163, 171 n. 5
Malinowski, Bronisław 20
Mandelstam, Osip 137 n. 78
maskil(a), *see* Haskalah
Margolin, Anna 67, 69, 70
Margoshes, Samuel 164, 170, 171
Markish, Peretz 123, 125, 127
Marx, Karl 32 n. 6
Marxism 2, 19, 20, 22, 24, 25, 31, 34 n. 52
Mayzel, Nakhmen 164
Maze, Ida 61
Mendele Moykher-Sforim 80, 86, 134
Mestre 16
Mickiewicz, Adam 101–03

Midrash 11, 12, 17 n. 11, 18 n. 27, 83, 86, 90, 111, 127
Miron, Dan 80
Mishna 11, 12, 17 n. 21, 18 n. 27, 83, 86, 90, 111, 117
Morgan, Lewis H. 20, 22, 28–31
Moscow 132, 164
mysticism 111, 115

Nabokov, Vladimir 108
Nadir, Moishe 141, 142, 148
nationalism 3, 24, 93–95, 97, 98, 101–05, 106 n. 12, 107 n. 43, 118
Nealon, Christopher 65, 76
Neamț, Piatra 167
New York 22, 24, 68–70, 81, 100, 102, 108, 112, 140, 144, 149 n. 2, 154, 155, 159, 164–67
Nezvizh 84
Niger, Shmuel 16 n. 2, 81, 125, 131, 164
Norich, Anita 3, 71, 120 n. 5
Novershtern, Avraham 3, 71, 72
Novogrodek 63 n. 35

Old Yiddish literature 7–19, 71
Opatoshu, Joseph 125, 164
Ozick, Cynthia 149 n. 4

Palestine 5, 78 n. 59, 79 n. 61, 126, 132, 154–56, 159, 160, 164, 165
Paris 165, 167, 170
Paryszewski, Marcus 172 n. 22
Passover 18 n. 31, 41, 42
Patagonia 5, 171 n. 4
Peckerar, Robert 81
Peretz, Y. L. 101–03, 134
Philippson, Ludwig 98, 106 n. 22
Picasso, Pablo 127
Pinsky, David 88, 97, 98, 106 n. 12
Pogrom 2, 37, 42, 44, 125, 136 n. 45
Poland 3, 84, 99, 100, 103, 104, 110, 111, 114, 118, 164, 165, 167, 182
Poltava 153
Portugal 98, 99
prostitution 142, 152, 157, 158, 167–69
Purim 12, 13, 18 n. 29, 183
Pushkin, Alexander 124

rape 44, 46, 95–97, 168
Ravitch, Melech 3, 69
Rembrandt, Rijn van 127, 136 n. 35
Remenik, Hersh 124
Renaissance 2, 13, 17 n. 17
Reuveni, Aharon 5, 152–60
Rich, Adrienne 3, 66–69, 73–75, 78 n. 56 and n. 58, 79 n. 61
Rio de Janeiro 165, 167, 170
Rivkin, Borekh 5, 144, 165, 166, 172 n. 15
Romania 163, 164, 167, 168, 171 n. 9

Roskies, David G. 81
Ryback, Issachar Ber 125

Sadan, Sadan 82
Sappho 69
Seidman, Naomi 107 n. 14
sexual identity 6, 174, 182
sexual violence 96, 99, 153, 168
sexuality 3, 4, 38, 39, 50, 53, 55, 56, 75, 93, 94, 96, 103, 104, 116, 129, 132, 140, 158, 173, 175, 177, 179, 181, 184, 186, 187
Shanghai 152, 153
Shemen, Nachman 19, 29–31
Shmeruk, Chone 3, 94, 99, 100, 105 n. 3
Schneerson, Fishl 108, 114
Sholem Aleichem 3, 80–83, 89, 109
Shomer 3, 4, 80–90, 94, 95, 99
Shriftn 118, 143, 151 n. 38
Shumiatcher, Esther 69
Sigal, Itskhac 48
Singer, Isaac Bashevis 4, 6, 108–20, 173–87
Slaughter, Frank G. 112
Sloan, Jacob 110
socialism 20, 22, 23, 25, 28, 31, 125, 126
Sommo, Yehuda 13
Song of Songs 116, 129, 130
South Africa 70, 164
Soviet Union 70, 116, 124, 132, 165
Spain 98
Steiner, George 134
Steinsaltz, Adin 175
Sue, Eugène 81
Szeintuch, Yehiel 100, 101
Szold, Henrietta 69
Szwarc, Marek 125

Talmud 6, 24, 31, 36, 83, 86, 88, 90, 108, 117, 119, 173–81, 184, 185, 186
territorialism 165
Tierra del Fuego 5, 162–64
Tokyo 153
Torah 13, 27, 30, 43, 162, 183
translation into English 8, 66, 73–75, 108–10, 114, 116, 125, 175, 181, 184, 185
translation into French 113
translation into Hebrew 81, 95–98, 154, 155
translation into Russian 109, 114
translation into Yiddish 7, 15, 22–24, 117
Turgenev, Ivan 86
Turniansky, Chava 17 n. 10

Ukraine 44, 125, 153
Ulinover, Miriam 2, 48, 49, 69, 71
United States 121 n. 18, 152, 153
Untermann, Ernest 32 n. 2 and n. 6

Varhayt 63 n. 35
Vays, Yisroel-Dovid 28, 29
Vilna 82, 89, 164
virginity 48, 49, 96, 177, 181
Vrubel, Mikhail 127

Walkowitz, Rebecca L. 160 n. 9
Warsaw 5, 61, 69, 72, 75, 84, 100–02, 110, 115, 116, 118, 125, 140, 151 n. 38, 162, 164–68, 171 n. 12, 179
Weber, Max 124, 135 n. 16
Weininger, Otto 4, 117, 140
Weinreich, Max 7, 8, 75
Weinstein, Laurie 168
Whitman, Ruth 70
Whitman, Walt 163

Wiener, Leo 80, 81
women's rights 19, 22, 28, 29, 110
Woolf, Virginia 78 n. 51
World War I 5, 154–56, 160 n. 6
World War II 93, 110, 118

Yakubovitsh, Rosa 2, 41, 42
Yiddish PEN Club 110
Yiddishism 29, 97
Yidish-bukh 29

Zeitlin, Aaron 3, 93, 100–04, 117
Zimmerman, Bonnie 72
Zinberg, Israel 14
Zionism 5, 29, 76, 96, 97, 104, 140, 156, 159, 165
Znamenski, Andrei A. 20

www.ingramcontent.com/pod-product-compliance
Lightning Source LLC
LaVergne TN
LVHW061251060426
835507LV00017B/2013